Progressive Myths

Michael Huemer

Table of Contents

Acknowledgements

I would like to thank Ari Armstrong, Jonathan Anomaly, Kyle York, Ross Levatter, Nathan Cofnas, and David Barnett for their helpful comments on the manuscript, which resulted in numerous improvements, large and small. None of these brave souls are responsible for any of the errors or cancellable offenses contained in this book. Any such misdeeds are due to my inherently evil nature as a cis-hetero white man.

Introduction

I have written this book because I think truth matters. Society cannot be reliably improved through lies, exaggerations, and misleading stories; it requires knowledge of the real, factual situation we face, in whatever area we seek to improve matters. I also believe that contemporary progressive political ideology is a deeply misguided belief system that causes great harm to society.

Are all progressive positions completely misguided? Of course not; don't be ridiculous. Racism and sexism really are bad, gays should be allowed to get married, global warming is real, etc. But contemporary progressivism goes far beyond these well-known points. Progressivism as I understand it—at least, the kind of progressivism that I take issue with—sees contemporary America as a deeply unjust society, filled with prejudice and systematically designed to harm and oppress. I consider this viewpoint thoroughly out of touch with reality. For more, see the rest of this book.

To be clear, my problem is not that progressives have *bad values*, nor is it that I *don't like* them or that they don't belong to *my tribe*. My problem is that they are *factually mistaken*. They hold beliefs that objectively conflict with

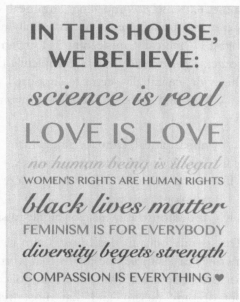

IN THIS HOUSE,
WE BELIEVE:

science is real

LOVE IS LOVE

no human being is illegal

WOMEN'S RIGHTS ARE HUMAN RIGHTS

black lives matter

FEMINISM IS FOR EVERYBODY

diversity begets strength

COMPASSION IS EVERYTHING ♥

Figure 1: Popular sign displayed by American progressives.

the way the world is in many respects; they misunderstand the current state of society, the causes of social problems, and the effects of social policies. This leads them to advocate policies and behaviors that worsen society and even undermine their own values.

"Progressive beliefs" is a broad category covering many issues. It would be impossible to rebut progressive beliefs *in general* in a single book. Plus, as with any ideology, there are many progressives who are not open to persuasion, no matter what I might say. So I cannot undermine all progressive ideas for all people.

Instead, I aim to address those people, however many they may be, who have an open mind about progressive ideology. If you're a committed woke progressive, you'll probably hate this book. If you're a committed rightist, then you'll probably love it. I assume, however, that there are some people who are neither of those things—people who are uncommitted but could be persuaded one way or the other by hearing evidence.

Sometimes, I believe, people adopt progressive ideology for rational reasons: They hear what appear to be compelling pieces of evidence for progressivism from sources whom they trust. My contention is that when this happens, that evidence is almost always bogus. If you hear some extremely compelling empirical evidence supporting left-wing ideas, that putative evidence is usually either false or radically misleading. By "radically misleading", I mean that if you knew the whole context, you would draw a completely different conclusion from what the evidence initially seems to support.

Which brings me to the idea of *progressive myths*. A progressive myth is

   i. an empirical, factual claim, which
   ii. is believed by many progressives,
   iii. seems to obviously, strongly support an element of progressive ideology, and yet
   iv. is demonstrably false or highly misleading.

That is my focus in this book: I aim to debunk a series of progressive myths. For example, the myths that women get paid 30% less than men for the same work, that American police frequently murder black men out of pure racism, and that most rich people in America got rich through inheritance, all will be discussed in later chapters. In each case, I'll state the myth, then cite some evidence that the myth has really influenced some people (else some critics would claim not to know what I'm talking about). Then I'll explain what is wrong with it.

I will not give a *neutral* presentation in the following chapters, but I *do* aim to give an *objective* presentation. I am a philosopher, not a lawyer or a campaign manager. My task is not to replace left-wing propaganda with right-wing propaganda. My task is to replace propaganda with a fair and accurate account. Hence, though the myths herein are chosen for being incorrect in some way, I will mention when I think there is something in the vicinity of the myth that is correct.

Some of these myths will probably be things you believe or are tempted to believe. If so, I hope you'll come to see their falsity. If this happens repeatedly, I hope you'll start to question whether progressivism in general is on the right track.

I have selected beliefs that can be debunked fairly quickly and forcefully. Many other progressive beliefs require long argumentation and subjective judgment calls to assess. About these more difficult issues, I have nothing to say directly here, apart from the suggestion that if progressive sources are bad at reporting simple matters of fact, then maybe the odds of their getting much more difficult matters right are none too encouraging.

I expect some critics to accuse me of attacking straw men, either because *they personally* haven't been taken in by the myths I debunk, or because the myths are not propounded by the *most* informed, sophisticated, academic progressives. (As an aside, I suspect these sophisticated partisans are much rarer than you might hope. Plenty of people with PhD's are radically wrong and unsophisticated about tons of things, especially outside their areas of specialization.) That is the nature of a book devoted to debunking myths—naturally, the most informed people don't embrace most myths, but presumably that doesn't mean that debunking myths is useless. I am quite certain that there are many people who believe each of these myths. I know this partly because *I myself* was taken in by some of these before doing the research, and I *would* believe many others if I had not long ago acquired a general skepticism of the news media and persuasive political content. I don't particularly care whether the people taken in by the myths are academics or ordinary people; I am not one of those academics who wishes only to talk to other academics.

But, you might wonder, if the *most sophisticated* progressive thinkers don't subscribe to the myths, then why would debunking them undermine progressivism? Shouldn't we focus on what the most sophisticated progressives say?

While that seems like a reasonable challenge on its face, I think it treats intellectuals as more rational than we really are. The way we work is typically more like this: We adopt a political ideology when we're 20 years old and know practically nothing, based mainly on our emotional temperament and a smattering of misleading factoids. We spend the next several years rationalizing that ideology, which we cling to ever after. If our original reasons for adopting the ideology are undermined by later evidence, we invent new reasons for holding on to the same beliefs. If you're clever enough, you can rationalize nearly any ideological belief in the face of nearly any body of evidence. The most sophisticated progressives are not the ones who are the best at pursuing the truth or even at persuading third parties; they are the ones who are the best at protecting their belief system from falsification. Often, this involves constructing elaborate systems of mutually-reinforcing claims, none of which can be rebutted without taking on the whole rest of the system.

At least, that's how things look to me. So I've concluded that the best way to promote accurate political beliefs (or at least one way that's worth trying) is to stop people from adopting false ideologies to begin with, by intercepting common myths that might appeal to naïve readers who have not yet adopted a firm ideological orientation.

The myths I address herein are about relatively circumscribed, objective points of fact. I do not address such big-picture issues as "Can socialism really work?" or "Is wealth inequality unjust?" Those sorts of questions would take much longer to address, and it is difficult to answer them decisively. Instead, I address simpler questions such as, "Do women really earn 30% less than men do for the same work?", because there we are much more likely to make actual progress.

I have one request for readers, whether you are left-wing, right-wing, or other. Please do not make up views that I didn't assert and ascribe them to me. Do not assume that I am a stereotypical "right wing" extremist or that I agree with right wing people where I haven't explicitly said so. (I have found, by the way, that leftists tend to be extremely bad at understanding what rightists think anyway.) Do not "read between the lines" to infer what I "must be implying". If you think of some ridiculous or horrible political view that you think I'm implying, that is almost certainly just in your imagination. I am not the sort of writer who likes to *imply* his point.

Now you might be wondering: "If you're not a typical right-wing extremist, then why did you write a book only about *progressive* myths? What about all the *conservative* myths out there? Surely those are the bigger problem."

In reply, there are four reasons why I am not discussing conservative myths here. One is that there is only so much ground that one book can cover, and the progressive myths are more than enough to fill this one.

Another reason is that the right-wing myths that I have run into have not generally struck me as persuasive on their face (e.g., "the 2020 election was stolen", "global warming doesn't exist"), so there seemed less need for debunking. The left today is much better at creating the kind of myths that I am interested in debunking, ones that sound to most educated readers like reports of empirical facts.

Third, as I shall explain later (Chapter 24), I am particularly concerned about the harm that progressive ideology is doing to America.

Finally, it seems to me that the left has taken over America's cultural institutions, including nearly every field of study in academia, all of the arts, most of the news media, corporate HR departments, and nearly all of the major tech companies. Rightists hold their own only in the realm of government, where they control roughly half of elected offices. This means that in the long run (assuming that the right does not bring down democracy in the near term), the left is the greater threat. It is *their* ideas that have been taught to the last three generations, and it is their errors and deceptions that will be taught to the next.

Part I: Myths About Individuals

In this part, we review events involving specific individuals who received widespread news coverage in the last several years. This coverage tended to have a distinctly leftward slant. If you watched mainstream media coverage or listened to woke social media, you probably absorbed these myths.

If you didn't follow these cases, you may wonder why these cases are important for understanding our society. The answer is that these are case studies in the sort of distortions found in prominent information sources. These cases are particularly useful because it is usually more straightforward to determine the truth about a single episode than it is to determine the truth about some generalization about society. Once we see how media and activists treat relatively straightforward matters of fact, we will know better how to receive their claims about more complex issues.

1 Trayvon Martin

Myth

Trayvon Martin was murdered due to racism, and his killer was then acquitted due to racism.

Background

On February 26, 2012, Trayvon Martin, a black 17-year-old male, was walking through a neighborhood in Sanford, Florida, heading from a store to the house of his father, whom he was visiting.[1] He was spotted by George Zimmerman, a 28-year-old Hispanic man who was the captain of the local neighborhood watch. Zimmerman was licensed to carry a gun and was armed at the time.

Zimmerman found Martin suspicious and so started following Martin while calling the police. Zimmerman talked for a few minutes with the police dispatcher, who assured him that the police were on their way. By the time he hung up, Zimmerman seemed to have lost Martin. Between the time he hung up and when the police arrived, however, Zimmerman had an altercation with Martin, during which Zimmerman shot Martin once in the chest, killing him.

The police arrived shortly after, took Zimmerman into custody, and questioned him. Zimmerman said that Martin had attacked him and that Zimmerman had shot Martin in self-defense. The police released Zimmerman without charges.

A few days later, a media firestorm erupted around the case, largely due to the publicity efforts of Martin's parents and their lawyer. Many saw Zimmerman as a racist murderer, though Zimmerman denies that race played any role in the events. Accusations included: that Zimmer-

---

[1] Wikipedia, "Killing of Trayvon Martin".

man racially profiled Martin, that Zimmerman disobeyed a police dispatcher's order not to follow Martin, and that Zimmerman started the fight between the two. Some witnesses heard calls for help while the two were fighting. Martin's parents say it was Trayvon calling for help, but Zimmerman says it was himself.

2.2 million people signed an online petition on change.org to have George Zimmerman prosecuted, the most signatures for any petition in the history of the website.[2] The governor of Florida appointed a special prosecutor for the case, and Zimmerman was prosecuted for second-degree murder.

The trial took place in 2013. A key prosecution witness was Rachel Jeantel, who stated that she was Martin's girlfriend and was on the phone with Martin moments before his death. Jeantel testified that Martin had been afraid of Zimmerman, that she heard Martin ask Zimmerman, "What are you following me for?", to which Zimmerman replied, "What are you doing around here?"; then she heard the sound of Martin's earpiece falling to the ground, followed by Martin saying "Get off! Get off!", before the phone went dead.

Zimmerman was found not guilty. Protests erupted in cities across the country. Some black activists called (unsuccessfully) for Zimmerman to be prosecuted in federal court. The case inspired the influential Black Lives Matter movement, which continues to this day.

Examples

#BlackLivesMatter was founded in 2013 in response to the acquittal of Trayvon Martin's murderer. [...] We are working for a world where Black lives are no longer systematically targeted for demise.
—Black Lives Matter website

Testimony at the trial revealed that law enforcement ordered Zimmerman not to pursue the teen and to stand down until police arrived. Zimmerman continued to pursue Trayvon.
—Benjamin Crump, lawyer for Martin's parents

As we all watched every day of the trial, there was not even the hint that Trayvon Martin did anything wrong.
—Rev. Al Sharpton, black activist and political commentator

---

[2] Martin and Fulton 2012.

You know, when Trayvon Martin was first shot I said that this could have been my son. Another way of saying that is that Trayvon Martin could have been me 35 years ago.

—President Barack Obama

"This guy looks like he's up to no good. He looks black."
—NBC edited version of audio clip from Zimmerman's call to police, portraying Zimmerman as a racist

A police surveillance video taken the night that Trayvon Martin was shot dead shows no blood or bruises on George Zimmerman, the neighborhood watch captain who says he shot Martin after he was punched in the nose, knocked down and had his head slammed into the ground.

—ABC News report

Trayvon was running for his life. He was screaming for help, fighting for his life. And then, he was *murdered.*
—Congresswoman Frederica Wilson (D-FL)[3]

After Zimmerman's acquittal, Americans were surveyed for their opinions on the case (figure 2). Half of whites were satisfied with the verdict, while blacks were overwhelmingly dissatisfied (86%). Democrats and young people were also especially dissatisfied.[4]

Reality

Let me start with a trivial observation that nonetheless appears to be necessary. The guilt or innocence of George Zimmerman depends on the particular *factual details of the case.* It cannot be determined based on the *races* of the two parties involved, nor can it be determined based on your political affiliation. The fact that Trayvon Martin was black does not prove that he was the aggressor, *nor does it prove that he wasn't the aggressor,* and nor does it prove that Zimmerman was a racist. None of that can be known without looking at the specific facts.

I say this because it looks as if many people rushed to judgment about the case, presuming that it must be a racist murder because the victim was black or because left-leaning media elites and celebrities

---

[3] Sources: BLM website (a); Crump 2019, p. 58; Sharpton 2015, 3:48-3:57; Obama 2013, 2:22-2:37; Wemple 2012; Gutman 2012; Wilson 2012, 2:42-2:52.
[4] Pew Research Center 2013.

were saying that.

So let's look at the evidence.

(1) Did Zimmerman diso-bey a police order not to pursue Trayvon?

Not really. The audio re-cording of Zimmerman's call with the police reveals that Zimmerman told the police dispatcher that he was following Martin. The dispatcher said, "We don't need you to do that", to which Zimmerman replied, "Okay." A little later, the dispatcher asks for Zim-merman's location. Zim-merman isn't sure of the address. He asks for the police to call him when they get near. The dispatcher agrees, and they hang up.

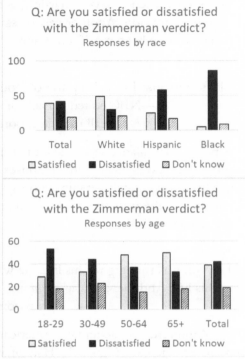

Figure 2

According to Zimmerman, he then walked around looking for an address to give to the police. That was when he says Trayvon reap-peared and confronted him.

(2) Is Zimmerman a racist?

NBC News played an edited clip from the police call in which Zim-merman is heard to say, "This guy looks like he's up to no good. He looks black"—creating the impression that Zimmerman thought Trayvon was up to no good because he was black.

In fact, Zimmerman only mentioned Martin's race in response to a direct question from the dispatcher. The entire exchange went like this:

> Zimmerman: Hey, we've had some break-ins in my neighborhood, and there's a real suspicious guy, uh, [near] Retreat View Circle, um, the best address I can give you is 111 Retreat View Circle. **This guy looks like he's up to no good**, or he's on drugs or

something. It's raining and he's just walking around, looking about.

Dispatcher: Okay, and this guy, is he white, black, or Hispanic?

Zimmerman: **He looks black**.[5]

NBC kept the part in bold and cut out the rest. Why did Zimmerman think Martin was suspicious? There had been a string of crimes in the neighborhood in the preceding year, including break-ins near where Martin was walking. Zimmerman didn't recognize Martin (which is understandable since Martin did not live there). He says that he found Martin suspicious since Martin was walking around in the rain, looking at the houses. When Martin fled between two of the houses, Zimmerman probably found that doubly suspicious.

It is doubtful that Zimmerman was a virulent racist, because he was an Obama voter who had previously served as a mentor to two black youths.[6] Nevertheless, race might have played some role in the events of February 26, 2012. One of Zimmerman's African American neighbors told a reporter:

Let's talk about the elephant in the room. I'm black, OK? There were black boys robbing houses in this neighborhood. That's why George was suspicious of Trayvon Martin.

On one previous occasion, a woman had her house broken into by two black men while she was home with her infant child. She called the police; the burglars fled as police arrived. Later, Zimmerman came to the woman's house, gave her his contact information, and gave her a stronger lock for her door to prevent further break-ins. That woman stated that "People were freaked out. It wasn't just George calling police ... we were calling police at least once a week."[7]

In light of this, it would be unsurprising if Martin's race was a factor in Zimmerman's suspicion of him. I leave it to the reader to judge whether this would constitute an objectionable kind of racism. But note that, if Martin's race played a role, this would not be due to a general, a priori belief on Zimmerman's part that black people are suspicious; it would be due to his knowledge of the actual descriptions of the individuals who were victimizing his neighborhood.

---

[5] Trayvon Martin Shooting Call 2012.
[6] Gilbert 2019, 4:33–5:48.
[7] Francescani 2012.

(3) What the heck was Zimmerman doing following Martin or calling the cops on him? Is this some sort of trigger-happy vigilante?

Neighborhood Watch is a crime-prevention program active in many neighborhoods across the U.S. Neighbors hold meetings and agree to be on the watch for suspicious activity in the neighborhood. They usually receive training and support from their local sheriff's office. Members are encouraged to report all suspicious activity to the police immediately (but not to directly confront suspects). Figure 3 shows signs commonly posted in neighborhoods with this program.

In 2011, in response to the crime wave they were experiencing, George Zimmerman and his neighbors created a Neighborhood Watch program. Zimmerman was selected by his neighbors as the program's coordinator.

So Zimmerman probably just saw himself as doing his part to help make his community safer. He probably started following Martin out of frustration at previous incidents in which criminals had gotten away and a desire to be able to tell the police where Martin had gone. The police call records Zimmerman muttering "These assholes always get away."

Figure 3

Trayvon Martin knew none of this, as he had only recently arrived in the neighborhood. He just knew some stranger was watching him and may even have thought that Zimmerman was looking for a fight.

(4) Were the police racist for not initially charging Zimmerman?

No. The police had no legal basis for charging Zimmerman. Based on his account of events, the shooting was legally justified, and they had no evidence at the time to contradict this. Even with evidence that was later gathered by the prosecutors in the case, Zimmerman was still acquitted. This vindicates the initial decision; police should not file charges that they do not have evidence to support. (We discuss the evidence below.)

The detective who investigated the case thought that all the evidence added up to the conclusion that Zimmerman was telling the truth, but his colleagues pressured him to file charges anyway.[8] The police chief similarly reports that city officials pressured him to arrest Zimmerman, despite the lack of evidence. He tried to tell them that this was illegal, but they didn't care. "They just wanted an arrest; they didn't care if it got dismissed later", he reports. The chief refused and was fired as a result.[9]

What appears to have happened is this: The police knew that they had no basis for charging Zimmerman, so they let him go. The parents of Trayvon Martin were distraught over the death of their son, and they refused to believe that his killing was in any way justified. So they started a media campaign to represent the case as a racist murder.

Millions of people who knew nothing of the case other than the family's assertions signed on, including major media outlets. The case played too well into progressive narratives for people to spoil things by examining the facts. The government caved under political pressure to file charges against Zimmerman, then did their best prosecuting a losing case. Despite the acquittal, however, Zimmerman had already been convicted in the media, and thus tens of millions of people to this day continue to believe that he got away with murder.

Figure 4

(5) Was Zimmerman injured?

An ABC news story claimed that, after his altercation with Martin, Zimmerman showed no signs of blood or bruises, despite allegedly having been beaten by Martin.

That was false. In fact, police photographs from that night show Zimmerman with blood on his nose and mouth, where he said Martin punched him, and on the back of his head, which he said Martin had

---

[8] Stutzman and Pavuk 2012; Alvarez 2012.
[9] McLaughlin 2013.

slammed into the concrete (figure 4).[10]

(6) Who attacked whom?

Now to the central question of the case. Zimmerman says that after he hung up with the police, Trayvon Martin reappeared and confronted him:[11]

> Trayvon: Yo, you got a problem?
> Zimmerman: No, I don't have a problem, man.
> Trayvon: Well, you got a problem now.

Then Trayvon punched Zimmerman in the face. Zimmerman fell down. Trayvon got on top of him and started slamming his head into the concrete sidewalk and punching him. Zimmerman screamed for help.

A neighbor came out of a nearby building. Zimmerman pleaded for help, but the neighbor just promised to call 911 and retreated. As Zimmerman was squirming to get his head off the concrete, his jacket slid up, which revealed the gun strapped to his side. Martin saw the gun, said, "You're gonna die tonight, motherfucker", and reached for Zimmerman's gun. At that point, Zimmerman pulled the gun and shot Martin.

Since Martin is dead, we don't have his version of events; we only have Zimmerman's version, as given above. But all the available evidence fits with the general outlines of Zimmerman's story, leaving the shooting both legally and morally justified.

There is audio available of a neighbor's 911 call, in which screams for help can be heard in the background. Zimmerman's family say the screams are definitely from George Zimmerman. Trayvon Martin's father initially said that these screams were *not* from his son, then later changed his mind to agree with Trayvon's mother, claiming that the screams *were* from Trayvon.[12]

It's easy to see why George's and Trayvon's families might lie. For both, their first loyalty is doubtless to their family member. Fortunately, however, the police located the one third-party witness who saw the two men struggling on the ground. That witness told police that he saw Martin on top of Zimmerman, beating him, while Zimmerman was

---

[10] Wikipedia, "Killing of Trayvon Martin".
[11] See Zimmerman's (2012) video reenactment for the police.
[12] Kovaleski and Campbell 2012.

calling for help.[13] There is no obvious reason for this witness to lie; therefore, it is highly probable that Martin was in fact on top of Zimmerman, beating him, at the time that Zimmerman shot him.

Forensic evidence corroborated this. In the trial, a forensic expert testified that the gun was in contact with Martin's *shirt* but two to four inches away from Martin's *skin* at the time it was fired. This suggests that Martin was above Zimmerman, leaning forward with his shirt hanging down, at the time he was shot; it is not consistent with the idea that Zimmerman was on top of Martin.[14]

Many commentators have focused on Zimmerman's decision to follow Martin to see where he had gone. One lesson from this case is that if you see a person you suspect may be a criminal, *do not follow that person*. Just report them to the police. Zimmerman's choice in this case was unwise and ultimately ended in tragedy. That, however, is quite different from his being a racist murderer.

Another lesson is that if you see a strange man watching you, do not confront that man or try to fight with him. Just call the police. Also, do not ever try to grab a man's gun; he will definitely shoot you.

(7) What did Rachel Jeantel hear?

There was one important witness for the prosecution whom we haven't yet discussed. Shortly before his death, Trayvon Martin was on the phone with his girlfriend. After the shooting, she gave a one-page, handwritten note to Trayvon's mother, recording what she had heard. My best attempt to transcribe it from a photo on the internet is as follows (leaving language errors intact):[15]

March 19, 2012

I was on the phone when Trevon decided to go to the Cornerstore. It started to rain so he decided to walk through another complex because it was raining to hard. He started walking then noticed someone was following him. Then he decided to find a shortcut cause the man wouldn't follow him. Then he said the man didn't follow him again. Then he looked back and saw the man again. The man started getting closer. Then Trevon turned around and said why are you following me!! Then I hear him fall, then the phone hung up.

[13] Weiner and Stutzman 2012.
[14] Winter et al. 2013, reporting the testimony of Dr. Vincent Di Maio.
[15] Eugene 2012.

I called back, and text no reponse. In my mind I thought it was just a fight. Then I found out this tragic story.

Thank you,
Diamond Eugene

During the trial, a witness named Rachel Jeantel testified for the prosecution. She said that she was the girlfriend who had been on the phone with Trayvon and had given the letter to Trayvon's mother. She said that she had heard Martin say "Get off! Get off!" before the phone call cut off. Notice that this last bit is crucial to the prosecution, since it suggests that *Zimmerman* was on top of *Martin*. This is the key piece of evidence for claiming that Zimmerman was the aggressor and for denying his claim of self-defense. Notice also that that bit was not mentioned in the letter above, and thus it relies entirely on Jeantel's verbal testimony.

You may also have noticed something odd about this story: The letter was signed "Diamond Eugene", yet the witness who claimed to have written it was named "Rachel Jeantel". (Some news stories from the time show pictures of the letter, but with the signature blacked out.[16] They don't mention the name discrepancy.) Jeantel claimed that she had signed the letter "Diamond Eugene" because that was her *nickname*. The defense attorney asked her to read the letter in court, and she was unable to do so. She explained that she could not read cursive handwriting, and that she had had a friend write the letter for her. Nevertheless, she supposedly signed it (the signature is printed, not cursive).

All of this apparently sounded perfectly legitimate to the journalists who covered the case at the time. If it sounds completely reasonable to you as well, I have several bridges I would like to sell you.

In 2019, the conspiracy theorist and filmmaker Joel Gilbert published his documentary *The Trayvon Hoax*, which details the fraud that he says was carried out by the prosecution in the Zimmerman trial, with the help of Rachel Jeantel, Trayvon Martin's mother, and the family's lawyer. Despite some credibility issues about the filmmaker's past work, the documentary is highly

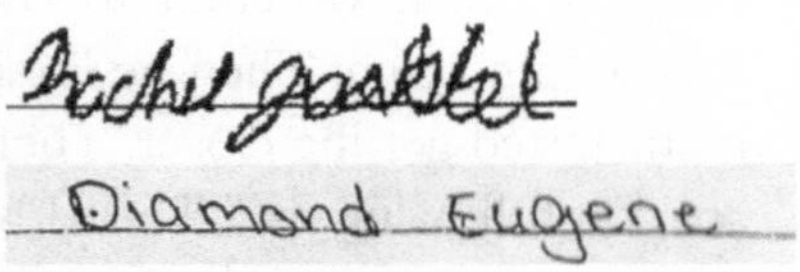

Figure 5

---

[16] Kaye 2013, 2:55; NBC News 2013.

persuasive, and the main claims are supported with photographs and video and audio clips that appear in the film. (You know the saying, "Just because you're paranoid, doesn't mean they're not out to get you"? Just because Joel Gilbert is a conspiracy theorist, doesn't mean that he didn't find an actual conspiracy this time.) In figure 5, I reproduce photos of Rachel Jeantel's signature, which Gilbert got from a traffic ticket Jeantel had gotten, and the signature on the letter from Diamond Eugene. The writing is about as different as it could possibly be.

Gilbert got a copy of Martin's phone records, which helped him identify a woman named Brittany Diamond Eugene. Gilbert gives exhaustive evidence that this is the real Diamond Eugene to whom Martin had been talking on the day he died. The evidence includes photos of Brittany Diamond Eugene on Martin's phone, which look nothing like Jeantel. It also includes a recording of Diamond Eugene's voice that was made by the Martins' attorney and played for the media, which sounds like Brittany Diamond Eugene and not like Rachel Jeantel. The attorney had stated that his witness, Diamond Eugene, was 16 years old. Brittany Diamond Eugene was 16 years old, whereas Rachel Jeantel was 19. (Jeantel said that she had lied about her age, pretending to be 16 for some reason.)

All this matters because, again, the courtroom testimony of Jeantel was crucial to the case against Zimmerman. It now appears that that testimony was all lies; Jeantel had not heard *any* of what she said she heard because she was not the one who was on the phone with Martin. Gilbert suggests that Martin's mother and the prosecutor coached Jeantel to impersonate Eugene when the real Eugene refused to testify. Whoever is responsible, it remains the case that there is no credible basis for disputing Zimmerman's self-defense claim.

Consequences of the Trayvon Martin Hoax

Race relations in America have deteriorated since 2012 and continue to do so today, largely due to the progressive campaign to convince us that black people are in constant danger from white racists who go about murdering blacks out of pure hate. Many young Democrats have been taken in by this campaign, but it is particularly effective with blacks. A shocking proportion of black Americans believe radically distorted accounts of cases such as that of Trayvon Martin, which feed the impression that whites are the enemy of blacks.

To state the obvious, this is good for no one. It is no good for whites to be hated, and it is no good for blacks to have suspicion and anger toward the majority of their society. It is nearly impossible to succeed in any society if you regard the majority of that society as your enemy.

In an apparent effort to stoke this racial animosity, the Martin family's lawyer, Benjamin Crump, wrote a book titled *Open Season: Legalized Genocide of Colored People*. In it, he describes George Zimmerman as "a white man who asserted that he was Hispanic because his mother was born in Peru".[17] This is similar to calling Barack Obama "a white man who claimed to be black because his father was born in Kenya".

The progressive narrative about racism seems calculated to sow rage and division, of the kind that has led to riots during the last several years. If the narrative were *true*, we would need to know about it so that we could stop the epidemic of white racist violence. But since it is not true, the problem is unsolvable. One cannot address a grievance based on fundamentally false assumptions; we cannot stop a genocide that doesn't exist. All that can come of this is more tension and violence, until people stop lying.

---

[17] Crump 2019, p. 57.

2 Michael Brown

Myth

Michael Brown was murdered due to racism, after he had surrendered and held his hands up.

Background

In Ferguson, Missouri in 2014, a white police officer named Darren Wilson had an altercation with an 18-year-old black man named Michael Brown, which resulted in Wilson shooting and killing Brown.[18] There are conflicting accounts of what happened, but here is what is agreed upon:

Brown had just stolen some cigarillos from a nearby store and was carrying them in his hand while walking down the middle of the street with his friend, Dorian Johnson. Officer Wilson drove by them heading in the opposite direction and told them to get off the street and onto the sidewalk. Johnson replied that they were almost to their destination, and the two continued. Wilson backed his patrol SUV up and positioned it in the path of Brown and Johnson. Brown and Wilson then had a physical altercation, which resulted in Wilson shooting twice at Brown, hitting him once in the right hand.

Johnson hid behind a car while Brown fled down the street. Wilson chased Brown while calling for backup. When Brown was near the corner, he did something that is disputed among witnesses (see below). Wilson then shot six rounds at him. After about a three second delay, Wilson shot four more times. In total, Brown was hit at least six times, including one bullet that went through the top of his head, killing him instantly.

---

[18] For details of the case, see Wikipedia, "Killing of Michael Brown"; U.S. Department of Justice 2015.

Accounts differ over how the altercation started and what happened just before Wilson shot Brown to death. Brown's friend, Johnson, said that when Wilson was in his patrol vehicle, he tried to open his door aggressively, and it bounced off Johnson and Brown's bodies, closing again. Then Wilson reached through his window, grabbed Brown by the throat and tried to pull Brown in. While Brown struggled to get away, Wilson shot him. Then Brown fled down the street. Wilson shot Brown in the back as he was fleeing. Brown then held his hands up, turned around, and said "Don't shoot!" Wilson fired multiple more rounds at him anyway, killing him.

Wilson, on the other hand, said that when he was in his patrol vehicle, he tried to open the door, but Michael Brown pushed it closed. Then Brown started punching Wilson through the window. Wilson drew his gun and warned Brown to stop or he would shoot. Brown grabbed Wilson's gun hand and pointed the gun toward Wilson's hip. Wilson used both hands to aim the gun toward Brown, then fired twice. Brown fled down the street, and Wilson gave chase. He did not shoot as Brown was fleeing. But then Brown turned around and charged at Wilson. That was when Wilson fired a volley of shots. Brown paused, then started to charge again, at which point Wilson fired more shots, this time killing Brown.

There were many conflicting witness reports about the incident, with some supporting Wilson's account and a larger number broadly supporting Johnson's account.[19] The case was referred to a grand jury, which reviewed all the evidence before deciding *not* to indict Officer Wilson. The case was also investigated by the FBI and the Justice Department, who also decided not to file charges.

The incumbent local prosecutor was voted out of office after this case after having served in that post for 28 years. His successor promised to review the Michael Brown case with an eye toward prosecuting Wilson. After reviewing it, the new prosecutor also decided not to prosecute.

Examples

This case led to protests and riots across the country. There was widespread vandalism, looting, and arson in Ferguson. Wilson was

---

[19] Santhanam et al. (2014) provide a chart listing witness takes on several key issues.

widely portrayed as a racist murderer. Black Lives Matter protestors
adopted the slogan "Hands up!" or "Hands up, don't shoot!", alluding
to Michael Brown's alleged surrender before he was shot.

According to polling
data, after the grand jury
decided against indicting
Darren Wilson, a large
portion of Americans, in-
cluding a third of whites
and *four fifths* of blacks,
were disappointed or an-
gry with the decision (figure 6).[20] Years later, many
people still remembered
the case as a racist mur-
der. Some quotations:

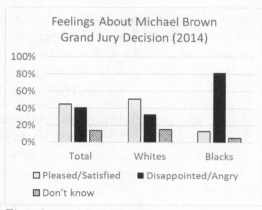

Figure 6

> This is a boy who did everything right, who never got into a fight,
> who stayed in school.
>
> —Cornell Brooks, president, NAACP (referring to Michael Brown)

> The assumption that black people must be guilty of something lies
> behind the Ferguson shooting, and the police reaction … Brown's
> prosecutors in the court of public opinion will nonetheless demand
> he defend himself against these charges because he was a black teen-
> ager. His killer will remain presumed innocent.
>
> —Steven Thrasher, journalism professor, Northwestern University

> It is at once horrific and predictable that a law enforcement officer
> may never have to answer for his crimes in criminal court … This
> reality check simply locates another officer in the context of the
> white supremacist law-enforcement apparatus that defends him in
> lieu of protecting its (black) citizens.
>
> —Hannah Giorgis, columnist, *The Guardian*

> In 2014, Mike Brown was murdered by Ferguson police officer Dar-
> ren Wilson. It was a guttural response to be with our people, our
> family—in support of the brave and courageous community of Fer-
> guson and St. Louis as they were being brutalized by law enforce-

[20] De Pinto et al. 2014.

ment, criticized by media, tear gassed, and pepper sprayed night after night.

—Black Lives Matter website

Michael Brown's murder forever changed Ferguson and America. His tragic death sparked a desperately needed conversation and a nationwide movement. We must fight for stronger accountability and racial equity in our justice system.

—Kamala Harris, U.S. Presidential candidate, 2019

5 years ago Michael Brown was murdered by a white police officer in Ferguson, Missouri. Michael was unarmed yet he was shot 6 times. I stand with activists and organizers who continue the fight for justice for Michael. We must confront systemic racism and police violence head on.

—Elizabeth Warren, U.S. Presidential candidate, 2019

It's been six years since Michael Brown's life was taken in Ferguson—reigniting a movement. We must continue the work of tackling systemic racism and reforming policing.

—Joe Biden, U.S. Presidential candidate (later President)[21]

The street where he was shot is now the site of a memorial to Michael Brown that activists visit every year on the anniversary of his death.[22]

Reality

(1) Intrinsic plausibility

There is overwhelming evidence that Dorian Johnson was lying about the circumstances of Michael Brown's death.[23] The most compelling evidence is forensic (discussed below). But let's start with general plausibility considerations.

Johnson was Brown's personal friend, who stood by his side when he stole the cigarillos and had the altercation with Wilson, so it is easy to see why he might lie. He probably wished to portray his friend in a more positive light and to exact revenge on the cop who killed his

---

[21] Sources: Swaine 2014; Thrasher 2014; Giorgis 2014; BLM website (b); Harris 2019; Warren 2019; Biden 2020.
[22] Carson 2022.
[23] For the evidence discussed below, see U.S. Department of Justice 2015.

friend. This alone doesn't mean that he lied, but it means that we should be cautious about taking his testimony at face value.

Johnson's story also included intrinsically implausible elements, such as that Wilson, *from inside his vehicle*, grabbed Brown by the throat and started a "tug-of-war", trying to pull Brown toward him. It is nearly impossible to grab a standing person's throat while seated inside a car, unless the other person is leaning down very close to your window. There is also no reason to pull a suspect toward you. If Wilson's aim was to shoot Brown, it would have made more sense to do so while out of Brown's reach, rather than trying to pull Brown close enough that Brown might be able to hit Wilson or grab his gun. It is also implausible that Wilson could have had a tug of war from his seated position, using only his left hand, with a man who outweighed him by 80 pounds. So it seems extremely unlikely that Johnson's account of the start of the altercation was at all accurate. That, in turn, makes it more likely that Johnson also lied about the rest.

These points should have been obvious to anyone hearing Johnson's account, even before looking at the forensic evidence. Yet they escaped many activists and reporters, who uncritically latched onto Johnson's story.

(2) Did Brown attack Wilson while Wilson was in his vehicle?

Yes. There was a red mark on Wilson's face, and Wilson's DNA was found on Brown's hand. Brown's DNA was also found on Wilson's gun, collar, pants, and the inside of the driver's side of Wilson's vehicle. This is all consistent with Wilson's story and not with Johnson's story: Brown's DNA got on Wilson's gun when Brown grabbed the gun, Brown's DNA got on Wilson's collar when Brown hit Wilson, etc.

(3) Did Wilson shoot Brown in the back?

No. The medical examiners found no entry wounds in the back. All the wounds in Brown's body were from the front.

(4) Was Brown charging Wilson when Wilson shot him?

Yes. All sources agree that, when Wilson was chasing Brown, the two were moving down the street to the *east*. After the shooting, investigators found blood stains from Brown on the street along with ten shell casings from Wilson's gun, arrayed to the west of the first blood stains. Michael Brown's body lay on the ground to the *west* of most of the shell casings—meaning that Brown and Wilson had moved westward after Wilson started firing. Wilson must have been backing up, and Brown must have continued moving in Wilson's direction. This fits with Wilson's account of events and contradicts Dorian Johnson's account. Several eyewitnesses interviewed by the FBI corroborated this aspect of Wilson's account.

(5) Did Brown hold his hands up in surrender?

No. First note that it is highly unlikely that Brown *both* held his hands up in surrender *and* charged toward Brown as indicated above.

Though several witnesses claimed that Brown surrendered, the FBI found serious credibility problems with twenty-four of the witnesses they interviewed. That part of the Justice Department report reads like a rogue's gallery of comically bad witnesses. Some witnesses admitted that their accounts were influenced by media reports; some admitted to having lied to the FBI or the local police; many contradicted themselves, the forensic evidence, or undisputed facts about the case. Several witnesses had prior convictions for crimes of dishonesty. One witness, who suffers from memory loss and was under psychiatric care, gave an account inconsistent with the objective evidence; when asked about this, she grabbed the recording device and refused to give it back. After the agents retrieved the device, she admitted that she had lied.[24]

After taking account of this, the Justice Department found that there were eight credible witnesses who corroborated Wilson's self-defense claim and *no* credible witnesses who maintained that Brown had surrendered or who disputed the self-defense claim.

Questions and Objections

(1) Were the investigations biased?

Perhaps the grand jury, the St. Louis County prosecutor in 2014, that prosecutor's successor, the FBI, and the Justice Department were all biased against Michael Brown because of his race, and *that* is why all those people claimed that there was insufficient evidence to charge Officer Wilson.

Reply: Admittedly, the local prosecutor at the time was white. The grand jury had three black members and nine white members. Howev-

---

[24] Witness 126, U.S. Department of Justice 2015, p. 66.

er, the Justice Department at the time was run by Eric Holder, the first African American attorney general, who had been appointed by Barack Obama, the first African American President. Both Holder and Obama stood by the Justice Department's investigation, so it is unlikely that it was a racist process.[25] After the first St. Louis County prosecutor was voted out of office, the position was taken over by Wesley Bell, who, as it happens, was the first African American to hold that position. He promised to look into prosecuting Darren Wilson. When he looked into it, though, he came to the same conclusion as everyone else: There was no legal basis to prosecute Wilson.

It is not credible that all these people were biased. If you still think Wilson was guilty of murder, you'll have to explain why everyone who investigates the case in detail, including left-wing black people, comes to the opposite conclusion.

(2) Why would so many people lie?

One of the disturbing things about the story is the number of people who were prepared to lie about the events, claiming to have witnessed a white cop murder a black man. Had there been less forensic evidence available, and had they been better liars, they might have gotten an innocent man convicted of murder. Not that these witnesses were all malicious; most probably were not present at the scene but believed the "Hands up" myth and assumed that they were only lying in the service of justice.

By my count, there were two witnesses (one black, one white) who lied in an effort to *exculpate* Darren Wilson, while another twenty witnesses, eighteen of whom were black, lied in an effort to *incriminate* Wilson.[26] Most of them claimed to have seen Brown hold his hands up in surrender. If this never happened, where did they all get this idea?

The answer is: Dorian Johnson. He went around telling the media and local residents his fabricated story shortly after the shooting. It appears that local residents then pressured each other to support the narrative about a white cop murdering a harmless black teen.

Multiple witnesses reported feeling pressure from the community and fearing reprisals if their neighbors should learn that they had given

---

[25] Larotonda and Good 2015; CBS News 2015.
[26] Lied to exculpate: Witnesses 140, 142. Lied to incriminate: Witnesses 101, 118-128, 130-133, 137-139, 148. Witnesses 112 and 135 are hard to classify. See U.S. Department of Justice 2015, pp. 44-77.

the police evidence corroborating Wilson's account of events.[27] One cited signs in the neighborhood that said, "Snitches get stitches" (slang for "People who report crimes to the authorities will be injured"). Another witness who had initially told police that the shooting was justified refused to be interviewed for the record later. He cited community sentiment in favor of the "Hands up" narrative and stated that he would rather go to jail than testify.

(3) It doesn't matter; "Hands up" is just a metaphor

In 2014, activists who were interviewed after the factual accuracy of the "Hands up" narrative had come under question stated that its literal truth or falsity was irrelevant, as the slogan was just a metaphor for the larger problem of racist police violence, or even for helplessness in the face of inequality in general.[28]

It would be difficult to find a better illustration of ideological dogmatism. Progressives were (and some still are) happy to cite the Michael Brown case as evidence of the deep racism in American society. But when their beliefs about the case turn out to be radically erroneous, they declare the case irrelevant and refuse to draw any lessons from it. So we only "learn" from cases that conform to our pre-existing narrative. If a case fails to fit, we ignore it. This is the definition of confirmation bias, and it makes one insensitive to the truth.

Perhaps if Michael Brown were an isolated case, progressives would be right to discount it. But it isn't. Time and again, false accusations of racism spread like wildfire through the media and activist networks. When the deception is exposed, progressive media elites and political activists sweep the case aside, scarcely even acknowledging the falsehoods. We have already seen the deception present in the Trayvon Martin case, and we will see more cases in the coming chapters.

The real lesson of such cases is not one concerning the prevalence of racist violence, but one concerning the prevalence of false accusations of racism, along with the sheer gullibility and mendacity of the news media. As we saw earlier, some people claimed that Michael Brown was unfairly presumed guilty because of his race.[29] The truth was precisely the opposite: Darren Wilson was presumed guilty because of his race

---

[27] Witnesses 102, 103, 105, 108, 109, 113, and 139; see U.S. Department of Justice 2015, pp. 28-34, 72-3.
[28] Lieb and Holbrook 2014.
[29] Thrasher 2014.

and his occupation. Indeed, it is worse than that: *Even after being proved innocent*, he is still widely assumed to be guilty, based on the progressive stereotype that "White cops are racists." Judging Wilson based on stereotypes about his race and occupation is as foolish and prejudiced as judging Brown based on stereotypes about his race.

3 Amy Cooper

Myth

Amy Cooper, the "Central Park Karen", was a racist who tried to harm an innocent black man by making a false complaint to the police, using the well-known tendency of police to assume the worst about any black man.

Background

In May of 2020, Amy Cooper and Christian Cooper (no relation) had a disagreement in New York's Central Park. Amy was walking her dog, unleashed, in a part of the park where dogs are required to be on a leash. Christian was birdwatching in the same area. Birdwatchers tend to be annoyed by unleashed dogs, because they tend to scare the birds away. Christian asked Amy to put her dog on a leash, but she refused.

Christian then recorded a video of her on his phone, subsequently posted to social media.[30] The beginning of the video shows Amy approaching Christian and telling him to stop recording her. In a frightened voice, he says "Please don't come close to me. Please don't come close to me." She stops and threatens to call the police. He replies, "*Please* call the cops." She does so, and tells them, in a frightened voice, that there is an African American man threatening her and her dog. She repeats herself in an increasingly desperate tone. At the end, she leashes the dog, and Christian says, "Thank you."

Christian and his sister both posted the video on social media, where it went viral, provoking nationwide outrage against Amy Cooper.

Examples

Racism in the ornithology world reared its head in 2020 when Amy

---

[30] Cooper and Cooper 2020.

Cooper called the police on ... Christian Cooper ... The park visitor ... had falsely accused him of threatening her when he asked her to keep her cocker spaniel on a leash.

—New York Post

[T]he incident is a reminder of larger ills in American society: the willingness of white people to call the police on black people, and the epidemic of violence against black Americans by both police and white civilians.

—Vox News

Black Americans often face terrible daily dangers in outdoor spaces, where they are subjected to unwarranted suspicion, confrontation, and violence. ... We are grateful Christian Cooper is safe.

—Rebeccah Sanders, senior vice president
for state programs at the Audubon Society

And now here you have this woman who—we've all seen the video now—blatantly, blatantly knew how to use the power of her whiteness to threaten the life of another man and his blackness.

—Trevor Noah, comedian

The video out of Central Park is racism, plain and simple. She called the police BECAUSE he was a Black man. Even though she was the one breaking the rules. She decided he was the criminal and we know why. This kind of hatred has no place in our city.

—Bill de Blasio, New York City Mayor

Filling a false police report is a crime. Being racist is reprehensible. There needs to be accountability for this. Disgusting.

—Mark Levine, New York City Council member[31]

Reality

(1) Did Christian Cooper threaten Amy Cooper?

It was widely reported that Christian had not threatened Amy, and thus she was making a false police report. In fact, he *did* threaten her; that part just wasn't in the video. He started recording after he threatened

---

[31] Sources: Cost 2023; North 2020; North 2020; Noah 2020, 2:20-2:39; de Blasio 2020; Levine 2020.

her. This is *by his own admission*: By his own account, Christian had said, "if you're going to do what you want, I'm going to do what I want, but you're not going to like it."[32]

This left Amy to wonder what it was that he wanted to do that she wasn't going to like. Rape her? Injure her? Injure her dog? When you make such an open-ended threat to a woman, in a place where you and she are the only people around, you can't really be offended if she gets scared. That really is not an odd or unwarranted reaction. In addition, Amy Cooper says that Christian's manner was radically different before he started recording. In the recording, he sounds as if *he* is frightened of *her*; however, before he started recording, he had been aggressively shouting at her about the dog.

After his verbal threat, Christian took some dog treats out and tried to feed them to Amy's dog. Reflect now on the oddness of a man who doesn't have a dog pulling dog treats out, right after expressing dismay about your unleashed dog and promising to do something that you're not going to like. What is the reasonable interpretation of that? The most natural interpretation seems to be that he is trying to poison your dog or lure the dog over to harm it in some other way. After poisoning your dog, it can't be ruled out that he has some further harm in store for you. These are not crazy, "racist" interpretations. It is not unreasonable to be afraid, and it would not be inaccurate to report that the man has threatened you and your dog.

As it turns out, Christian was not trying to poison the dog; he was merely trying to use Amy's fear of that possibility to make her put the dog on a leash. But she could not know that at the time, which of course is what Christian was counting on.

(2) Was Amy Cooper really afraid?

In her call to the police, Amy's voice becomes increasingly desperate-sounding. Some viewers thought that she was putting on a performance, pretending to be afraid so that the cops would come and hurt Christian. However, there is no reason to think this.

We can know that Amy's perception of Christian's threatening behavior wasn't unusual, because Christian had had similar encounters with other people in the park. By his own account, he had a habit of doing the same thing to other dog-walkers, and this had led to other

---

[32] Nir 2020a. For the following details about the case, see Weiss' (2021) podcast.

dog-walkers' physically assaulting him twice that spring before he ran into Amy.

One dog-walker, who happened to be a black man, reported feeling threatened after Christian shouted at him and started following him. That case led to a physical altercation between the two. That dog-owner also said that he knew two other dog-owners who had had similar experiences with Christian Cooper, but they were afraid to come forward because they were white. All of this makes it very plausible that Christian's manner really was aggressive and threatening before he started recording. While some people (mainly men) respond to threatening behavior by physically fighting the person who is threatening them, other people respond with fear and calling the police.

The reason for the increasing desperation in Amy Cooper's voice in her 911 call is that when she first tells the operator that Christian is threatening her, the 911 operator can't hear her; they have a bad connection. She repeats it louder. The 911 operator still can't hear her. Getting increasingly desperate, she says it a third time.

All of these details—about Christian's threat against Amy, about his history with other dog-owners, about the bad connection—were generally missing from the very extensive media reports, which painted the event as a simple case of a "Karen" trying to use her white privilege and pretending to be afraid in order to have a completely harmless and innocent black man attacked by the police.

(3) Is Amy Cooper a racist?

Well, she *could* be, but this incident hardly proves it. Race might have been a factor in Amy's fear of Christian, but as explained above, there is enough about Christian's behavior to explain her fear without invoking race.

She mentioned Christian's race three times on the phone with police. But this is not especially odd or racist either. When you report threatening or suspicious behavior to the police, it is common to include a physical description of the suspect, including the suspect's race. This helps the police find the suspect. If the 911 operator tells you that she can't hear you, it is then normal to repeat that description.

(4) Is there an epidemic of violence against black Americans by police and white citizens?

No, there isn't. As discussed in Chapter 7, the police are more prone to shooting *white* suspects than black suspects. As to civilians, the over-whelming majority of homicides are *intra*-racial—that is, people killing other members of their own race. Of course, in a country of over 300 million people, there are going to be some inter-racial homicides. But homicides committed by blacks against whites are more than twice as common as homicides by whites against blacks in the U.S.,[33] despite that there are 5.6 times more white people than black people in the U.S. A randomly chosen black person is thus 13 times more likely to kill a white person than a random white person is to kill a black person.

(5) Does this case illustrate white privilege and black disadvantage?

Based on the general progressive narrative about race in America, as well as the specific claims people were making in discussing the Amy Cooper case (see above), one would predict that when the white woman reported the black man to the police, something ranging from very unpleasant to deadly would happen to the black man, while nothing bad would happen to the white woman. Let's see how that prediction plays out.

What happened to Amy Cooper? First, she was mobbed by thou-sands of people on social media condemning her, demanding that she be fired, etc. She was doxed and received death threats. The New York City Commission on Human Rights launched an investigation of her. The police filed criminal charges against her for making a false police report. (The charges were later dropped after she completed an "educa-tional" program focused on racial identity.) There were demands that she be banned from the park. She was immediately fired from her high-powered job in finance. She was unable to live a normal life due to the notoriety and eventually fled the country, returning to her native Canada. In the end, even Christian Cooper thought things had gotten out of hand.[34]

Now, what happened to Christian Cooper?

Nothing—except that he was celebrated on social media, and there were glowing profiles of him in the news media.

---

[33] U.S. Department of Justice 2020.
[34] Nir 2020a; 2020b; Daniel Johnson 2021; Aggeler 2020.

4 Jacob Blake

Myth

Jacob Blake was yet another victim of racist police violence.

Background

Jacob Blake was a black man who was shot in the back by a white cop in Kenosha, Wisconsin on August 23, 2020.[35] Police were responding to a call from Blake's girlfriend, who told them that Blake was not allowed to be on the premises and that he had taken her car keys. Cellphone video of the shooting, taken by a neighbor, surfaced on the internet. The video shows Blake walking around an SUV with two police officers following him, guns drawn. He calmly walks around the front of the SUV to the driver's side, ignoring the cops, and opens the door. As he leans into the SUV, with his body obscured by the door, the cop immediately behind him grabs his shirt from behind, then fires seven shots at him. The video ends with a man's voice repeatedly screaming, "Why the fuck did you all just shoot him?" as police gather around Blake, who lies on the ground.

Blake's stomach, kidney, and liver were damaged by the shooting. He survived but was left paralyzed from the waist down. The Wisconsin Division of Criminal Investigation and the U.S. Department of Justice conducted investigations into the officer who shot Blake, Rusten Sheskey. In the end, no charges were filed against Sheskey, and he was returned to duty.

This case led to protests across the country and riots in Kenosha, where vehicles were set on fire, buildings vandalized and burned, and businesses looted for three nights.

---

[35] See Wikipedia, "Shooting of Jacob Blake".

Examples

Sports stars, celebrities, scholars, and politicians weighed in right after the shooting:

> It's just the compounded grief, the compounded trauma of these horrific murders, these lynchings.
>
> —Alexis Hoag, legal scholar, Columbia Law School

> With yet another example of racial discrimination with the shooting of Jacob Blake, and the unlawful abuse of peaceful protesters, we MUST unify as a society. It is imperative that all people ... come together to say, 'Enough is enough!'
>
> —Baltimore Ravens (football team) official statement

> All you hear is Donald Trump and all of them talking about fear. We're the ones getting killed. We're the ones getting shot. ... It's amazing to me ... why we keep loving this country, and this country does not love us back.
>
> —Doc Rivers, coach, Los Angeles Clippers (basketball team)

> [I]t's only the brown faces ... the brown-toned people that get treated in this way.
>
> —Jacob Blake's father

> The nation wakes up yet again with grief and outrage that yet another Black American is a victim of excessive force. This calls for an immediate, full and transparent investigation and the officers must be held accountable. ... Equal justice has not been real for Black Americans and so many others. ... We must dismantle systemic racism.
>
> —Joe Biden, U.S. Presidential candidate (later President)

> The police who shot Jacob Blake in the back seven times must be fired, arrested and prosecuted to the fullest extent of the law. Congress cannot wait any longer to act forcefully to end the horrific violence against Black Americans at the hands of police.
>
> —Bernie Sanders, Presidential candidate

> So when millions of us have seen with our own eyes the execution of unarmed black men, can someone explain how any policeman still feels permitted to do dastardly deeds like what was done to Jacob

Blake tonight? (And don't dare anyone say that we don't have all the facts yet)

—Marianne Williamson, Presidential candidate

Wow this is SICKENING ! I can't believe it ! What's going to be the excuse now ?

—Cardi B, rap artist[36]

Reality

The video on its face *looks* like an unjustified shooting. Blake does not appear to be doing anything especially threatening at the time he is shot. But, *pace* Marianne Williamson, those who rushed to judgment did not have all the facts. Let's add some of those facts.[37]

(1) Blake had an outstanding arrest warrant.

There was an arrest warrant outstanding for Jacob Blake, for charges involving domestic violence and felony sexual assault, which he had allegedly committed at the same address where the police found him on August 23, 2020. The responding officers were aware of this at the time. Under Wisconsin law, this meant that they were *legally obligated* to arrest Jacob Blake if they encountered him.

(2) Blake was armed.

In the video, one can just make out that Blake is holding a small, black object in his left hand as he comes around the vehicle.[38] That object is a knife. The person who took the video heard the cops yelling "Drop the knife!" Blake ignored them. In his police interview after the shooting, Blake said that he didn't drop the knife because it was a gift with sentimental value, which he wanted to put in the car. In a later media interview, Blake instead claimed that he didn't hear the officers' orders.[39] I find these explanations inadequate.

---

[36] Sources: Sanchez 2020; Baltimore Ravens 2020; Rivers 2020; Sanchez 2020; Radcliffe 2020; Sanders 2020; Williamson 2020; N. Saad 2020.

[37] For detailed discussion of all these facts, see Graveley 2021.

[38] KARE 2020. Freeze the frame partway through second 0:13, when Blake's hand is momentarily in front of his shirt. The knife is a "bear claw" folding knife, which was open at the time.

[39] Blake and Strahan 2021, 3:52-4:00.

(3) Police tried non-lethal force.

Blake resisted when the police tried to arrest him. The police tried physically restraining him, but he struggled with them and got away. They hit him with Tasers twice. Both times, he just pulled the prongs out and continued. They tried applying the Taser directly to his neck; this also was ineffective.

In his *Nightline* interview, Blake explained that he didn't know the police wanted to arrest him. I find this unlikely.

(4) Three children were in the car.

There were three children in the car at the time Blake tried to get into the driver's seat. His girlfriend who had called 911 shouted that her kids were in the car. (They were the children she had had with Jacob Blake.)

(5) Blake may have been about to stab the officer.

The officers involved said that, just before he was shot, Blake started to twist his body in a manner suggesting that he was about to stab Officer Sheskey. Two civilian witnesses corroborated this, and it is consistent with the location of the bullet wounds in his side. It is also made plausible by the fact that, in a previous incident, Blake had resisted arrest and slashed at two cops with a knife. (That time, officers managed to take him into custody without anyone being hurt.)

To sum up: Say you're a police officer. You are legally required to arrest the individual in front of you. He struggles with you to avoid arrest and breaks away. The Taser has no effect on him. He holds a knife that he refuses to drop. He walks away from you and tries to get into a car with three children in it. If you don't stop him in the next few seconds, he will drive away. As you grab his shirt, he looks like he's about to stab at you with the knife. What options do you have at this point? To let him drive away? And, what, follow him in a high-speed chase with the children in the car? This doesn't seem viable.

In this case, it really is hard to see how the cop had any other choice but to shoot.[40]

---

[40] But why shoot Blake seven times? Why not just shoot once and then pause to see if that stops him? Because in real life, unlike the movies, one shot typically does not immediately stop a criminal, and if not stopped immediately, Blake could have stabbed Sheskey, gotten in the car and closed the door, or done something else dangerous in a fraction of a second.

5 Kyle Rittenhouse

Myth

Kyle Rittenhouse was a white supremacist who drove to Kenosha from far away to get involved in trouble and provoke protestors. He murdered two people, and he got away with it due to the racism of American society.

Background

The Jacob Blake shooting (see Chapter 4) touched off civil unrest in Kenosha, Wisconsin, from August 23-25, 2020. Vehicles were set on fire, buildings vandalized and burned, and stores looted. The town suffered tens of millions of dollars in damages over the three nights.[41]

17-year-old Kyle Rittenhouse showed up to the scene of the riots on the night of August 25 armed with an AR-15 style rifle (similar to that carried by American soldiers).[42] In reaction to the previous nights' violence, citizens had formed militias to protect the town, an effort Rittenhouse wanted to join. He wound up in altercations that resulted in his shooting three people that night, killing two of them. The people killed were Joseph Rosenbaum and Anthony Huber. Gaige Grosskreutz was hit in the arm and survived. Video surfaced on the internet of the shootings of Huber and Grosskreutz. Another video surfaced during the resulting court case showing the Rosenbaum shooting.

News media and social media coverage portrayed Rittenhouse as a white supremacist murderer. Media outlets repeated many times that Rittenhouse had "crossed state lines" to get to Kenosha, perhaps suggesting that he had no business there and went far out of his way looking for trouble.

---

[41] McAdams 2020.
[42] See Wikipedia, "Kenosha Unrest Shooting".

Rittenhouse was charged with two counts of murder and one of attempted murder. At trial, Rittenhouse was found not guilty of all charges. Reactions were split along party lines. Many on the left called this a victory for "white supremacy", leaving many people with the impression that Rittenhouse had shot black people.

Examples

During the trial, 45% of Americans surveyed—including overwhelming majorities of Democrats and black people—thought that Rittenhouse should be found guilty (figure 7).[43]

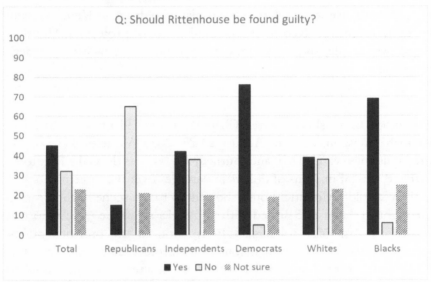

Figure 7

Facebook deactivated Rittenhouse's account and blocked searches for his name before the not-guilty verdict came in:

> We've designated this shooting as a mass murder and have removed the shooter's accounts from Facebook and Instagram.
>   —Facebook official announcement[44]

On the belief that Rittenhouse had shot black people:

> "I assumed the guys he shot were Black guys," said a neighbor when

---

[43] Frankovic 2021.
[44] Brandom 2020.

the Kyle Rittenhouse homicide trial came up in casual conversation. Others seconded that opinion as an informal poll conducted by the MSR found most people, like our White neighbor, holding this assumption.

—*The Minnesota Spokesman-Recorder*[45]

As soon as the trial verdict came out, activists, politicians, and entertainers reacted:

The verdict in the #KyleRittenhouseTrial is a reminder of the treacherous role that white supremacy and privilege play within our justice system.

—Derrick Johnson, President & CEO, NAACP

These continue to be dark days for black people killed at the hands of people that believe our lives do not matter.

—Rev. Al Sharpton, Civil Rights Activist

The judge. The jury. The defendant. It's white supremacy in action. This system isn't built to hold white supremacists accountable. It's why Black and brown folks are brutalized and put in cages while white supremacist murderers walk free.

—Congresswoman Cori Bush (D-MO)

Carrying a loaded gun into a community 20 miles from your home and shooting unarmed citizens is fundamentally wrong.

—J.B. Pritzger, governor of Illinois

The system is not broken. It works. In the favor of white supremacy.

—Lizzo, rap artist

#kylerittenhouse found not guilty tho we SAW HIM kill two. Fundamentally stupid […] A tragic, tragic day for decent, THINKING, feeling, ethical people everywhere.

—Bette Midler, actress

I hope Kyle Rittnehouse [*sic*] car crashes on his way home . I hope the car flips and he can't get out while it's on fire and dies in it . This is a genuine wish

—Guap, rap artist[46]

---

[45] Reeves 2021.

Reality

(1) Did Rittenhouse shoot black people?

No. Joseph Rosenbaum, Anthony Huber, and Gaige Grosskreutz were all white men. This makes it puzzling on its face how the case came to framed as centering on race or "black people killed at the hands of people that believe our lives do not matter", as Al Sharpton put it.

There was one black man (Maurice Freeland) who jump kicked Rittenhouse in the head while Rittenhouse was on the ground. Rittenhouse fired at him and missed. It would be difficult, however, to argue that Rittenhouse shot at Freeland because Freeland was *black* rather than, say, because Freeland *was attacking him*, given that Rittenhouse also shot the three white men who attacked him.

(2) Was the verdict fundamentally stupid?

No. *Pace* Governor Pritzger and Bette Midler, the case was not as simple as "Did Rittenhouse shoot those people or not?" In the law and most ethical views, use of deadly force can be justified in self-defense; this is not stupid. Both sides in the trial agreed that Rittenhouse really shot three people. The issue was whether he fired in self-defense.

(3) Did Rittenhouse shoot Joseph Rosenbaum in self-defense?

Yes. Let's start with some background.[47] Witnesses described Rosenbaum as "hyperaggressive and acting out in a violent manner" on the night of August 25, 2020. Rosenbaum had said, to a group of people that included Rittenhouse, "If I catch any of you guys alone tonight, I'm going to fucking kill you."[48]

Later that night, Rosenbaum caught Rittenhouse alone and apparently moved to carry out his threat. He threw a plastic bag (containing socks, underwear, and deodorant) at Rittenhouse and then chased Rittenhouse as Rittenhouse fled. Another nearby rioter shouted, "Get him and kill him!" and fired a pistol into the air. As Rosenbaum caught up to Rittenhouse, Rittenhouse turned. Rosenbaum lunged forward, apparently trying to grab Rittenhouse's gun. That's when Rittenhouse

---

[46] Sources: Derick Johnson 2021; Sharpton 2021; Bush 2021; Pritzger 2021; Jefferson 2021; Midler 2021; Hayes 2021.

[47] For details of the case, see Wikipedia, "Kenosha Unrest Shooting".

[48] Forliti et al. 2021.

shot him. The chase and shooting were captured on grainy drone video, which was played at the trial, leaving no doubt that Rosenbaum was chasing Rittenhouse and was either lunging or falling forward when he was shot.[49] Rittenhouse said that Rosenbaum grabbed the gun; a nearby witness saw Rosenbaum grab for the gun but wasn't sure whether Rosenbaum's hand made contact with the gun.[50]

Does this add up to a case for self-defense? Yes. Given these facts, it was completely reasonable for Rittenhouse to believe that Rosenbaum intended to inflict serious bodily harm or death on Rittenhouse. Rittenhouse attempted to escape without using violence, but Rosenbaum chased him down. If Rittenhouse had not fired when he did, Rosenbaum would have attempted to take the gun away and, very plausibly, kill Rittenhouse with it. It is difficult to see how Rittenhouse had any other choice but to shoot at that point. Keep in mind that all of this happens very fast; if Rittenhouse had hesitated another fraction of a second, Rosenbaum would have been on him. A second later, Rosenbaum might well have been the one shooting Rittenhouse.

In online discussions, some speculated that Rittenhouse had earlier *provoked* Rosenbaum. There is no evidence for this, but in any case, this is irrelevant. The video clearly shows Rittenhouse fleeing and Rosenbaum chasing; that suffices to make Rosenbaum the aggressor.

If you don't yet see this, try imagining that video surfaced of some right-wing figure chasing someone down and grabbing that person's weapon. Would you be tempted to propose that the person being chased was the aggressor?

(4) Did Rittenhouse shoot Anthony Huber in self-defense?

Yes. After shooting Rosenbaum, Rittenhouse fled down the street in the direction of a group of police. He was chased by a large group of rioters/protestors, which included Anthony Huber and Gaige Grosskreutz.

This is captured in the viral video that made the Rittenhouse case famous.[51] The video shows Rittenhouse stumbling and falling to the ground. A few other men catch up with him. Everything happens very quickly, but it is possible to make out what happened by freezing

---

[49] Piwowarczyk 2021; Daley 2021.
[50] McGinnis 2021.
[51] Chicago Sun-Times 2020.

frames of the video, as was done in the trial (figure 8). First, Maurice Freeland jump kicks Rittenhouse in the head and shoulder. Rittenhouse fires twice at him but misses. Then Anthony Huber hits Rittenhouse in the head with a skateboard. Rittenhouse shoots him and he falls to the ground. Gaige Grosskreutz, who was approaching with a pistol in his hand, holds his hands up. Rittenhouse points his gun but doesn't fire. Then Grosskreutz moves to the side while lowering his hands and starting to point the pistol toward Rittenhouse. Rittenhouse fires, hitting Grosskreutz in his right arm.

Figure 8

Focus now on Anthony Huber. It might at first seem that there was no need to shoot him, as a skateboard is not a deadly weapon. Also, Huber seems to be moving away, right after hitting Rittenhouse, at the time he is shot. Why did Rittenhouse shoot him?

Note three important points. First, even though Huber was moving away, he was also at the same time reaching for or grabbing the barrel of Rittenhouse's gun. This is visible in the video. If someone physically attacks you and then tries to take your gun, it is rational to assume that that person will kill you if he gets the weapon.

Second, although a skateboard is not typically a deadly weapon, being hit in the head with any heavy, hard object can be dangerous.

Third, bear in mind the context. Rittenhouse is on the ground, surrounded by multiple men attacking him or about to attack him (besides Freeland, Huber, and Grosskreutz, a couple more are in the immediate vicinity). One of the men is holding a gun. A large, angry mob is just behind them, approaching Rittenhouse. Again, everything is happening very quickly; you can barely distinguish the above-described events if you play the video at normal speed. What Rittenhouse should expect at this point is to be overwhelmed and possibly shot within the next one to two seconds, and then to have the mob beating him while he lies helplessly on the ground a second later. He needs to immediately stop the attack so he can get up and get away.

One of the prosecutors suggested that it wasn't so bad because "everybody takes a beating sometimes."[52] A beating by one person is one thing. But a beating by a mob full of angry rioters, one of whom is holding a handgun, is not just a minor scuffle. It is an imminent threat to your life.

Some people proposed that Rittenhouse had provoked the mob and therefore lacked the right to defend himself. But again, Rittenhouse was the one fleeing toward the police; the mob was chasing him down and physically attacking him. That makes them the aggressors.

(5) Did Rittenhouse shoot Gaige Grosskreutz in self-defense?

Yes. Grosskreutz was holding a pistol in his right hand, which he was pointing at Rittenhouse when he was shot. Grosskreutz confirmed this on the stand, under questioning by Rittenhouse's lawyer (discussing a zoomed-in version of the third photo from figure 8):

Lawyer: So, Mr. Grosskreutz, I'm gonna show you what has been marked as exhibit 67. That's a photo of you, yes?

Grosskreutz: Yes.

Lawyer: Okay. That's Mr. Rittenhouse?

Grosskreutz: Correct.

Lawyer: Okay. Now, you'd agree your firearm is pointed at Mr. Rittenhouse, correct?

Grosskreutz: Yes.

Lawyer: Okay. And once your firearm is pointed at Mr. Rittenhouse, *that's* when he fires his gun. Yes?

Grosskreutz: No.

Lawyer: [Referring to photo.] Sir, look I don't wanna ... does this look like right now your arm is being shot?

Grosskreutz: That looks like my bicep being vaporized, yes.

Lawyer: Okay. And it's being vaporized as you're pointing your gun directly at him. Yes?

---

[52] Kraus 2021, 51:43.

Grosskreutz: Yes.

Lawyer: Okay, so when you were standing 3-5 feet from him with your arms up in the air, he never fired. Right?

Grosskreutz: Correct.

Lawyer: It wasn't until you pointed your gun at him, advanced on him, with your gun, now your hand's down, pointed at him, that he fired. Right?

Grosskreutz: Correct.[53]

(6) Did Rittenhouse go far out of his way to get to Kenosha?

Journalists covering the case repeated over and over, often with a tone of outrage, that Rittenhouse had "crossed state lines" to get to Kenosha.[54] As it is not illegal in the U.S. to cross state lines, it was not always obvious what the reporters were outraged about. Some may have thought that Rittenhouse illegally transported a gun across state lines. This would be wrong; it is not illegal to transport a gun across state lines, nor did Rittenhouse do so (the gun was stored in Kenosha to begin with).

In at least some cases, the suggestion seemed to be that Rittenhouse had no ties to Kenosha and had gone a long way to get there, which somehow indicates bad behavior.

In fact, the town Rittenhouse lived in, Antioch, is adjacent to the Illinois-Wisconsin border, on the Illinois side. Kenosha is just a half hour drive away, on the Wisconsin side. Rittenhouse regularly drove there for work. His father, grandmother, aunt, uncle, and cousins all lived in Kenosha.

(7) Did Rittenhouse go to Kenosha to cause trouble?

No, all indications are to the contrary. Rittenhouse had a history of interest in protecting and helping people. In high school, he joined the Explorers program at the nearby Grayslake Police Department, as well as a cadet program at the Antioch Fire Department. He worked as a lifeguard in Kenosha. On August 25, 2020, he was cleaning graffiti off a school during the day, just a few hours before the riots.[55] During the riots, he carried around a first aid kit, offering medical attention to

---

[53] Grosskreutz 2021, 2:51:44-2:52:59.

[54] Orfalea (2021) collects dozens of examples.

[55] Williams 2021; Barone 2020.

people. Before Rosenbaum attacked him, he was carrying a fire extinguisher to put out a fire; that is what brought him near Rosenbaum. After the shootings, he immediately approached police with his hands up and tried to turn himself in (they just told him to get out of the way and drove past). So everything we know about Rittenhouse is consistent with his going to the scene of the riots to prevent damage and help people, not to commit crimes. The police on the scene realized this too; there is video footage of police giving water to a group of militia members (including Rittenhouse), thanking the militia members, and saying "We appreciate you guys, we really do."[56]

The same cannot be said of the people Rittenhouse shot. News reports portrayed them sympathetically, but all three had a troubled past. Rosenbaum was a convicted child molester who was out on bail for an assault in Wisconsin. On the day of the shootings, he had just been released from a hospital for a suicide attempt. That night, he was filmed trying to start fights with militia members and shouting, "Shoot me, [*n-word*]."[57]

Anthony Huber, the skateboard wielder, had previously been convicted for disorderly conduct, domestic abuse, strangulation, and felony false imprisonment with a dangerous weapon. In one case, Huber held a knife to his brother's stomach and threatened to gut his brother like a pig. He also choked his brother for about ten seconds and cut his ear with a knife.[58]

Gaige Grosskreutz had a previous felony conviction that was expunged, plus a misdemeanor conviction for intoxicated use of a firearm. He was carrying his handgun illegally on the night of August 25 (his concealed carry permit was expired). He also has a long arrest record for a variety of crimes, including disorderly conduct, criminal damage to property, burglary, criminal trespass, and theft.[59]

All of this adds to the plausibility of what we already know: All three men aggressively attacked Kyle Rittenhouse on that night.

---

[56] Kavanagh 2020.
[57] McBride 2021c; Based Logic 2020.
[58] McBride 2021b.
[59] McBride 2021a; Wisconsin Department of Justice 2020.

6 Three Non-Myths

The preceding chapters might give the impression that there are no problems with police violence. This is not the case. Sometimes, the police use excessive force and wrongfully kill people, including black people. The correct conclusion is neither "Police are always in the right" nor "Police are always in the wrong." The correct conclusion is "One must examine the facts of each individual case." To add some balance, I mention in this chapter three wrongful police killings of black people.

Eric Garner

Incident

On July 17, 2014, a black man named Eric Garner was killed by a white police officer, Daniel Pantaleo.[60] Garner was suspected of selling "loose cigarettes"—i.e., selling single cigarettes (rather than whole packs) to people without charging tax on them. When Officer Pantaleo tried grabbing Garner's arms, Garner pulled his arms away, saying, "Don't touch me." Pantaleo then put a chokehold on Garner and wrestled him to the ground, aided by a few other officers. He held the chokehold for several seconds while Garner lay helpless on the ground, then forcefully pressed Garner's head against the sidewalk, leaning on Garner's head with his body weight, while other officers swarmed around Garner. Garner repeated "I can't breathe" eleven times. All of this is visible in a video taken by a bystander and posted to the internet.[61] At the end of the video, another cop moves the bystander away so he can't film the scene anymore.

Garner fell unconscious and lay on the ground for several minutes

---

[60] For details of the case, see Wikipedia, "Killing of Eric Garner".
[61] Castanet News 2014.

before an ambulance arrived to take him away. He died during the ride to the hospital.

Aftermath

A New York grand jury reviewed the case and decided not to indict Pantaleo. The proceedings were kept secret, so we may never know what charges they were asked to consider or what their reasoning was.

The U.S. Justice Department also investigated the case. In 2019, five years after the event, William Barr, Attorney General under President Trump, finally decided that the Justice Department would not pursue any charges against Pantaleo, citing the difficulty of proving that Pantaleo had *willfully* violated Garner's civil rights. This decision went against the recommendation of the Justice Department's Civil Rights Division.[62]

In the same year, Pantaleo was finally fired from the police force after an NYPD investigation found, in the words of the Police Commissioner, that "Officer Pantaleo's use of a prohibited chokehold was reckless and constituted a gross deviation from the standard of conduct established for a New York City police officer."[63]

Evaluation

There are a few problems with the police conduct in this case, especially that of Officer Pantaleo but also that of the other officers who stood by and allowed the excessive force to occur.

To begin with, arresting someone for selling single cigarettes without charging tax on them seems like overkill. This must be among the most trivial offenses for which anyone has ever been arrested.

Second, the idea that the violence against Garner was justified because he was "resisting arrest" is farcical. This case was not like that of Michael Brown or Jacob Blake—Garner never attacked anyone, nor was he armed. All he did was pull his arms forward when Pantaleo grabbed them from behind as he was talking to another officer. This technically counts as resisting arrest, but it is not the kind of dangerous resistance that requires extreme force.

Third, Pantaleo's smashing Garner's face into the ground while Garner lay helpless shows malicious intent and should have been

---

[62] Shortell 2019.
[63] CBS News 2019.

grounds for a battery charge against Pantaleo independent of the choke hold.

Fourth and most importantly, the use of choke holds was and is forbidden by New York Police Department regulations. The city medical examiner found that Garner's death was caused by the choke hold as well as the compression of his chest by the police. Garner's family ordered an independent autopsy, which concurred that the compression of Garner's neck was the primary cause of death. While Pantaleo presumably did not *intend* to kill Garner, the police department's investigation found his behavior reckless. Reckless behavior leading to the death of another human being is standardly classified as involuntary manslaughter, which is a felony under New York law. So Pantaleo should have been prosecuted for manslaughter, as you or I certainly would have been if we did the same thing. Police officers should be held to a *higher* standard of conduct than ordinary civilians, not lower.

Congressman Peter King (R-NY) praised the decision not to charge Officer Pantaleo, arguing that Garner would not have died if Garner had not been obese, had asthma, and had a heart condition. This is probably true.[64] However, the police were well aware of Garner's weight; therefore, they should have taken it into account. In addition, they should know that some people have asthma, heart conditions, or other medical problems. *Most* people would not have been killed by that choke hold, but *some* non-negligible portion of people would be. Again, *that is why choke holds were prohibited.* To be guilty of manslaughter, it isn't necessary that Pantaleo knew that Garner was *definitely* going to die. It is enough that Pantaleo created an unnecessary high *risk* of death.

One good thing came out of the case: In 2020, New York state passed the Eric Garner Anti-Chokehold Act, which made it a felony, punishable by up to 15 years in prison, for a police officer to use a choke hold in a way that leads to serious injury or death.[65]

Breonna Taylor

Incident

On March 13, 2020, police in Louisville, Kentucky, served a search

---

[64] Levine 2014.
[65] New York State Assembly 2020.

warrant at the apartment of a black, 26-year-old medical technician named Breonna Taylor.[66] The warrant was for suspected drug activity by Taylor's former boyfriend. The former boyfriend was known *not* to be at the apartment, but police suspected that he had been using Taylor's address to receive drug packages.

Breonna and her then-current boyfriend, Kenneth Walker (not suspected of any crime), were in bed when three officers broke down the door with a battering ram and entered the apartment shortly before 1:00 in the morning. The police say they identified themselves, but Walker says that he and Breonna heard no such announcement. Walker fired a single shot at the intruders. The police fired 32 shots in return. They missed Walker but hit Taylor six times, killing her.

Aftermath

One of the officers involved in the raid was fired, not for killing Taylor, but for shooting recklessly in such a way that some of his bullets entered neighboring apartments. That officer was also indicted by a grand jury for the same action, but he was acquitted at trial.

Some background: A grand jury is a group of ordinary citizens (in Kentucky, 12 citizens) who evaluate evidence presented by a prosecutor to determine whether the evidence is good enough to bring charges against a particular suspect. In Kentucky, grand juries are regularly used in felony cases. If the grand jury thinks there is enough evidence, then the prosecutor proceeds to prosecute that suspect.

In the Breonna Taylor case, the grand jury did not indict any of the officers other than the one who fired bullets into other apartments. There were no charges for killing Breonna Taylor. Two members of the grand jury later came forward, accusing the prosecutor of mischaracterizing the grand jury proceedings to the public, failing to give the grand jury all the evidence, and "using grand jurors as a shield to deflect accountability and responsibility". The prosecutor admitted that he did not present homicide charges to the grand jury because he didn't think such charges were warranted; he thought the officers had acted in self-defense. The grand jurors, however, said that there *was* enough evidence to prosecute the officers for killing Taylor, but the prosecutor did not give them that option. They stated that there was an uproar in the room when the grand jury members found out that they were only there to

---

[66] For details of the case, see Wikipedia, "Killing of Breonna Taylor".

consider charges against the one officer for endangering the neighbors.[67]

That was at the state level. At the federal level, one officer was prosecuted for shooting bullets into neighboring apartments. His first trial ended in a hung jury, and he is set to be retried. In addition, three other officers who were not present at the raid were charged with lying to a judge on the application to obtain the search warrant and/or trying to cover up the false search warrant application. To obtain the search warrant for Breonna Taylor's apartment, the police claimed to have verified with the Post Office that Taylor's ex-boyfriend had received packages at Taylor's address—but they had not in fact verified that.[68] One officer has pled guilty for the false search warrant application. The other cases are still pending as of this writing.

The other two officers on the raid, who killed Breonna Taylor, are still not being charged with anything because they were not aware of the false search warrant application and the Justice Department considers them to have been acting in self-defense.

The six officers most involved in the case—the three who shot into Taylor's apartment plus the three involved in the false search warrant application—all either resigned or were fired, although the one who fired the fatal shot was then hired by a neighboring sheriff's office.

The city paid $12 million to Breonna Taylor's mother to settle a wrongful death lawsuit, then passed a law banning the use of no-knock warrants. They also paid $2 million to Taylor's boyfriend to settle another lawsuit.

Evaluation

The federal charges mentioned above seem justified. But what people find most outrageous is the fact that, still, no one is being prosecuted for actually shooting Breonna Taylor. The reason is that (a) the officers were acting on a search warrant, which they reasonably *believed* was valid, and (b) Kenneth Walker fired at them first. Those facts are not in dispute, and they would make it hard to convict the police officers in court.

Nevertheless, morally speaking, the officers who shot Taylor are probably guilty of murder. Why? Let's review some of the background

---

[67] Knowles and Iati 2020; King 2020.
[68] U.S. Department of Justice 2022.

facts.

a. The officers knew the apartment they were raiding was *not* that of the actual suspect who was being investigated and that the suspect was elsewhere. So anyone they encountered in that apartment would probably be an innocent person. In addition to Taylor, there could be any number of innocent people present—friends, family members, children, etc. (This is a general problem with no-knock raids.)
b. If a person is awakened in the middle of the night by the sound of someone smashing down their door, that person is likely to be both disoriented and terrified.
c. In America, about 44% of households own a gun.[69]
d. If someone in the apartment shot at the intruders, standard police practice would be to respond with overwhelming violence, emptying their guns in the direction of the threat.

From these facts, the police should have predicted that breaking down Breonna Taylor's door at 1:00 in the morning created a high risk of causing the deaths of innocent people. There was no emergency that required them to do so at that time. So this was objectively reckless behavior, endangering the lives of innocent people.

This makes the police officers the aggressors on that night, which invalidates their self-defense claim. Since the officers have no valid self-defense claim, their actions constitute murder. If you or I acted similarly, we would most certainly go to prison for many years.[70] Police officers should not get a pass for behavior that would qualify as murder if you or I did it. Again, police should be held to a higher standard of conduct than the rest of us, not lower.

Objection: The police say that they announced themselves repeatedly; therefore, Walker should have stood down.

Reply: The police most likely did *not* announce themselves or did not do so sufficiently loudly and clearly. Walker attested that he heard no announcement and had no idea what was going on. He suspected that it

---

[69] L. Saad 2020.
[70] Of course, we would go to prison just for breaking into a house since we are not in general legally permitted to do so, but that is not my point. My point is that if we unnecessarily created a serious risk of death for innocent people, even if our behavior was *otherwise* legal, if it led to our having to kill an innocent person, we would go to prison for that death.

was Taylor's ex-boyfriend breaking in.[71] Under Kentucky's "stand your ground" law, he was exercising his right to use deadly force to defend against home invaders. If he knew it was the police, it is highly unlikely that he would have responded by firing one shot at them. During the raid, Walker called 911 to report the break-in and shooting. It is highly unlikely that he would have called the police to report the intruders if he knew that the intruders *were* the police.

The grand jury members who spoke to the press agreed with this assessment and found the testimony of the police officers inconsistent and not credible.[72] The *New York Times* interviewed nearly a dozen neighbors, only one of whom (who was outside at the time) reported hearing the police identify themselves, just once.[73] It is likely that the police made a mistake, then later lied about it to evade criminal liability.

As mentioned above, the local prosecutor sided with the police. Why might there be a disagreement between a grand jury and a prosecutor? One reason is that prosecutors are biased in favor of police. Besides the general phenomenon that government officials tend to side with other government officials, prosecutors work with the police department in all of their cases and depend upon the police to provide evidence; therefore, they need to maintain good relations with the police. By contrast, grand jury members are ordinary, impartial citizens. Therefore, if a grand jury disagrees with a prosecutor about whether the police should be prosecuted, the grand jury is probably right. For similar reasons, if a local prosecutor disagrees with federal investigators, the federal investigators are more likely to be right.

George Floyd

Incident

We turn to the most notorious case of police violence in recent years. On May 25, 2020, a white police officer named Derek Chauvin killed a black man named George Floyd.[74] Floyd was accused of using a counterfeit $20 bill at a store. The police decided to arrest him. They wrestled him to the ground, then Officer Chauvin knelt on Floyd's neck for about nine minutes, while two other officers helped to restrain him

---

[71] Callimachi 2020.
[72] King 2020.
[73] Callimachi 2020.
[74] For details of the case, see Wikipedia, "Murder of George Floyd".

and a fourth prevented bystanders from interfering. Floyd told the officers sixteen times that he couldn't breathe. Floyd stopped moving, then eventually went silent. Another police officer checked his pulse and found none. The police called for an ambulance and waited till it arrived. During this entire time, Chauvin kept his knee on Floyd's neck. None of the other officers tried to stop Chauvin, and none tried to provide medical aid. This was captured on video taken by bystanders, which led to nationwide outrage, protests, and riots.

The ambulance took Floyd away, but medics were unable to revive him. He was pronounced dead at the hospital an hour later.

Aftermath

In this case, justice descended swiftly on the perpetrators. All four officers were fired the same day. Chauvin was prosecuted for felony murder, found guilty, and sentenced to 22½ years of confinement. The other three officers were convicted of aiding and abetting manslaughter and sentenced to 3–3½ years.

Evaluation

Controversy has since arisen about the case, with right-wing commentators such as Tucker Carlson and Candace Owens declaring Chauvin innocent. Floyd died from a drug overdose and a preexisting heart condition, they say (echoing Chauvin's lawyers).[75] A recent documentary, *The Fall of Minneapolis* by producer Liz Collin, reinforces this theory.[76] Collin includes body camera footage from the arrest, which she claims exonerates Chauvin. She contends that Chauvin was using an approved police restraint technique, that police witnesses lied about this during the trial, and that it was Floyd's drug use, rather than Chauvin's use of force, that killed George Floyd. This alternative theory even temporarily persuaded the eminently reasonable academic podcasters Glenn Loury and John McWhorter, who expressed surprise to learn that Derek Chauvin didn't kill George Floyd.[77]

The truth, I believe, is something in between what the BLM activists say (that Chauvin deliberately murdered Floyd due to racial hate) and what the right-wing commentators say (that Chauvin is completely

---

[75] Carlson and Baker 2021; Baker 2021.
[76] Collin 2023.
[77] Loury and McWhorter 2023. They later changed their minds; see Loury and McWhorter 2024.

innocent). The truth is that Derek Chauvin killed George Floyd *accidentally but culpably*.

(1) Did Derek Chauvin kill George Floyd at all?

The county medical examiner found that Floyd had a large amount of fentanyl and methamphetamine in his system and a preexisting heart condition. Nevertheless, *pace* Carlson and Owens, the medical examiner did not say that that was the primary cause of death. Rather, the two autopsies on George Floyd both concluded that the major cause of death was the restraint by the police officers.

Collin's documentary also shows that Floyd first complained of difficulty breathing *before* the police put him on the ground and before anyone compressed his neck. Does this show that Chauvin didn't kill him?

No. The simplest explanation is that the heart condition and the drugs put Floyd in a vulnerable condition, such that a restraint technique that would have left most people unharmed actually killed him. He was already having difficulty breathing, and Chauvin's aggressive restraint technique with compression of his airway pushed him over the edge.

The alternative theory is that George Floyd was about to die from independent causes and that, purely by coincidence, he just happened to die right when Derek Chauvin was kneeling on his neck. This strains credulity.

(2) Was it intentional?

Surely not. Even if Chauvin was an evil racist just itching for a chance to kill a black man, why would he choose to commit his murder on camera, in broad daylight, in front of a crowd of witnesses? The most plausible account is that Chauvin killed Floyd by accident. He had used the same restraint technique before (as shown in video from his arrests of earlier suspects[78]) without anyone dying. When Floyd became unresponsive, Chauvin probably assumed that Floyd was merely unconscious (which can result from restricted blood flow to the brain) and would soon recover.

---

[78] FOX 9 Minneapolis-St. Paul 2023.

(3) Was Chauvin using an approved police technique?

Collin's documentary claims that Chauvin was merely using the "maximal restraint technique" (MRT) that Minneapolis police officers were taught. Her film shows images from police training materials depicting this technique. They show a suspect lying on the ground and an officer kneeling with his knee on the suspect's shoulder or neck, in a position very similar to what Derek Chauvin used on George Floyd.[79] Collin claims that police witnesses lied about this during the trial, falsely denying that Chauvin was using an approved technique. Collin also claims that, in the police bodycam footage, one can see that Chauvin is kneeling on the shoulder, rather than the neck.

I find this unpersuasive. Rather than supposing that the police lied in court, it is more plausible that the police saw that Chauvin was not using the MRT correctly, and that is why they said he was not using an approved police technique. The MRT calls for the officer to kneel on the suspect's *shoulder*, not his *neck*. Although these superficially appear similar, the difference is crucial for a suspect who is having difficulty breathing. *Pace* Liz Collin, I am unable to see what she sees in the bodycam footage; on viewing her documentary, I could not make out exactly where Chauvin's knee was. However, in the

Figure 9

bystander cellphone video that originally went viral on the internet, one can clearly see Chauvin's knee on Floyd's neck (figure 9). Even if there was a moment when it was placed on the shoulder, it was on the neck when he was filmed by the bystanders.

Minneapolis police guidelines allow for neck restraints in some conditions, but only for suspects who are actively resisting. Floyd was not actively resisting during the several minutes that Chauvin knelt on his neck, as seen in the bystander video.

Minneapolis police guidelines also call for the suspect, after being

---

[79] Collin 2023, 1:01:46, 1:04:55.

restrained, to be turned on his side to avoid positional asphyxia. One of
the images that Collin shows of the Maximal Restraint Technique is
from a PowerPoint training presentation (figure 10). The slide contains
an image of an officer kneeling with his knee on a suspect's shoulder
and neck (so it is misplaced). That same slide also contains the following bullet points:

· Sudden cardiac arrest typically occurs immediately following a
violent struggle
· Place the subject in the recovery position to alleviate positional
asphyxia[80]

Chauvin did not place Floyd in the recovery position (on his side),
despite prompting by one of the other officers on the scene.

All of this suffices to conclude that Chauvin violated police department guidelines.

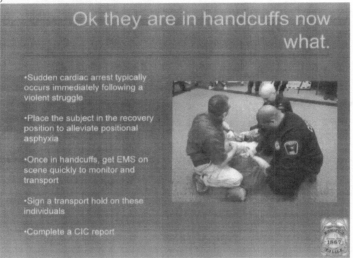

Figure 10

(4) Was Chauvin culpable for Floyd's death?

Yes. To be culpable for someone's death, it is not necessary that one
kill the person *deliberately* or *knowingly*. One may become culpable by
taking actions that unreasonably *risk* causing death. That was the case
with Chauvin and Floyd. Death was a somewhat improbable but not
bizarre result of Chauvin's excess use of force. Given Floyd's com-

---

[80] Collin 2023, 1:04:55.

plaints about difficulty breathing, plus his appearance of being under the influence of drugs, Chauvin could have anticipated that Floyd would be at elevated risk of cardiac arrest and/or asphyxia. Since there was no need to kneel on his neck for an extended period of time and this created a predictably elevated risk of death, Chauvin is to blame for George Floyd's death.

In the wake of Floyd's death, many states passed laws banning or restricting chokeholds and other neck restraints. Twenty-five states now have bans or serious restrictions on choke holds. The other states should follow suit.

(5) Was it murder?

If Chauvin killed Floyd *accidentally*, why was he convicted of murder? Doesn't murder require intent to kill? Was this an error by prosecutors and the jury, perhaps influenced by fear of riots?

Legally speaking, no, it wasn't an error. Chauvin was charged under the "felony murder" rule. This is a legal rule whereby, if you commit a felony and someone dies as a result, you can be charged with murder, even if you did not intend the death; it is enough that the *other* felony was intentional. In this case, Chauvin's excess use of force was classified as assault, which is a felony. Since Chauvin intentionally assaulted Floyd, and this assault caused Floyd's death, Chauvin was guilty of felony murder under the law.

One can certainly question the justice of the felony murder rule. It enables criminals with the same degree of blameworthiness, who acted in the same way in indistinguishable circumstances, to get very different punishments as a result of luck. Be that as it may, the felony murder rule has been in effect for centuries, many non-police defendants have been charged and convicted under this rule, and it applied to the facts of Derek Chauvin's case. So as far as that goes, Chauvin was treated like a normal defendant.

Chauvin's sentence (22.5 years) initially appears excessive for an accidental (though culpable) killing. The typical sentence for felony murder is 12.5 years for a first offense. In this case, the judge held that an especially harsh sentence was justified in view of two aggravating factors: (i) that Chauvin had abused a position of public trust (the position of police officer) and (ii) that Chauvin had killed Floyd in an unusually cruel way (relative to typical felony murder cases). These are reasonable arguments, though there is room for debate about what was the just sentence for this crime. This appears to be a rare case in which government agents were treated according to the same rules that would be applied to anyone else.

Lessons

(1) Are the police angels or devils?

Some right-wing pundits appear to believe that all homicides by police are justified. Some left-wing pundits appear to believe that all homicides by police are *un*justified. Both of these are foolish, dogmatic positions. The truth, obviously, is that some police homicides are justified and others are unjustified—and distinguishing the two requires careful attention to *the factual evidence in the specific case.* One cannot judge a case based on the identities of the people involved. Knowing the race and occupation of two people does not tell you whether the one was justified in killing the other. Justice is inherently individual.

(2) Pundit vs. jury

Fortunately, we have a pretty good system for determining guilt or innocence: the jury trial. Juries of unbiased citizens must spend many hours listening to all the evidence and arguments on both sides of a case, then deliberate until they reach a unanimous verdict. Political pundits don't have to do any of that; they can just say whatever pops into their heads, whenever they want. Therefore, if a political pundit disagrees with a jury verdict, the pundit is probably wrong.

(3) The role of race

Eric Garner, Breonna Taylor, and George Floyd were all African Americans, and all were killed by white cops. Can we therefore conclude that their deaths were due to racism?

Again, no. One can't conclude "racism" merely by looking at the races of the perpetrator and the victim of a crime. In these three cases, no one presented any evidence that race had anything to do with why those individuals were killed.

"But then," you might wonder, "are we to believe it is just a *coincidence* that all the victims were black and all the perpetrators white?"

No, it isn't a coincidence; it is a selection effect. In fact, the police kill far more whites than blacks.[81] Here are some more unarmed people who were killed by police recently:

Timothy Randall
Tyler Woodburn
Matthew Mitchell
John Bomar
Richard Poulin
Joseph Nagle
Jeffrie Glover
Clesslynn Crawford
Nicholas Rodin

Those are all just from the year 2022.[82] I bet you don't know any of those names. Why not? Because they are all white people, so their deaths did not contribute to a progressive narrative about racism in America, and so they did not make the national news.

There is a problem of police using excessive force. But it isn't a racial problem. The appearance of a race-specific problem is an illusion created by media and activist indifference to non-black victims.

---

[81] See discussion in Ch. 7.
[82] Mapping Police Violence 2023.

Part II: Racial Myths

The loudest strand of contemporary progressivism is what is sometimes called "woke" ideology or "wokism", whose central tenet is that American society is filled with unjust prejudice and that this is among the worst problems, if not *the* worst problem, facing our society. The two most influential branches of wokism are feminism and "anti-racism". In this part of the book, we discuss "anti-racism". (I use scare quotes because I do not think this movement actually combats racism.) This is an ideology which holds that America is a deeply racist society and that this racism is the main cause of black disadvantage in America.

7 Racist Police Shootings

Myth

Many unarmed black people are shot by American police every year. Blacks are regularly killed by police due to racism.

Examples

It is hard to find published sources that directly state the first part of the myth, concerning unarmed black men, though there are many sources that devote extensive attention to police shootings of unarmed black men while ignoring victims from other races.

In 2021, *Skeptic* magazine published survey results indicating people's answers to the following questions:

Q1: "If you had to guess, how many unarmed Black men were killed by police in 2019?" (Available answers: About 10, about 100, about 1000, about 10,000, more than 10,000.)

Q2: "If you had to guess, in 2019 what percentage of people killed by police were Black?" (Respondents could choose any number from 0 to 100.) [83]

In answer to Q1, 29% of people answered "about 1,000" or more (1,000: 19%; 10,000: 6%; over 10,000: 4%). In answer to Q2, the average estimate was 48%.

This doesn't tell the whole story, though. The answers differed greatly by political orientation. Respondents who self-identified as "liberal" or "very liberal" were much less accurate than moderates or conservatives. Among liberal or very liberal respondents, nearly half (46%) thought that the number of unarmed black men killed by police was about 1,000 or more. This same group on average estimated that

---

[83] Saide & McCaffree 2021a. See also Skeptic Research Center 2021.

58% of people killed by police were black.

Misconceptions were correlated with trust in the media—people who reported greater trust in the media were more misinformed about police shootings.[84] This may be because media sources give misleading impressions about this particular issue. Alternately, it may be because "racist police shootings are a huge problem" and "the mainstream media are trustworthy" both have independent appeal to liberals.

Concerning the second part of the myth, that police killings show racial bias: The main argument for this is that a *higher percentage* of the people killed by the police are black than the percentage of the general population who are black:

> Police disproportionately shoot and kill black Americans ... black Americans were twice as likely to be shot and killed by police officers, compared with their representation in the population.
>
> —ABC News

> Black people, who account for 13 percent of the U.S. population, accounted for 27 percent of those fatally shot and killed by police in 2021.... That means Black people are twice as likely as white people to be shot and killed by police officers.
>
> —NBC News

> #BlackLivesMatter was founded in 2013 in response to the acquittal of Trayvon Martin's murderer. [...] We are working for a world where Black lives are no longer systematically targeted for demise.
>
> —Black Lives Matter website[85]

Reality

There *is* evidence that American police are unnecessarily violent.[86] However, that is not my topic here. My topic here is whether police violence shows a widespread *racial bias*.

(1) How often are unarmed black people killed by police?

Start with the number of unarmed black people killed by police. Again, half of liberal respondents estimated this at 1,000 or more for 2019. The correct figure was 36. (The *total* number of blacks killed by police

---

[84] Saide & McCaffree 2021b.
[85] Sources: Schumaker 2020; Bunn 2022; BLM website (a).
[86] Huemer 2021, §7.2.

in that year was 286, of whom just 36 were unarmed, 32 men and 4 women.) In the same year, police killed 54 unarmed white people (46 men and 8 women).[87]

Does this still represent a major problem? Bear in mind that this was in a country of 330 million, which included 47 million blacks. It would not be shocking if, of 47 million black people, a total of 36, despite being unarmed, did something sufficiently threatening to cause them to be killed by police. In any case, the risk of this happening to a given black person is extremely small; they are literally more likely to be struck by lightning.[88]

(2) The racial disproportion

Let's turn to the total numbers of blacks and other Americans (whether armed or unarmed) killed by police. The statistics in the quotes above are accurate, based on the best available data: Blacks comprise about an eighth of the population but a *quarter* of the police shooting victims. Hence, you are more likely to be shot if black than otherwise. Does this indicate racism?

Consider another, even more shocking disproportion: Males make up only 50% of the population but *95.5%* of the police shooting victims.[89] Men are thus *twenty-one times* more likely to be shot by police than women. One *could* claim that this indicates an extraordinary degree of sexism, many times worse than the racism shown by police departments.

But most of us would reject this inference. To determine whether the shooting statistics indicate sexism, we must first consider such things as: How often do police make contact with male suspects? How

---

[87] Mapping Police Violence 2023. These numbers may be undercounts due to underreporting. Incidentally, conservative activist Charlie Kirk incorrectly reported the number of unarmed blacks killed by police as *eight*, apparently based on an incomplete database (Stellino 2020).

[88] 400-500 Americans are struck by lightning per year, and 79% of the fatalities are among men (Dayton n.d.). I don't have lightning strike statistics by race, but assuming that lightning is race neutral, the average black person's risk of being struck should be about 1.3×10^{-6}, while their probability of being unarmed and shot by police is about 7.7×10^{-7}. For black *men*, the probability of a lightning strike is probably about 2.2×10^{-6} (given that men are about four times more likely to be struck than women), while the probability of being shot by police while unarmed is about 1.5×10^{-6} (32 out of 22 million black men).

[89] Statista 2023b.

often do men commit violent crimes, compared to women? How often do men commit violence against police officers, compared to women? Those questions would be relevant because they are proxies for the tendency of men to engage in threatening behavior toward police of the sort that could plausibly lead to a violent police response even in the absence of sexism. As it turns out, about 88% of all murderers and *nearly all* cop-killers are men. In 2013-14, for example, there were 66 men who killed police officers and *one* woman who aided her husband in killing a pair of police officers.[90]

This would undercut the narrative of anti-male bias among police. Police may well be killing too many men, but we cannot infer *sexism*, since the gender disparity can as well be explained by greater numbers of aggressive male suspects as compared to females.

An exactly parallel point applies to the racial disparity. To assess the amount of racial bias, we need to consider such things as number of police contacts, violent crime rates, and rates of violence against police officers.

Begin with numbers of police contacts. Usually, when police make contact with a suspect, this is because a member of the community has called the police to report some apparent criminal behavior. These community members usually give a description of a suspect whom they believe to be committing or about to commit a crime. As it turns out, the racial composition of the group of suspects reported to the police by members of the community matches the racial composition of people shot by the police, leaving no evidence of racial bias on the part of the police.[91]

You could hypothesize that racism by *members of the community* causes them to disproportionately report black people to the police. But the simpler explanation is that the higher rates at which black individuals are reported to the police are due to the higher *crime rates* by black individuals.

Apropos of that, recall that, per the quotations above, blacks comprise about 13% of the U.S. population but 27% of police shooting victims. However, blacks also comprise about *40%* of murderers in the U.S., and *43%* of cop-killers.[92] Therefore, just as in the case of the

---

[90] Homicide statistics: FBI 2020. Cop killers: Kutner 2015.
[91] Selby et al. 2016.
[92] Homicide data: FBI 2020. Cop-killers: Lee 2015.

gender disparity, the racial disparity in police shootings could plausibly be explained by a disparity in threatening behavior. It's still *possible* that racism plays a role, just as it's still possible that sexism plays a role, but the statistics give us *no reason* to posit racism or sexism. If anything, the statistics suggest a *pro-black* bias by police, since the rate at which blacks are shot by police is *disproportionately low* compared to the rate at which black people kill police officers.

(3) Experimental evidence

The above sort of evidence has limitations. The database of homicides committed by the police does not have information about all the aspects of suspects and their behavior that may have influenced a decision to use lethal force. In brief, one cannot tell how threateningly each suspect was behaving.

Experimental evidence may address this shortcoming, since a laboratory experiment can control essentially all plausibly relevant factors other than race. This was the task of Lois James et al.'s (2016) study, which observed police behavior in simulators of the sort used during police training.[93] The simulations involve video enactments, using actors, of the sorts of scenarios that police often encounter that have a risk of leading to a shooting. Sometimes, the suspect in the video pulls a gun and shoots at the camera; other times, the suspect pulls out an innocuous object such as a wallet. As the scenario unfolds, officers must decide whether and when to draw their guns and shoot at the suspect in the video. For the experiment, officers were equipped with Glock 22's (like those used in many police departments), modified to emit infrared light rather than shooting real bullets, to detect when and where officers had shot.

Researchers prepared two versions of each of several scenarios: a version using a white actor, and a version using a black actor with everything else held the same. The purpose was to test whether officers would be quicker to shoot at black suspects.

This sort of experiment admittedly has its own limitations. Since officers know that they are not in any genuine danger, they may not react in the same way that they would in real life (even though they were instructed to do so). Nevertheless, the simulations were highly realistic, subjects showed signs of immersion, and simulations of this

---

[93] James et al. 2016.

kind are widely taken to be the best way of preparing for real-world encounters. If officers were quicker to shoot black suspects in the simulations, progressive commentators would surely be quick to cite this as powerful evidence of racism, and rightly so.

In fact, the *reverse* turned out to be the case. In the scenarios in which the suspect pulls a gun, officers took 1.1 seconds to shoot if the suspect was white, and *1.3* seconds if the suspect was black. In scenarios in which the suspect pulls out a harmless object, officers wrongly shot the suspect 14% of the time if the suspect was white, and only 1% of the time if the suspect was black. This dovetails with the other evidence cited above for a pro-black or anti-white bias in police shootings.

Objections

(1) How could there possibly be an anti-white bias in police shootings? That's ridiculous.

Reply: The most likely explanation is an effect of media coverage and public attention. In recent years, enormous attention has focused on shootings of black suspects, which causes problems for the police department and the individual officers involved. By contrast, the other three quarters of police shootings, which are of non-black suspects, receive almost no attention. Thus, police officers are much more reluctant to shoot black suspects than suspects of other races.

This is supported by the statements of actual police officers. In 2015, a white Birmingham police detective was attacked by a black suspect, pistol whipped with his own gun, and left unconscious and bleeding on the ground while the suspect drove away. The detective later explained that the suspect was able to do this in part because the detective had hesitated to use force. "A lot of officers are being too cautious because of what's going on in the media," he said. "I hesitated because I didn't want to be in the media like I am right now." Another cop in the same police department explained that police are "walking on eggshells because of how they're scrutinized in the media".[94]

Perhaps this is as it should be—if you could be deterred from using deadly force against someone by fear of your actions' being scrutinized, then you probably should not use deadly force against that person. Granted, this entails some risk to officers, as the above case illustrates.

---

[94] Valencia 2015.

But perhaps the risk to officers is worth it to reduce the risk of unnecessarily killing civilians.

In that case, the problem is that the media *don't* scrutinize shootings of white, Asian, Hispanic, or other non-black suspects. Fewer people would probably be killed if they did.

(2) This doesn't address all other forms of racial bias in policing or the justice system.

Reply: That's right, it doesn't. The above discussion is only about homicides by police. This is worth addressing because it is the most momentous action taken by police or the justice system, as well as the most discussed. This issue was the cause of the protests and riots in many American cities in the last few years.

The hypothesis cited in reply to Objection 1 is consistent with the possibility that other aspects of the justice system show more racial bias, since they are much less scrutinized by the media and the public. If police rough up a suspect on the street, or a judge hands out an overly harsh punishment, there will normally be no public scrutiny. This is also consistent with Roland Fryer's well-known (2019) study, which found that police are more likely to use *nonlethal* force against minority members than against whites, but *not* more likely to use *lethal* force.[95] An obvious explanation for the difference in nonlethal force is that police officers engage in racial profiling.

---

[95] Fryer 2019. For a list of studies of racial bias in policing and the justice system, see Balko 2020. For a contrary view, see Langan 1994.

8 Implicit Bias

Myth

Psychology has proved that most people have implicit racist attitudes that cause them to unfairly discriminate. These biases can be addressed through implicit bias training.

Background

In the 1960's and earlier, racism in America was explicit. Nobody had to *argue* that there was racism, because the racists, which at one time included nearly everyone, would tell you openly that they thought whites were superior to blacks. Laws explicitly prohibited whites and blacks from intermarrying, eating in the same restaurant, or attending the same schools. Other laws tried to stop blacks from voting without explicitly forbidding it.

The Civil Rights Movement of the 1960's fought this racism, and won—all of those laws were repealed, new laws prohibiting racial and other discrimination were passed, and virtually everyone with a public voice came to agree that racism was wrong. The change has been so dramatic that the laws and commonplace sentiments of the past are shocking to modern eyes.

It took longer for people's personal, non-political attitudes to change. Though interracial marriage had been legalized nationwide by a 1967 Supreme Court decision,[96] in 1990, 63% of non-black Americans still said they would be opposed to a close relative marrying a black person. By 2016, that number had dropped to 14%.[97]

What do you do when your political movement wins? You could celebrate and then move on. Or ... you could find ways of denying that

---

[96] *Loving v. Virginia*, 388 U.S. 1 (1967).
[97] Livingston and Brown 2017.

you really won, so you can continue the movement.

Enter the concept of "implicit bias". This is the idea that even people who sincerely affirm ideals of equality have *unconscious* prejudices, which can subtly influence their behavior, making them discriminate against minorities without realizing it.

This bias is thought to be measurable using the Implicit Association Test (IAT; sometimes mistakenly called the "Implicit Attitude Test").[98] In this test, subjects are sequentially shown images, each of which is associated with either (a) white people, (b) black people, (c) goodness, or (d) badness. For instance, they might see (a) a picture of a white person, (b) a map of Africa, (c) the word "happiness", or (d) the word "pain". (The test can also of course be done using other categories to detect other kinds of associations; these examples are just to illustrate how you could detect implicit racism.)

In one condition, the subject is supposed to press one button whenever he sees something that is related to *either* white people or goodness, and a different button for things that are either black-person-related or badness-related. You're supposed to press the buttons as quickly as you can. This tests the ability to form associations between "white" and "good", and between "black" and "bad".

In another condition, the subject is supposed to press one button whenever he sees something that is related to either black people or goodness, and a different button when he sees something that is either white-related or badness-related. Again, you press the buttons as quickly as you can.

Most people make more errors and take longer to press the buttons in the latter condition, when they are asked to associate *blackness* with goodness, as compared to the condition that asks them to associate *whiteness* with goodness. The reaction time difference is generally in the neighborhood of 0.2 seconds. Many believe that this reflects bias against blacks. Since this result often occurs even for those with explicit egalitarian beliefs, it is thought to indicate *unconscious* bias.

Millions of people have now taken the IAT, many companies are giving workshops to employees to make them aware of implicit bias and how to fight it, and some courts in America now give instructions on implicit bias to jurors.

---

[98] See Greenwald et al.'s seminal (1998) article.

Examples

The pervasiveness of prejudice, affecting 90 to 95 percent of people, was demonstrated today in a Seattle press conference at the University of Washington by psychologists who developed a new tool that measures the unconscious roots of prejudice. [...] [T]he test has been used to show the unconscious roots of prejudice toward a variety of racial, ethnic and religious groups, as well as to illuminate automatic gender and age discrimination.

—University of Washington News

How is it, then, that the data continues to show results [in the justice system] unduly differentiated by race or other group-identity? [...] Emerging social science offers a partial answer as it turns from a focus on *explicit* bias [...] to a focus on *implicit* bias, which is unconsciously generated [...] While these implicit associations are made without our express knowledge, and often contrary to our honestly held beliefs, they nevertheless influence our responses and decisions.

—American Bar Association

[T]he automatic White preference expressed on the Race IAT is now established as signaling discriminatory behavior.

—Banaji and Greenwald, psychologists & IAT pioneers

[I]t is reasonable to conclude not only that implicit bias is a cause of Black disadvantage but also that it plausibly plays a greater role than does explicit bias in explaining the discrimination that contributes to Black disadvantage.

—Banaji and Greenwald

Allowing implicit biases and negative stereotypes to run rampant in the workplace is harmful and very likely to reduce the diversity of the workforce.

—Description from corporate DEI training website

When people ask if [implicit bias training] works, I can say without question that it works better than saying nothing.

—Jeffery Robinson, deputy legal director, ACLU[99]

---

[99] Sources: Schwarz 1998; American Bar Association n.d.; Banaji and Greenwald 2013, p. 47; Banaji and Greenwald 2013, appendix 2; Ahmad 2017; Gayla 2017.

Reality

(1) What can we learn from the gender IAT?

If there is one thing that progressives know, it is that America is prejudiced against women and racial minorities. The race IAT is cited to demonstrate our preference for whites over blacks. The IAT has also been used to show that we naturally associate women with the home and men with work.

What happens if the race IAT is modified to replace race with gender, so that people are alternately asked to associate men and women with goodness and badness? It is interesting that one almost never hears about this version of the IAT.

The reason one does not hear about this may be that it does not give the "correct" result, i.e., the result predicted by progressive ideology. The gender IAT indicates that people have an automatic preference for *women over men:* On average, people take longer to press the button and make more errors when they are asked to associate men with good things and women with bad things, as compared with the condition where they are asked to associate women with good things and men with bad things.[100] The IAT also shows that people more readily associate males with violence and threats.[101]

In other words, precisely the methodology that is supposed to demonstrate that Americans are prejudiced against blacks implies, when applied to the categories of male versus female, that Americans are also prejudiced against males. Indeed, the effect is about 50% *stronger* for gender than for race, apparently indicating that anti-male prejudice is stronger than anti-black prejudice.[102]

Another IAT experiment investigated the effects of combinations of categories. IAT's were used to measure subjects' implicit positive or negative associations with images of particular people. The people in the images differed visibly in age, race, sex, and social class. The researchers found that subjects tended to have more positive associations with whites, women, and upper-class people. They also found that

---

[100] Carpenter 2000; Nosek 2005.

[101] Rudman and Goodwin (2004) find that men show an overall slight preference for men, while women show a much stronger preference for women, though both sexes associate men with threat.

[102] Nosek 2005, p. 572.

the effect of sex dominated the other effects—i.e., the gender of the person in the image was a much stronger predictor of people's positive or negative associations than the other factors.[103]

Progressives thus face a dilemma: Either the IAT does not measure prejudice, or our society is even more prejudiced against men than it is against blacks.

(2) What else might it mean?

The conventional interpretation is that the IAT measures a person's degree of unconscious prejudice. However, psychologists have thought of a number of alternative interpretations. One alternative is that the IAT measures a person's *awareness of* stereotypes and social disadvantage.

Uhlmann et al. tested this by introducing subjects to two fictional groups, the Noffians and the Fasites, where the Fasites were associated with privilege and the Noffians with victimization.[104] This was enough to induce reaction-time differences on the IAT so that subjects scored as having "implicit bias" against Noffians. Since the subjects had no knowledge about Noffians other than that they were an oppressed group, it is plausible that the IAT scores merely indicate a perception of Noffians as *badly treated*, rather than reflecting actual antipathy toward Noffians.

Alternately, it could be that people actually started to dislike Noffians merely because Noffians were oppressed (perhaps we tend to dislike all oppressed groups). In that case, to reduce prejudice against oppressed groups, we would probably have to stop associating them with oppression, which would require *not* talking so much about how oppressed these groups are.

(3) Is it reliable?

If you're trying to test some stable characteristic, you want a test that, when the same group of people take it and then retake it, generally gives the same results both times as to who scores higher than whom. If I take an IQ test on Tuesday and then again on Friday, my Tuesday score should be a strong predictor of my Friday score.[105]

---

[103] Connor et al. 2023.

[104] Uhlmann et al. 2006.

[105] My Friday score need not be *the same* as my Tuesday score; perhaps I improve with practice. But the *ordering* of people in terms of IQ should not vary much as a

In psychology, "test-retest reliability" refers to this tendency of a test to give similar results when taken by the same person, i.e., the correlation between a person's scores on different occasions. Reliability varies from 0 (scores are completely unrelated) to 1 (the first score perfectly predicts the second score). In statistics, a reliability of 0.8 or more is considered good, while reliability under 0.5 is considered unacceptable.[106]

The test-retest reliability of the IAT in general, averaged across 20 studies, is about 0.5.[107] The reliability of the *race* IAT in particular, averaged across 13 studies, is about 0.33, suggesting that this test does not measure any stable psychological trait.[108]

(4) Does it predict discrimination?

It is common in psychology and social science for studies to contradict each other—one study finds that A contributes to B, another that A inhibits B, and another that A and B are unrelated. The reasons why this happens are interesting but too complex to discuss right now.[109] But because of this phenomenon, it is particularly useful to look at *meta-analyses*, articles that review the findings of many different studies on a particular question to try to determine the overall conclusion supported by the literature.

A few meta-analyses have been published on the subject of the IAT's ability to predict discrimination. Greenwald et al. reviewed research reports pertaining to how scores on various versions of the IAT were related to various forms of "discrimination". (I use scare quotes because not all the measures were really about discrimination; see below.) They found that IAT scores in general were positively correlated with measures of "discrimination". For the race IAT in particular, the correlation was 0.24—meaning that if you show "implicit bias" per the test, then you're a little bit more likely to engage in

---

group of people retake the test.

[106] Statistics How-To n.d.

[107] Lane et al. 2007, p. 70. They try to spin this by focusing attention specifically on IAT's for *self-esteem*, which show acceptable reliability.

[108] I averaged Gawronski et al.'s (2017, p. 303) own reliability estimate with the numbers they report from other studies (p. 308). Weighting according to study size does not significantly change the average.

[109] For discussion, see Alexander 2014; Huemer 2022, §18.3.

"discriminatory behavior".[110]

Explanatory note: Correlation coefficients like this are used in social science to express how closely two variables are connected, i.e., to what degree knowing the value of one lets you predict the value of the other. Correlations can vary from 1 to -1 (negative correlations indicate that as one variable increases, the other tends to *decrease*). Roughly speaking, a correlation of x means that x^2 of the variation in one variable can be predicted from variations in the other, so a correlation of 0.24 means that 5.8% (=0.24^2) of the variance in one variable can be predicted from the other variable. In social science, it is very hard to find correlations above 0.5, except for variables that are pretty much the same thing (like a person's score on the same test on different days). So a correlation of only 0.24, while it sounds low, is not unusual for this area of research.

To continue: A few years later, Oswald et al. conducted an updated and improved meta-analysis of IAT's used to predict "discrimination", which included some additional studies that Greenwald et al. did not have access to and corrected some omissions and mistakes by Greenwald et al. Oswald et al.'s updated meta-analysis found that the race IAT has only a *0.15* correlation with "discrimination". This is really very small; furthermore, this correlation was biased upward by the inclusion of functional neuroimaging studies in which the measure of "discrimination" consisted in having *brain scans* that look different, without any outward discriminatory *behavior*.[111] By the way, measures of *explicit* bias (where you just ask people about their attitudes) did about as well at predicting "discrimination". The authors conclude: "[T]he IAT provides little insight into who will discriminate against whom, and provides no more insight than explicit measures of bias."[112]

A few years later, a third meta-analysis was conducted, by Carlsson and Agerström, who decided to be more precise about what counts as discrimination. The previous analyses (both Greenwald and Oswald) had been very generous about "discrimination", including, e.g., brain scans as indicating discrimination even with no behavioral manifestation. Some of the included studies also used political preferences as measures of discrimination, e.g., subjects' views about Barack Obama,

---

[110] Greenwald et al. 2009, p. 24. This was based on 32 samples of people. They also report a correlation of 0.27 for IAT's *in general*, which includes IAT's used to predict consumer preferences, political choices, and various other things.
[111] Oswald et al. 2013, p. 182.
[112] Oswald et al. 2013, p. 188.

which is obviously dubious. Carlsson and Agerström thus decided to only include for analysis studies that measured paradigmatic discrimination—for instance, rating white students better in academic ability than otherwise similar black students, or being more cooperative with white partners than black partners in a trust game. They found 13 samples in the literature for which both implicit bias and discriminatory (no scare quotes this time!) behavior had been tested. For this group of samples, Carlsson and Agerström again found a tiny correlation of 0.15 between IAT scores and discrimination.[113]

More importantly, however, Carlsson and Agerström found this correlation unimportant because the *total amount* of discrimination discovered in the studies taken as a whole was tiny and statistically insignificant. A few studies found anti-black discrimination, a few found *anti-white* discrimination, and most found no statistically significant overall discrimination. As Carlsson and Agerström conclude, "there is no evidence of reliable discrimination to be predicted by the IAT. Indeed, the average effect of discrimination is zero, and the results are widely inconsistent between different studies."[114]

This does not prove that there is no discrimination in society. But we should at least question whether there is really very widespread, severe discrimination in society, given the difficulty of detecting it in controlled environments.

(5) Does implicit bias training work?

Finally, Forscher et al. conducted a meta-analysis of 492 studies bearing on the effects of procedures to change people's implicit biases. They found that measures of implicit bias *can* be changed. For example, exposing subjects to images of admired black people and despised white people can influence their scores on a race IAT. However, there was no evidence that changing implicit bias measures had any effect either on people's explicit attitudes or on their behavior. The authors conclude, "We found no evidence that changes in implicit measures mediate changes in explicit measures and behavior."[115]

My conclusion: Implicit bias training is snake oil. There is no reason to think it produces any benefits.

---

[113] Carlsson and Agerström 2016, p. 284.
[114] Carlsson and Agerström 2016, pp. 285.
[115] Forscher et al. 2019, p. 541.

The Appeal of the IAT

It's easy to see why the theory of implicit bias has taken the country by storm. It plays into the woke worldview in which minorities continue to be held back by rampant racism. It provides the perfect explanation for why we don't seem to *see* or *feel* this racism on a daily basis, why by all obvious measures racism *seems* to have drastically declined. At the same time, the claim that you're a racist is rendered more palatable by the assurance that this is all unconscious and outside your direct control. It helps that the theory comes with an easily administered, picturesque, "scientific test" by which almost anyone can supposedly measure their own racism. Upon taking the test, one is assured that *science proves* that you have hidden racism. Since actual social scientists have more or less said this, the people offering implicit bias training probably do not even think that they are being deceptive. In short, the theory of implicit bias and the IAT are tailor-made for the woke era.

Social scientists love the IAT, because it is both easy to administer and incredibly flexible, seemingly enabling one to study all kinds of hidden attitudes and associations. Social psychologists tend to be overwhelmingly left-wing,[116] so it doesn't hurt that some versions of the IAT play into left-wing views about modern society. Social psychologists and social scientists are loathe to criticize the test since to do so would be disloyal to the cause.

Journalist Olivia Goldhill has written about the limitations of the IAT. She reports that Greenwald, one of the test's leading proponents, explicitly discouraged her from writing on that subject. "Debates about scientific interpretation belong in scientific journals, not popular press", he told her[117]—though he seemingly has no objections to *positive* coverage of the IAT in the popular press and has himself co-authored a popular book on the subject with Mahzarin Banaji.[118]

Journalist Jesse Singal has written a long and trenchant piece on the limitations of the IAT. He reports that in correspondence, Banaji indicated that she was not interested in hearing criticisms from non-experts. She characterized critics of the IAT as "a small group of aggrieved individuals who think that Black people have it easy in American society and that the IAT work might make their lives easier",

---

[116] See Duarte et al. 2015.
[117] Goldhill 2017.
[118] Banaji and Greenwald 2013.

she claimed that "the IAT scares people who say things like 'look, the water fountains are desegregated, what's your problem'", and she speculated about the psychological infirmities of her critics: "the fetish with Black-White race relations in some folks is something that science won't be able to answer because it seems not to be about the evidence. It will need to be dealt with by them in the presence of their psycho-therapists or church leaders."[119]

If you're wondering how deeply scientifically flawed ideas could come to be widely propounded by smart, highly-trained social scientists, the answer, at least in this case, is: politics. The boosters of the IAT see themselves as fighters for the cause of social justice. Almost everyone else in their field is on the same side politically, so they don't want to question an idea that seems to support the cause. They fear to give comfort to the enemy (i.e., conservatives); as well, they fear that any criticisms of the idea would be met with personal attacks, *as they in fact have been.*

All of that is part of the story of how the IAT and the theory of widespread implicit racism has become entrenched in our society. It also explains why it is impossible to trust scientists on politically relevant questions. The very fact that scientists are concerned with public opinion is precisely why the public should not trust them.

---

[119] Singal 2017.

9 Stereotype Threat

Myth

Stereotype threat is a major cause of cognitive performance differences between demographic groups.

Background

Different demographic groups often show different academic performance, both in classes and in standardized tests. Asians tend to outperform whites, who outperform Hispanics, who outperform blacks.[120] Girls tend to outperform boys in language abilities and in school in general, though boys slightly outperform girls in some mathematics tests.[121] These sorts of differences are a cause of concern to progressives, especially the race differences, which have proved recalcitrant in recent years and which seem to align with racial stereotypes that progressives find offensive.[122] Black-white test score differences are typically in the neighborhood of one standard deviation, meaning that an average white student scores better than about 84% of blacks.[123]

As you might guess, there is no consensus on the cause of these

---

[120] Jencks and Philips 1998; Reeves 2017.

[121] Reeves and Smith 2022; Ganley 2018; Brown and Alexandersen 2020. The mathematics gap (including which sex is favored) varies by country, by state in the U.S., and by the type of mathematics test, e.g., boys are favored with spatial reasoning tasks, tests of material not covered in school, and more advanced material, while girls do better on the rest.

[122] Though progressives tend to assume that stereotypes are inaccurate, academic research generally finds the opposite: Commonly-held beliefs about particular groups of people tend to be roughly accurate and are more likely to *understate* group differences than to overstate them (Jussim et al. 2015).

[123] Roth et al. (2001, pp. 310-12) estimate the IQ gap at 1.1 standard deviations, which slightly exceeds the gap for standardized scholastic tests such as the SAT.

differences. Some conservatives, for instance, blame the breakdown of the traditional family structure and rise of out-of-wedlock births, which have been much more pronounced among black Americans.[124] Others argue that black America has developed an oppositional culture that devalues academic achievement.[125] For progressives, the ideal explanation would be that the differences are caused by racism and sexism. The stereotypes don't reflect an independently existing reality; rather, the stereotypes *create* the differences in performance.

Enter the concept of "stereotype threat". This is the idea that the existence of a negative stereotype causes people to perform worse, particularly in conditions that make the stereotype more salient to the individual.[126] For instance, if you remind a black person of their race before giving them a test of academic performance, it is said, that person will tend to perform worse than they otherwise would. If you remind a girl of her gender before giving her a math test, she too will tend to perform worse.

Many psychological studies have found effects in this neighborhood. Many people now believe, because of this research, that the existence of stereotypes is a major factor, perhaps the sole factor, in explaining the academic underperformance of blacks and the mathematical underperformance of girls in some tests. This is a favorite topic of DEI trainers, and many universities now give instruction about the problem of stereotype threat to faculty members.[127]

Examples

> When activated, stereotype threat causes students to perform worse on assignments than they might otherwise. This reaction is neurobiological in nature—the perceived threat stimulates cortisol production in the brain having the effect of reducing the available working memory for completing tasks. Stereotype threat affects members of any group about whom there exists some negative stereotype.
> —Science Education Research Center, Carleton College

Stereotype threat is understood to be a primary cause of achieve-

---

[124] Moynihan 1965; Krumholz 2019.
[125] Fryer 2006; McWhorter 2014.
[126] Steele and Aronson 1995.
[127] University of Colorado Boulder n.d.; Rutgers University n.d.; Brown University n.d.

ment gaps for students of color and female students in STEM fields.

       —Reinert Center for Transformative Teaching
and Learning, St. Louis University

In several experiments, [Steele and Aronson] showed that Black undergraduates performed more poorly on standardized tests than White students when their race was emphasized. When race was not emphasized, however, Black students performed better and equivalently with White students.

       —Reducingstereotypethreat.org

Claude Steele has spent several years investigating the large score gap between whites and blacks on standardized tests. ... In research conducted at Stanford, Steele administered a difficult version of the Graduate Record Exam... Blacks who believed the test was merely a research tool did the same as Whites. But Blacks who believed the test measured their abilities did half as well.

       —PBS *Frontline* special

Similar research found that African American participants' performance was impaired by making salient the stereotype that minorities perform poorly on diagnostic standardized tests (Steele & Aronson, 1995). African Americans performed equally to their White counterparts when the diagnostic use of the test was eliminated, thus eliminating stereotype threat.

       —Oswald & Harvey (academic journal article)[128]

Reality

(1) Does stereotype threat explain the entire black-white gap?

As the last three quotations illustrate, it is common to claim that stereotype threat explains the *entire* gap in test scores between blacks and whites. This idea appears in many popular presentations of the idea, in some psychology textbooks, and even in some academic articles.[129] If true, this would be an amazing discovery that should have paved the

---

[128] Sources: Carleton College n.d.; St. Louis University n.d.; Stroessner et al. n.d.; Chandler 1999, 22:28-24:03; Oswald & Harvey 2000, p. 340. The "reducingstereotypethreat" site is the product of a team of seven academic researchers in psychology, medicine, and law.

[129] Sackett et al. (2004) cite many examples.

way for pedagogical modifications that should have nearly eliminated that gap throughout the country by now.

As you may have guessed, it is not true. The misunderstanding derives from a bar graph in Steele and Aronson's original article (figure 11).[130] The graph shows the performance of black subjects and white subjects on a test in two different conditions, labeled "diagnostic" (the condition in which they were told that the test would diagnose their intellectual abilities) and "nondiagnostic" (in which they were told the test was merely a research tool). The graph appears to show the black and white students performing almost identically in the non-diagnostic condition, with a large gap appearing only in the diagnostic condition. Thus, it appears to indicate that removing stereotype threat equalizes student scores.

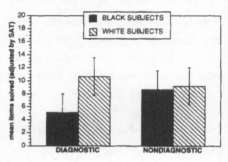

Figure 11

It is easy to overlook the caption on the *y*-axis, which reads "mean items solved (*adjusted by SAT*)" (my emphasis). What this means, as explained in the original article, is that the researchers (Steele and Aronson) asked the students what scores they had gotten on the SAT (the standardized test that students generally had to take before applying for college). The black students, on average, had lower SAT scores than the white students. The researchers then applied an *adjustment* to the black students' scores on the test they took in the lab to make up for their lower SAT scores. Essentially, the black students got a handicap. *That* is why in the non-diagnostic condition, the graph shows them equal to the white students. It does not mean that they actually scored equally to the white students; it just means that they underperformed the white students in the non-diagnostic condition of the experiment by about the same amount as they had underperformed on the SAT. By contrast, in the diagnostic condition (which was supposed to activate stereotype threat), they underperformed the white students *even more* than they had underperformed on the SAT. That is what Steele and Aronson's graph actually means.

---

[130] Steele and Aronson 1995, p. 802.

This makes a huge difference. Given this correct understanding of the experiment, it provides no support for the idea that we can eliminate the black-white gap merely by removing stereotype threat.

(2) Practical lesson: the harm of progressive ideology

Progressives tend to view the stereotype threat literature as supporting the benefits of progressive education: Progressive philosophy teaches people to reject stereotypes, which should help to reduce stereotype threat and improve the performance of minorities.

But another lesson is at least equally natural: Progressive ideology *harms* minorities by *activating* stereotype threat for them, in two ways. First, progressive teachings directly increase *awareness of stereotypes*. They seek to make everyone aware, for example, of how blacks and women have been discriminated against and what negative stereotypes our culture continues to harbor about them. According to the stereotype threat theory, it is not necessary that a person *subscribe to* negative stereotypes in order to suffer stereotype threat; it is enough that they be *aware* of the negative stereotypes.

Second, progressive ideology makes race, gender, and similar categories *salient* to people. In the stereotype threat literature, it is said that merely asking someone to identify their race can activate stereotype threat and thence hamper their cognitive performance. If this is true, then the progressive discussion of race and gender, including the frequent insistence that these are central, defining aspects of one's "identity", must be activating stereotype threat all the time. Anyone who believes the stereotype threat literature, therefore, has good reason to *oppose* progressive teachings about race, gender, and the like.

(3) The replication crisis

Before saying more about stereotype threat specifically, I need to give you some general background about replicability in psychology.

For many years, smart people have quoted results of published psychological studies as scientific facts. For example, if you spoke to someone educated in modern psychology during the past couple of decades, you might have learned that when people read words related to old age ("Florida", "old", etc.), this causes them to actually walk more slowly.[131]

---

[131] Bargh et al. 1996.

How are things like that established? Well, you have one group of people read the old-age words and a different group read other words not related to age. Then you have someone secretly time each person walking down the hallway after they leave the room. You find that, on average, the people who got the age-related words take more time.

But wait; given individual variation, that could just be due to chance. So you next do a "significance test" calculation, which tells you whether (given the amount of observed individual variation) the speed difference between the two groups is large enough that it would be unlikely to occur just by chance. By convention, in psychology, one normally uses a 5% significance level, which means that your result counts as significant only if there is less than a 5% probability that you would get a result of that magnitude purely by chance if the effect you're testing for didn't really exist. If you get a statistically significant result, then you get to publish it and then go around telling everybody that this is a real effect you discovered.

Importantly, with this method, you should expect to get positive results 5% of the time even when your hypotheses are false. That's what the 5% significance level *means*. (You could reduce the risk of false positives, but that would come at the cost of increasing the risk of false negatives, i.e., missing out on more *true* theories.)

Psychologists, social scientists, and medical researchers have been using this method for decades. Back in 2011, Cornell psychologist Daryl Bem used the method non-ironically to "establish" the existence of ESP and backwards causation (wherein an effect occurs *before* its cause).[132] He reported the results of *nine* studies that found effects in which subjects appeared to anticipate the future. The probability of his getting all these results by chance, if there really is no ESP, is supposedly about 0.000000000000000001.[133] However, subsequent attempts to replicate Bem's results failed,[134] and few people regard Bem's theory as viable. Thus, this episode served as a wake-up call to many, illustrating that one can use widely accepted methods in psychology to produce seemingly powerful support for false theories.

Then, between 2011 and 2015, a group of 270 psychologists decided to try to replicate 100 studies in psychology, all of which had been

---

[132] Bem 2011.
[133] That's 10^{-18}, multiplying the *p*-values from Bem 2011, Table 7, column 2.
[134] Galak et al. 2012.

published in leading journals in 2008.[135] Of the 100 studies, 97 had reported statistically significant results. Yet in the replication experiments, only *35* had statistically significant results, and the effects observed were on average about *half* the size reported in the original studies. *Social* psychology (the field to which stereotype threat and implicit bias research belong) fared particularly poorly: Only *25%* of social psychology results replicated.

Thus began the Replication Crisis in psychology. It now turns out that many results that psychologists have been teaching their students about for decades don't replicate. The study about age-related words making people walk slowly failed to replicate. Even famous and widely-studied phenomena are coming under suspicion. For instance, there is the phenomenon of "ego depletion", in which performing a task that requires effort leaves your willpower depleted, thus making it more difficult to resist temptations or perform other willpower-demanding tasks.[136] This phenomenon has (like stereotype threat) been the subject of over 300 studies since it was first allegedly discovered, and yet a recent replication effort using over 2000 subjects in 23 labs could not find the effect. Another effort involving 36 laboratories and over 3500 subjects around the world also found no evidence of ego depletion. The phenomenon seems to have simply vanished.[137]

How could this happen? A number of practices have developed in social psychology (and other fields) that lead to unreliable results. These include:

a. *Publication bias:* Journals are rarely interested in publishing negative results or replication studies. So if a lab looks for ego depletion and fails to find it, that result would typically go unpublished. Since academics need publications to keep their jobs and gain prestige, they find ways to get positive results.

b. *p-hacking:* Researchers can collect data, search for patterns in it, and when they find one, claim that it was their hypothesis. One in twenty hypotheses (5%) will pass a test of statistical significance even if the data is completely random. If you don't see the effect you were look-

[135] Open Science Collaboration 2015.

[136] Baumeister et al. 1998.

[137] Hagger and Chatzisarantis 2016; Vohs et al. 2021. However, Roy Baumeister, the originator of the ego depletion theory, still maintains that ego depletion is the best-replicated finding in all of social psychology (Baumeister 2022).

ing for, you can try slicing the data in different ways—maybe an effect will show up if you restrict your attention to women, or old people, or college-educated people born on Tuesdays. Introducing additional variables (age, sex, race, etc.) gives you *many* more potential hypotheses to test, which is why statistical studies often have conclusions mentioning multiple variables, e.g., "Soy may ease sleep problems in older women"[138] (notice the combination of four variables there).

c. *Conceptual replications:* In social psychology, it is common to attempt "conceptual replications", rather than strict replications. That is, one tries to test a hypothesis *in different ways*, rather than repeating the same tests that were already done. If a conceptual replication fails, the psychologist can simply conclude that *that particular way* of triggering the effect doesn't work, rather than that the effect he is looking for doesn't exist. That failure will generally go unpublished, while the psychologist moves on to other ways of trying to trigger whatever effect he is looking for.

d. *Multiple measures:* If you're looking for some effect, you can try multiple different ways of measuring it. If one of them gives you the result you want, you report that, then forget the measures that didn't work.

e. *Selective exclusion:* Sometimes, particular participants in a study should be excluded, e.g., because they did not appear to understand the instructions, they didn't fill out the entire survey they were given, or they were statistical outliers. Often, it is a matter of judgment whether someone should be excluded. In such cases, the researcher can first look at the effect that person has on the study's overall conclusion, and use that to decide whether to exclude the person.

f. *Selective termination:* Sometimes, data appears to show a pattern at the beginning, but the pattern washes out as you collect more data. To prevent this from happening, you can decide to stop data collection as soon as you have a pattern that reaches statistical significance.

One study that surveyed over 2000 academic psychologists concluded that questionable research practices of this sort are widespread in the field.[139] Given a list of ten questionable research practices, 94% of survey respondents admitted to having engaged in at least one of them

---

[138] Actual headline from Reuters Health (2010).
[139] John et al. 2012.

on at least one occasion. Respondents tended to judge their own behavior as defensible, possibly indicating a lack of understanding of how these practices undercut the reliability of the field.

The best explanation for psychology's replication crisis is that (*i*) most psychological theories are false and most proposed effects illusory, but (*ii*) questionable research practices in the field enable researchers to present seemingly compelling evidence for false theories.[140]

(4) Odd features of stereotype threat theory

I had to go through all of that to explain to you why it is not unreasonable or ad hoc to suspect that stereotype threat might be illusory, in spite of the hundreds of studies "confirming" it in the psychology literature. Even theories that have been conceptually replicated in many different ways over many years can turn out to be illusory (see ego depletion). The most cool, amazing, or interesting effects, the ones that you would most like to tell your friends about, tend to be the ones that fail to replicate. The idea that merely asking someone their race, or merely mentioning that a test measures their ability, causes a significant drop in their test score, is interesting in a way reminiscent of the fascinating idea that merely mentioning old age causes people to walk slower.

Then there are the ad hoc assumptions one must make to enable stereotype threat theory to explain the data. The underlying assumption is that, naturally enough, people fear confirming negative stereotypes about their group. Steele and Aronson hypothesize that this fear lowers people's performance, perhaps due to causing stress or distraction (though their subjects did not report any extra stress in the supposedly high-stereotype-threat condition). However, it would be equally natural to suppose that the fear of confirming stereotypes would *improve* performance by giving people a *stronger motivation* to succeed.

To explain why black subjects did worse in the "diagnostic" condition in the lab than their SAT scores would predict, Steele and Aronson must hold that stereotype threat was somehow *more* activated in the lab than it was *by the SAT*. They propose that this is true because the test in the lab was more difficult than the SAT. However, it would be at least equally natural to suppose that the students would experience greater

---

[140] For discussion, see Ioannidis 2005; Schimmack 2020.

stereotype-threat-related stress and distraction when sitting for the SAT, since they knew the SAT was actually being used to assess their suitability for college.

Steele and Aronson also posit that the stereotype threat effect is greatest for students who are most identified with the subject matter of the test, who tend to be the best students. But it would also be plausible to hypothesize that the effect would be greatest for the *worst* students, since they would have the most justified fear of performing poorly, and perhaps the best students would be unaffected since they would already know that they are excellent students.

My point is not that any of these alternative hypotheses are in fact correct. My point is that it is *indeterminate* what the underlying posit predicts. Given the existence of the central postulated causal factor— fear of confirming stereotypes—one could equally well predict the *opposite* of nearly everything that Steele and Aronson claim is explained by that factor. There is an extremely wide range of ways the data could have turned out such that one could have explained it in terms of a fear of confirming stereotypes.

Here are some more unpredictable things about how stereotype threat is said to work, from an academic review of the literature:

> [M]inority students and women (in mathematics) tend to receive lower grades than their SAT scores would predict, as compared to their nonstereotyped counterparts…[141]

This implies that people are more stereotype-threatened by *course grading* than by *the SAT*. Again, one might have predicted the reverse, since the SAT is a paradigm of a diagnostic test of intellectual ability.

> Interestingly, Nguyen & Ryan (2008) found that subtle cues triggered larger stereotype-threat effects for women in math than did blatant or moderate cues, whereas for minorities moderate cues created the largest stereotype-threat effects. These patterns, however, were reversed for strategies designed to lower stereotype-threat effects. That is, for women in math, blatant strategies aimed at eliminating threat reduced stereotype-threat effects sizes more than subtle strategies, whereas for minorities subtle strategies aimed at eliminating threat reduced effect sizes more than did blatant strategies. Nguyen & Ryan (2008) also found that stereotype-threat effects for women in math

---

[141] Spencer et al. 2016, p. 417.

were largest among women who moderately identified with math.[142]

It is unclear why any of these things should be the case. These sorts of seemingly arbitrary modifications are characteristic of cases in which researchers are over-interpreting random noise.

(5) Publication bias in the stereotype threat literature

Publication bias makes it difficult to assess the reality and magnitude of any effect in psychology. Published articles in psychology normally show positive results, whatever hypothesis the researchers were testing. But how many studies failed to find what they were looking for and therefore went unpublished?

Replicability experts have developed statistical tests for publication bias in a given body of literature. One sign of publication bias is that effects reported in the literature tend to cluster on one side of the statistical significance threshold. Starting from the "significant" side, as you approach the cutoff for statistical significance, you find more and more studies until you hit the threshold, after which suddenly the frequency of reported effects drops off a cliff. From the shape of the curve before the cutoff, you can estimate how many non-significant results there would probably be if the rest of the curve wasn't cut off by publication bias.

Another way of detecting publication bias is as follows: If you know (or can guess) the size that an effect would have and how many partici-pants are in a given study, you can calculate the probability that the study will succeed in finding the effect. Large effects can be detected with relatively small numbers of participants; for smaller effects, you need a larger number of participants to have a good chance of detecting the effect. So what you can do is to look at how big stereotype threat effects are hypothesized to be, then look at how big the studies typically are, and from that predict how often they should be succeeding in finding the effect. If the published studies find the effect more often than you would expect given their size, then you can infer that publica-tion bias is probably suppressing failed studies.

Researchers using these kinds of statistical tests have found strong evidence of publication bias in the stereotype threat literature,[143]

---

[142] Spencer et al. 2016, p. 419.
[143] Shewach et al. 2019, pp. 1524-5.

possibly inflating the rate of success from about 16% to 73%.[144] That is, probably only about 16% of the time do researchers succeed in finding stereotype threat effects, even though 73% of the *published* studies show effects.

The magnitude of the effect is probably also greatly overstated in the published literature. Most studies are small and find moderate effects; however, larger studies tend to find much smaller effects. This can be explained by random variation plus publication bias (small studies have to find a larger effect in order to qualify as statistically significant, so the ones that find small effects get excluded by publication bias). One meta-analysis found that the stereotype threat effect reported in the literature is about one quarter as large in large studies as it is in small studies (0.11 versus 0.38; note that 0.11 is a pretty minimal effect).[145]

(6) Failed replications

Psychologist Russell Warne looked for strict replication attempts in the literature on stereotype threat—that is, attempts to closely reproduce specific previous studies, as opposed to mere "conceptual replications". He found four such attempts. Only one marginally succeeded in reproducing the original effect; the other three unambiguously failed.[146]

A larger analysis by Stoet and Geary examined ten attempts to replicate an earlier study of stereotype threat in women taking mathematics exams. Seven of the replications failed; only three found the desired effect.[147]

(7) Does stereotype threat work in the real world?

Nearly all stereotype threat studies have been conducted in the lab, with conditions importantly different from real-world tests such as the SAT or college placement exams. Notably, subjects may be less motivated to perform in the lab than they are in real assessments that have an effect

---

[144] Schimmack 2022.

[145] Shewach et al. 2019, p. 1524 (reporting values of Cohen's *d*).

[146] Warne 2021.

[147] Stoet and Geary 2012, p. 97, examining replications of Spencer et al. 1999. Stoet and Geary list ten additional replication attempts, eight of which found an effect. However, they deem these latter ten attempts methodologically flawed, as all of them use a previous mathematics test score as a covariate; this is problematic if the previous score might be influenced by the effect being studied (Stoet and Geary, p. 96). Hence, they focus on studies without this flaw, of which only 30% replicate the desired effect.

on their future.

To find out whether stereotype threat occurs in real exams, researchers did an experiment using actual administrations of the AP calculus exam (taken by high school students seeking college credit for calculus). One group of 897 students was asked to list their race and gender before taking the test; another group, consisting of 755 students, was not asked these questions until after they had completed the test. Theoretically, this should have activated stereotype threat for the first group and lowered their performance. But the researchers found no differences in performance between the two groups, regardless of the test-takers' race or gender.[148] They went on to conduct an analogous study using the Computerized Placement Tests (commonly used to determine course placement for community college students). Again, asking students about their race and gender had no effect on anyone's performance. This suggests that the stereotype threat effect is mainly a laboratory phenomenon not relevant to real-world testing situations.

A 2019 meta-analysis confirmed this. Researchers looked at studies of stereotype threat effects in situations similar to real-world assessments. In this subset of studies (comprising a total of 45 samples), the stereotype threat effect was much smaller than for less realistic studies.[149] In the only four studies that used *actual* real-world assessments, the effect vanished. The authors conclude:

> [T]he size of the stereotype threat effect that can be experienced on cognitive ability tests in operational testing scenarios such as admissions tests and employment testing may range from negligible to small.[150]

---

[148] Stricker and Ward 2004. The study included 70 black students in the high-stereotype-threat condition and 52 black students in the low-threat condition. This is many more than Steele and Aronson had.

[149] $d = 0.01$ for the real-world tests and 0.14 for the realistic lab tests, compared to $d = 0.31$ for stereotype threat studies generally (Shewach et al. 2019, pp. 1521, 1523).

[150] Shewach et al. 2019, p. 1528.

10 Racist Drug Laws

Myth

America's war on drugs is fundamentally racist. A good example of this is that we punish crack cocaine more severely than powder cocaine.

Background

A central thesis of wokism is that America is "systemically racist". Roughly, this means that racism is built into institutions and laws ("systems"), rather than merely existing as attitudes in a person's mind. It is often said that social systems were established in the past with racist motives and that these systems continue to disadvantage minorities today, even without racist motives by the present-day people participating in those systems.

The notion of a "system" here is extremely vague and open-ended, so one cannot really refute a general claim of "systemic racism". One can only refute specific, concrete examples of alleged systemic racism. We also cannot here address every concrete example. But it's worth looking at one of the most popular and initially plausible examples.

The most common and most comprehensible example I have heard is that America's drug laws are racist, because they result in disproportionate imprisonment of black people. And the most common and seemingly compelling example of *that* that I have heard is the sentencing disparity between crack and powder cocaine.

These are two ways of preparing the same drug, with the same physiological effects, but crack cocaine is more popular among *black* drug users, whereas powder cocaine is more favored by white and Hispanic users. In the midst of a 1980's panic about the spread of crack cocaine, the Anti-Drug Abuse Act of 1986 was passed, creating draconian penalties for crack. Possession of 5 grams of crack incurred a minimum 5-year prison sentence; for comparison, one needed to have

500 grams of powder cocaine to merit the same sentence.[151] This 100:1 ratio is often quoted to suggest that crack sentences are vastly greater than powder cocaine sentences. A later law passed in 2010 (the Fair Sentencing Act) reduced but did not eliminate the sentencing disparity.

Examples

Racism has been embedded in the United State's [*sic*] war on drugs since its inception. ... For instance, cocaine comes in two forms, and the form that is more common in Black communities incurs much harsher minimum sentencing.

—The Gateway Foundation (drug treatment provider)

Systemic racism continued to play a part in national drug policy through the 20th century, epitomized by the 1986 Anti-Drug Abuse Act that authorized penalties 100 times harsher for crack, which tended to be more popular in communities of color, than cocaine, despite these substances having no pharmacological differences.

—University of Cincinnati News

The Nixon campaign in 1968, and the Nixon White House after that, had two enemies: the antiwar left and black people. ... We knew we couldn't make it illegal to be either against the war or black, but by getting the public to associate the hippies with marijuana and blacks with heroin, and then criminalizing both heavily, we could disrupt those communities.

—John Ehrlichman, White House Counsel and
Domestic Affairs Advisor for President Nixon

President Reagan took President Nixon's racist drug war to a new level, and the mass incarceration of Black and Brown bodies accelerated under the Bush (times two) and Clinton administrations, especially after Clinton's 1994 crime bill.

—Ibram X. Kendi, leading woke author and activist

The entire foundation of the War on Drugs was built on racial resentment and outgroup targeting by the government.

—John Hudak, The Brookings Institution[152]

---

[151] England and Martin 2022.
[152] Sources: Gateway Foundation 2022; Tedeschi 2022; Baum 2016; Kendi 2017;

Reality

(1) Did crack users get vastly harsher sentences than coke users?

Not really. A Justice Department report in 2002 found that the sentencing ratio varied between six-to-one and one-to-one, depending on the circumstances of the crime.[153] Just prior to the 2010 reform, people convicted for crack offenses got an average of 9.6 years in prison, while powder cocaine offenders got an average of 7.3 years, making a ratio of *1.3* to 1, not 100 to 1.[154]

(2) But is there any rationale for the sentencing difference other than racism?

Yes. The Justice Department report also noted that smoking crack tends to be more psychologically addictive than snorting cocaine (the primary way of using powder cocaine), and that crack users tend to engage in violent crime and weapons offenses more often than powder cocaine users. This is not due to the pharmacological properties of the drugs (which are the same) but, apparently, to differences between the crack and powder markets: crack sellers tend to make a larger number of small transactions, and the crack market has more small dealers competing for territory.[155]

It is open to debate whether these are *good* reasons for a sentencing disparity. But it is easy to see how legislators could *think* they were reasons to punish crack more harshly, without having to be racist.

(3) Okay, but come on, Richard Nixon was a racist.

Yes, he was.[156] And racism may well have played some role in his support for the drug war. But Paul Ehrlichman was probably either wrong or lying about its being the central motive. (Ehrlichman had some resentment toward Nixon after the Watergate scandal got Ehrlichman sent to jail.) Nixon personally hated drugs, which probably explained much of why he wanted to stamp them out.[157]

More importantly, Richard Nixon could not pass any laws by himself. Congress makes the laws in the U.S. So, before concluding as

---

Hudak 2021.

[153] U.S. Department of Justice 2002, p. iii.

[154] Kurtzleben 2010.

[155] U.S. Department of Justice 2002, pp. 3, 8-9.

[156] For more, see Nagourney 2010.

[157] Lopez 2016.

to the purpose of the drug laws, we should ask who supported the drug war in Congress and why.

(4) Who supported the drug war in Congress?

A few widely-discussed landmarks in the history of the war on drugs include:

i.   the Comprehensive Drug Abuse Prevention and Control Act of 1970 (passed during the Nixon administration and marking the start of the modern "war on drugs"),
ii. the Anti-Drug Abuse Act of 1986 (passed under Reagan), and
iii. the 1994 Crime Bill (passed under Clinton).

All of these are sometimes cited as contributing to the incarceration of black people for drug offenses, as in the quotations above. It is impossible to *prove* whether any of these laws had racist motivations, as we cannot see into the minds of the legislators. But we can collect some evidence.

According to most progressives, the main source of racism is Republicans and white people, not Democrats or black people. Therefore, it would be useful to look at whether, say, these laws were mainly supported by white Republicans and opposed by blacks and Democrats. Of course, many white Democrats were racist too, so it would be especially important to see whether *black* legislators opposed these laws. Surely if the answers to these questions were "yes", progressives would cite this as corroborating the accusation of racism.

Start with the 1970 law that kicked off Nixon's war on drugs. Who supported that? It was introduced into Congress by a Democrat (Harley Staggers). It passed both houses of Congress with overwhelming bipartisan support. No Senator from either party voted against it. In the House, it was opposed by just six Democrats and no Republicans, while 187 Democrats and 154 Republicans voted yes.[158] There were nine black House members and one black Senator in Congress at the time. Of these, the Senator and two House members voted yes, two House members voted no, and the other five abstained.[159] The following year, members of the Congressional Black Caucus met with President Nixon

---

[158] Govtrack (a); (b).
[159] Wikipedia, "List of African-American United States Representatives"; "List of African-American United States Senators"; Govtrack (b).

and urged him to ramp up the drug war.[160]

What about the 1986 drug law that created the infamous crack/powder cocaine disparity? That law was also introduced into Congress by a Democrat (James Wright), and it also passed with overwhelming bipartisan support. Only two Senators (one Republican and one Democrat) voted no, while 97 voted yes (46 Democrats and 51 Republicans). In the House, 222 Democrats and 170 Republicans voted yes, while just 15 Democrats and 1 Republican voted no. There were 18 black House members and zero black Senators at the time. Of these, 13 voted yes while only 5 voted no.[161]

What about the 1994 Crime Bill that Ibram Kendi complained about above, which provided more funding for police and prisons? It was also introduced into Congress by a Democrat (Jack Brooks). It passed with overwhelming Democratic (but not Republican) support. In the Senate, 54 Democrats and 7 Republicans voted yes, while 2 Democrats and 36 Republicans voted no. In the House, 188 Democrats and 46 Republicans votes yes, while 64 Democrats and 131 Republicans voted no. At the time, there were 35 black House members and 1 black Senator. Of these, the Senator and 24 House members voted yes, while only 9 House members voted no and 2 abstained.[162]

In sum: The drug war and the Crime Bill were overwhelmingly supported by Democrats and black leaders.[163] This is puzzling if these laws were really examples of systemic racism. It's easy to *assert* that the laws were racist, but where is the evidence?

(5) What? How can this be?

Why would black leaders support a policy that would disproportionately put black men in prison? Were these self-hating "Uncle Toms"?

Hardly. Suppose we consider the obvious explanation: *The drug war was supposed to help.* I.e., when Congress made these laws, they weren't thinking that the laws would be an abject failure. They were *thinking* that

---

[160] Venugopal 2013.

[161] Wikipedia, "List of African-American United States Representatives"; "List of African-American United States Senators"; Govtrack (c).

[162] Wikipedia, "List of African-American United States Representatives"; "List of African-American United States Senators"; Govtrack (d); Govtrack (e). The reason for the Republican opposition was probably that the law included a new gun control provision, the famous assault weapons ban.

[163] For more on this, see Venugopal 2013; Fortner 2013; Elder 2018.

the laws would stamp out drug abuse. (In general, by the way, very few laws are meant purely to cause harm out of sheer hate. Most are meant to produce some overall benefit. Politicians may be incompetent or corrupt, but they are not generally Satanic.) The Congressional Black Caucus wanted Nixon to escalate the drug war *to help black communities*, because drugs were devastating those communities. Similarly, black legislators supported the law that increased penalties for crack cocaine because crack was devastating black communities. That is the most simple, straightforward explanation; there is no need to posit an evil conspiracy to destroy black communities.

We now know that the drug war was a mistake. It has strengthened criminal organizations, made drugs more dangerous, increased corruption, increased theft and violence, precipitated erosion of civil liberties, disrupted poor communities, and sent millions to prison, all while having disappointingly little effect on drug consumption. It also violates the rights of individuals, but that is a story for another time.[164] But the drug war did not commit *every* sin. In particular, it was not racist. It was not *meant* to destroy black communities; it was meant to protect them.

Perhaps progressives miss this fact because they underestimate just how often government policies produce the opposite of their intended effects.

---

[164] See Huemer 2004; 2008.

Part III: Feminist Myths

We turn now to some myths supporting feminism, a movement that holds, roughly, that women in modern America and similar societies are victims of an oppressive patriarchy. The movement thus seeks to liberate women from this oppression while generally advancing women's interests in society.

11 The Gender Pay Gap

Myth

Women in the United States earn much less than men do for the same work, due to sexism.

Background

This is known as "the gender pay gap". The figure has changed over time: In 1963, women earned just *59 cents* for every dollar that men earned. The figure rose over the years (which is why you see different numbers quoted), eventually reaching 82 cents today, but it still sounds like some pretty serious sexism.[165] This is among the most commonly cited factoids, if not *the* most commonly cited, by feminists seeking to demonstrate the rampant sexism of American society.

Usually, the statistic is cited without further explanation. Many listeners assume that the statistic refers to pay *for the same work*, i.e., that it controls for occupation and other relevant features of the job. Sometimes that assumption is stated explicitly.

Figure 12

---

[165] Kochhar 2023; Haan 2023.

Examples

In the U.S. and U.K., there has been a movement to obtain "equal pay for equal work", which many believe we do not currently have. Figure 12 shows a female protestor with a sign reading "I earn £7K less than him for the same work."[166]

In one episode of the comedy SciFi series *Rick and Morty*, two of the protagonists, discussing Earth society with some aliens, have this exchange:

Rick: On Earth, men and women are equals.
Summer: Equals?! We make 70% of your salary for *the same job*![167]

It is not only fictional characters who believe this. Here are some more quotes:

The reality is that if we do nothing it will take 75 years, or for me to be nearly a hundred, before women can expect to be paid the same as men for the same work.

—Emma Watson, actress

You and I have to continue fighting for equal pay for equal work.

—Lilly Ledbetter, equal pay activist

I am committed to tearing down the barriers to full and equal participation in our economy and society that still exist for too many women. All women deserve equal pay for equal work.

—Barack Obama, U.S. President

If you aggregate everybody working in the economy in every job, women get paid 77 cents for every dollar that men get paid. For the same work, dudes get paid more.

—Rachel Maddow, journalist[168]

One feminist joke explains that "Men earn more than women because they tend to choose lucrative careers, such as doctor, scientist, or lawyer, while women choose lower-paid jobs, such as woman doctor, female scientist, or lady lawyer."

---

[166] Photo: "Gender Pay Gap" by Nick Efford, CC BY 2.0.
[167] Myers and Michels 2014 at 11:25.
[168] Sources: Watson 2014; Forbes 2018; Obama 2015; Maddow 2012, at 1:32.

Reality

The gender pay gap statistics *do not* control for occupation or other relevant factors. In other words, they are not, in fact, about *the same work* or *equal work*. Rather, almost all of the gap is due to men and women doing *different work*.

In the Rachel Maddow segment quoted above, Maddow points out that men frequently earn more than women with *the same job title*. However, job title does not capture all factors relevant to earnings. There are multiple other factors, such as experience, education, industry (e.g., "receptionists" get different pay in different industries), job level, and hours worked. After controlling for these sorts of factors, the pay gap shrinks from 18 cents to 1 cent—i.e., we find women earning *99 cents* for every dollar that men earn.[169] (Some sources cite slightly different numbers, such as 95 cents or 98 cents.)

You could still say that maybe sexism explains that last penny of difference. But it would clearly be deceptive to claim that women are paid less than men due to sexism and, in that context, to quote the "70 cents", "77 cents", or "82 cents" statistic.

Moreover, it is far from clear that even that last penny of difference is due to sexism. In his book *Why Men Earn More*, political scientist Warren Farrell investigates the pay gap more thoroughly than other authors.[170] By the way, just so you don't dismiss his findings as propaganda produced by some right-wing, misogynistic men's rights activist: Warren Farrell began his intellectual career as a hardcore feminist activist, the only man to be elected three times to the Board of Directors of the National Organization for Women, and the goal of his book is to *help women* earn more. Farrell was initially convinced, just as most people are when they first hear about it, that the gender pay gap indicated unacceptable discrimination by men against women. It was only when he started to do serious research on it that he began to realize that this was simply not true.

Farrell identifies 25 things that tend to get an employee more pay (though some of these are redundant). According to Farrell, one can expect to be paid more money for:

1.   Working in technology or the hard sciences, rather than arts or

---

[169] Haan 2023.
[170] Farrell 2005.

social sciences,

2. Working in a dangerous field, such as the military,
3. Being exposed to the weather, rather than working indoors,
4. Taking a job from which you can't psychologically check out at the end of the day,
5. Taking a less fulfilling job,
6. Taking higher financial and emotional risks,
7. Working undesirable hours,
8. Working in unpleasant environments or with little human contact,
9. Updating your skills for the latest market needs,
10. Choosing the most lucrative subfield within your field,
11. Working longer hours,
12. Having more years of experience in your current occupation,
13. Having more years of recent, uninterrupted experience with your current employer,
14. Working more weeks of the year,
15. Being absent less often from work,
16. Commuting farther,
17. Relocating at the company's behest,
18. Traveling extensively for the job,
19. Taking on different responsibilities from others with your job title,
20. Taking on bigger responsibilities from others with your job title,
21. Accepting less security,
22. Having more training in your current occupation,
23. Starting with higher career goals,
24. Doing more in-depth job searches, and
25. Being more productive.

All of these make intuitive sense, and none are on their face unjust or motivated by prejudice. They generally have to do with the employee either doing more for the company or doing something that most workers would find undesirable, such that one must offer workers more money to make them willing to do it. All of these things, Farrell says, men tend to do more than women.

It is not feasible to measure and control for all of these factors, so we do not have statistics on what happens to the pay gap when all these things are accounted for. But it is plausible that after controlling for all

25 factors, the gender pay gap is not only eliminated but even re-
versed—that is, that women actually earn *more* than men *for the same
work.*

One reason for thinking this is that the pay gap is found to be
eliminated or nearly eliminated when one controls for a small *subset* of
the above factors. Farrell writes:

> I discussed how a nationwide study found men and women profes-
> sional, administrative, technical, and clerical workers made the same
> pay when their titles were the same, and their responsibilities were
> both the same and of equal size. Had this study also taken into ac-
> count factors like the number of hours worked, years in the field,
> absences from the workplace, or willingness to move, all of which
> tend to lead to men earning more pay, it is probable the study would
> have revealed that had the women worked equal hours, and so on,
> they would have earned more than the men. And this was two dec-
> ades ago.[171] [Now four decades ago. –mh]

For another piece of evidence, if we just compare never-married,
college-educated people with no children, working full-time, women
earn about 18% *more* than men.[172] It is hard to square this with the
"anti-woman discrimination" theory. Are we to believe that the patriarchy discriminates against women in general but for some reason
discriminates in the opposite direction just in the case of never-married,
childless, educated women—the very women who are most defying
stereotypical gender roles?

Objections

*(1) How could there possibly be a reverse pay gap? Everyone knows that
society discriminates against women, not men.*

Reply: There are a few plausible explanations for how women could earn
more for comparable work. For one, there are many programs, both
governmental and private, designed specifically to help women. These
programs probably sometimes succeed in helping women. Since there
are no programs designed specifically to help men, men are at a relative
disadvantage. For example, the U.S. Small Business Administration has

---

[171] Farrell 2005, ch. 11, p. 173, citing Sieling 1984.
[172] Farrell 2005, introduction, figure 1.

an office that "Promotes women-owned businesses through business training and technical assistance and provides access to credit and capital, federal contracts, and international trade opportunities."[173] There is no comparable office for men-owned businesses. A second, related factor is that many companies and schools practice affirmative action for women. A third factor is that employers may fear being sued for discrimination by women employees but not by men employees. Since the "fair" pay for an employee is a matter of subjective judgment, it is not entirely predictable what one might be sued for, except that one is extremely unlikely to be sued for anti-*male* discrimination. Therefore, employers may wish to err on the side of slightly overpaying their women employees.

Finally, there is the fact that most people in contemporary society, including both men and women, *like women more than they like men*. This phenomenon, sometimes called the "Women Are Wonderful" effect, has been well documented in psychological studies, and it includes both explicit and implicit attitudes.[174] This makes it more prima facie plausible that there would be discrimination in favor of women rather than against them.

(2) You haven't refuted that we're living in an oppressive patriarchy, because you haven't refuted all the other examples of sexism that I can think of.

Reply: That's right, I haven't. And I couldn't possibly do that, because "we're living in an oppressive patriarchy" is too broad of a claim. I could not possibly address every alleged example of sexism, just as I could not address every alleged piece of evidence for progressivism. The best I can do is take some particularly prominent pieces of evidence and examine them one at a time.

But note that this particular one is hardly minor, nor have I unfairly chosen it to pick on. The gender pay gap is an extremely prominent, widely-used factoid in support of feminist views. As illustrated by the quotations cited earlier, the pay gap myth is endorsed by famous actresses, powerful politicians, and influential activists. So I think it's pretty important that it turns out to be a myth.

---

[173] See U.S. Department of Labor (n.d.), which lists many "Federal Resources for Women".

[174] Eagly & Mladinic 1994; Eagly & Mladinic 1989; Eagly, Mladinic, and Otto 1991; Carpenter 2000; Rudman and Goodwin 2004. For a popular summary of the evidence on anti-male discrimination, see Tierney 2023.

(3) Maybe it's just because of sexism that female-dominated professions tend to be paid less than male-dominated professions.

Reply: No, it isn't. Salaries are not determined like that—by employers conspiring to make one broad social group get more money than another. Businesses try to pay employees according to the amount of value the employee contributes to the business, along with how difficult it is to find employees to do a particular task. If a business *doesn't* set salaries in this way, then they will lose out in competition with more rational businesses. The most obvious, simple explanation for why many jobs are both male-dominated and highly paid is that men tend to value monetary income more than women do. Women tend to prioritize work-life balance and other non-monetary goods.

Look again at Warren Farrell's list of 25 pay-enhancing traits. All of those items are intrinsically rational on their face; none of them could be claimed to enhance pay merely because men tend to do them. It's obviously the reverse; men tend to do them because they get you more money.

For example, consider hazard pay. People don't like getting injured or killed; *that's* why you have to pay them more to take risks on the job. It's not because sexist employers wanted to pay men more and they realized that men were taking more risks.

(4) Maybe sexism causes women to value money less than men.

Maybe society teaches men but not women to pursue financial success, because society devalues women and doesn't want them to succeed.

Reply: This objection rests on a simplistic value system wherein money is all that matters. The way one earns more money is by *making sacrifices*—working longer hours, working in unpleasant conditions, moving to a less desirable location for the job, and so on. It is foolish to assume that those sacrifices are always worth it. Men and women on average have different preferences and therefore make different tradeoffs—more men than women consider these sacrifices to be worthwhile in exchange for the extra pay. So men wind up on average with more money, while women wind up on average with more pleasant jobs, living in more desirable locations, spending more time with their families, and so on. There is no reason to assume that men therefore wind up overall better off than women.

Why do women and men have different preferences? This likely has both biological and cultural causes. Just focusing on the possible cultural component, perhaps men are conditioned to value financial success more, relative to other life goals. One *could* interpret this as indicating that society values men's interests more and therefore cares more about their financial success. But one could just as well interpret it as indicating that society values *women's* interests more and therefore cares more about their *personal fulfilment.* The mere difference between men's and women's priorities doesn't tell us whether society has a preferred gender, nor which gender that might be.

It is common to lament how most of the jobs with the highest income, status, and power—jobs such as CEO or U.S. Senator—are male-dominated. We attend less often to society's *worst* jobs. But nearly all of the worst and most dangerous jobs in America—garbage collector, roofer, construction worker, and so on—are also overwhelmingly male-dominated.[175] For example, the most dangerous (legal) job in America, lumberjack, is about 95% staffed by men.[176] As a result of this pattern, men suffer over 90% of all workplace deaths in America each year.[177] That is not an indication of patriarchy. It is an indication that *men are, on average, willing to do more for money* than women are.

My own sense is that the sacrifices people make for the sake of money are very often not worth it; many are foolishly sacrificing safety and happiness for money. Women are prudently doing less of this than men are. To eliminate the gender pay gap, we would have to either convince women to make more foolish sacrifices, or convince employers to pay women more just for being women *without* their having to make those sacrifices. Neither of these is at all a reasonable option.

---

[175] Farrell (2005, pp. 6-7) reports that 20 of the 21 worst jobs in America are overwhelmingly male-dominated (citing the *Jobs Rated Almanac*). But note that the Almanac only lists legal jobs. The actual most dangerous job (including illegal jobs) is prostitute, which is female-dominated.

[176] Zippia 2019; CNBC 2019. Lumberjacks have about a 1 in 1000 chance of dying on the job each year.

[177] Statista 2023a.

12 Campus Rape Culture

Myth

One in four women are raped in college. Sometimes, the statistic is cited as the number who experience rape *or attempted rape*. Sometimes, it is given as the number who experience *sexual assault*.

Examples

1 in 4 College Women Will Be Victims of Rape

—FindLaw.com article title

A recent study from the Department of Justice estimated that 25 percent of college women will be victims of rape or attempted rape before they graduate within a four-year college period.

—ABC News

Among undergraduate students, 26.4% of females and 6.8% of males experience rape or sexual assault through physical force, violence, or incapacitation.

—Rape, Abuse, and Incest National Network

1 in 4 Women Experienced Sexual Assault While in College, Survey Finds

—*Newsweek* headline[178]

Some Problems

This statistic implies that American college campuses are ten times more dangerous for women than Detroit, the most crime-ridden city in

---

[178] Sources: Strachan 2010; McFadden 2010; RAINN 2023; Gorman 2015.

America.[179] If you believe this, you should advise any young women you know to stay the hell away from college campuses. I would suggest, however, that we should find this statistic surprising. What are American universities doing, recruiting students right out of the nation's prisons?

Where did this alarmingly high statistic come from? The rape statistic begins with the National College Women Sexual Victimization Survey conducted in 1997.[180] Four thousand college women were interviewed late in the academic year (an average of 6.9 months in) and asked about any incidents that had occurred during that academic year. About 2.8% of respondents reported being the target of a (successful or unsuccessful) rape attempt during the preceding 6.9 months. The study authors tried to calculate from this how many would experience such victimization during their entire college careers. They assumed that a college career lasts 5 years, that sexual misconduct is equally likely to occur at any time during those 5 years, and thus they multiplied the 2.8% by (5 years / 6.9 months). The result is: 2.8% × (5×12)/6.9 ≈ 24%, which is almost ¼. Hence, 1 in 4 college women are raped during their college years.

There are six problems with this.

1. First, the probability calculation is incorrect; probabilities do not add up in that way. Simple illustration: Suppose there is a 60% chance of rain on Saturday, and an independent 60% chance of rain on Sunday. What is the probability that it will rain during the weekend? The answer is not: 2×60%=120%. The correct calculation is: $1 - (1 - 60\%)^2 = 84\%$.[181] Similarly, for the rape statistic, the calculation would be $1 - (1 - 2.8\%)^{(5 \times 12/6.9)} \approx 22\%$.[182]

---

[179] As discussed below, the "1 in 4" statistic is based on 2.8% of college women being raped in a 6.9-month period. By comparison, the rape rate in Detroit is around 0.1% of the population per year (Hunter and Harding 2021). For the most dangerous cities in the U.S., see World Population Review 2023.

[180] Fisher et al. 2000.

[181] Explanation: Probabilities only add for *mutually exclusive* events, and rain on Saturday is not mutually exclusive with rain on Sunday. To calculate the probability of [Rain on weekend]: P(rain-on-weekend) = 1 − P(no-rain-on-weekend) = 1 − P(no-rain-on-Sat. & no-rain-on-Sun.) = 1 − P(no-rain-on-Sat.)×P(no-rain-on-Sun. given no-rain-on-Sat.) = 1 − 40%×40% = 84%.

[182] This assumes that the risks in separate time periods are probabilistically independent. If some women are more generally prone to sexual victimization than others, then the 22% figure would be an overestimate.

2. The three months of summer vacation, when students are generally not in school, should not be counted since they are not relevant to the danger of being in college, nor can one infer the risk of those months from the risk during the school year.
3. The average college career is 4.33 years, not 5 years.[183] (Notice, by the way, that one of the above quotations mentions "a four-year college period", even though the study they are relying on assumed a five-year period.)
4. The "1 in 4" statistic lumps together completed rape with *unsuccessful attempts*.

After correcting those four errors, the correct figure is that the probability of being raped in college is about 9%; I include the calculation in a footnote.[184] This is all without questioning any of the data in the study. It is remarkable that a study whose data actually supports a figure of 9% is commonly cited as supporting a figure of 25%. This is not at all unusual: On politically charged subjects, ideologues pull out every trick in the book to inflate or deflate statistics, depending on what point they want to make. Most ideologically interesting statistics are rank propaganda.

Moving on:

5. About half of the people whom the study authors classified as rape victims, when asked whether what they experienced was "rape", answered "no". Most also denied that they experienced any physical or emotional injuries.[185] The authors suggest explanations for why rape victims would not realize that they were raped. However, the simplest explanation would seem to be that respondents said they were not raped because they were not raped, in the ordinary English sense of the term—i.e., the study authors were overly broad in what they classified as rape. If we take respondents at their word, then the

---

[183] Post University Blog 2021.

[184] Per Fisher et al. (2000, p. 10), 1.7% of respondents had suffered completed rapes, giving us: $1 - (1 - 0.017)^{[(4.33 \text{ yrs.})(9 \text{ months/yr})/(6.9 \text{ months})]} \approx 1 - 0.9835^{5.65} \approx 0.0923$.

[185] 48.8% of the "rape victims" say that what they experienced was not rape (Fisher et al. 2000, p. 15). The report mentions "physical or emotional injuries" before noting that only one in five victims of rape or attempted rape report experiencing any injuries (p. 22). For similar criticisms, see May 2010; Gilbert 1997.

main statistic drops from 9% to 4.6%.[186]

6. Different results can be obtained using different survey methods. The authors of the National College Women Sexual Victimization Survey have *also* reported the results of a "comparison study" they did using different methods. These different methods produce numbers an *order of magnitude* lower—0.16% of respondents reported suffering a completed rape that academic year, as opposed to 1.7% in the NCWSVS. If we were to use the 0.16% figure, then the estimated number of women who are raped during their college years would be 0.9%.[187]

So what are the methodological differences between the "comparison study" and the main study, i.e., the National College Women Sexual Victimization Survey (NCWSVS)? First, the NCWSVS, the survey that gets the higher numbers, asks more detailed questions, graphically describing different kinds of sexual victimization that respondents might have experienced. This might cause respondents to report incidents that they would fail to report when given vaguer, more general questions.

However, the NCWSVS also might suffer from overreporting, i.e., respondents who give false reports. This is a problem with surveys designed to measure rare events—rare events are hard to measure because even a small number of deceptive respondents can greatly skew the numbers.

To see the point, it may help to consider a parallel problem affecting a right-wing cause. A number of surveys have been done to determine how often Americans use guns to defend themselves from criminals. These surveys regularly conclude that private citizens use guns to stop crimes *millions* of times every year in the U.S.[188] Left-leaning critics

---

[186] $1 - (1 - .488 \times .017)^{\wedge}(4.33 \times 9/6.9) = 0.0460$. Fisher et al. (p. 4) state that they classified cases as "rape" based on detailed incident reports, but they do not provide the exact questions in the incident reports. However, an earlier study that found similar results included the following question: "Have you had sexual intercourse when you didn't want to because a man gave you alcohol or drugs?" Respondents who answered "yes" were classified as rape victims (Koss et al. 1987, p. 165, 167). Notice that this could be construed to include cases of agreeing to have sex due to lowered inhibitions due to alcohol consumption.

[187] $1 - (1 - .0016)^{\wedge}(4.33 \times 9/6.9) = 0.00900$.

[188] Kleck 1997. Interestingly, though, the NCVS (which uses methods similar to that of the "comparison study" discussed in the text) is an outlier, giving estimates an order of magnitude lower than other surveys for defensive gun uses.

argue that these surveys may greatly overestimate the frequency of defensive gun uses.[189] Suppose, hypothetically, that only 0.1% of people have an actual defensive gun use each year, but that 1% of survey respondents are liars (which would not at all be an implausibly high number of liars). They might lie, say, because they want to portray themselves as heroes, or because they are conservative and want to promote the cause of gun rights. This 1% would be enough to inflate the estimated frequency of defensive gun uses by *ten times* the actual frequency. Since we can't rule out a small number of liars, we don't know the true frequency.

The same reasoning applies to other rare events, including rape. If just 1% of respondents to the NCWSVS were deceptive (perhaps because they wished to portray themselves as victims deserving of sympathy, or because they were feminists who wished to raise awareness of rape, or for some other reason), that would greatly skew the estimate of rape prevalence. Since we can't rule out a small number of false reports, we don't know the true frequency of rape.

Objections

(1) Women don't lie about rape; therefore, the concern raised above must be misplaced.

Reply: See Chapter 13 below. In addition, note that the commonly cited studies regarding false rape reports concern *police reports*, not responses to telephone surveys. Deception may be more common in responses to telephone surveys since the stakes are lower and no steps are taken to investigate anything one says to the interviewer. Note also that even a very small number of false reports would be enough to greatly skew the numbers, as explained above.

(2) Why think that lying would inflate the rape statistics, rather than lowering them? There could also be women who were raped but lied and said that they weren't.

Reply: This objection overlooks how the statistics work. It is agreed on all sides that only a small percentage of college students have been raped in any given year. This fact alone makes the survey more vulnerable to false positives than false negatives.

---

[189] Hemenway 1997.

For illustration, imagine a group of 10,000 people, of whom, say, 1% have been bitten by a shark. Imagine also that about 1% of people are liars: When asked whether they have been bitten, they say the opposite of the truth, whatever that is. Notice that this assumption is perfectly symmetrical: We do not assume that either group (shark victims or non-shark victims) is any more honest than the other or that there is any greater tendency to lie in one direction than the other. Someone now surveys these 10,000 people to find out how many have been bitten by sharks. What would happen?

100 of the respondents (1%) would actually have been bitten. Of these, 1% (i.e., one person) would lie and say that they were *not* bitten. The other 99 would tell the truth that they had been bitten.

Then there would be 9,900 people who had *not* been bitten. Of these, 1% (i.e., 99 people) would lie and say that they *had* been bitten. The other 99% (i.e., 9801 people) would tell the truth that they hadn't been bitten.

So overall, 198 people would answer "yes" to the survey question and 9902 would answer "no", giving an estimate for the prevalence of shark bites of 1.98%, when the true prevalence was 1%. So even though we assumed *99% accuracy* for the survey respondents, the estimate that comes out at the end is still off by *a factor of two*. This illustrates a general point: Surveys of rare traits are inherently more vulnerable to overestimates than to underestimates.

The Sexual Assault Statistic

Let's turn to the *sexual assault* statistic, which should differ from the rape statistic because sexual assault is a broader category than rape. It is said that the number of college women who suffer sexual assault is about 1 in 4. This derives from other surveys of college students, most notably the Association of American Universities' (AAU's) Campus Climate Survey on Sexual Assault and Misconduct, which was conducted most recently in 2019.[190] This was an online survey in which students at 33 American colleges and universities were invited to participate. 26% of undergraduate women (close to 1 in 4) reported having been sexually assaulted since the beginning of their college careers.

This might sound close to "one in four college women are raped."

---

[190] Cantor et al. 2020.

"Sexual assault", however, is a much broader category than rape; most sexual assaults involve unwanted sexual touching without penetration. The AAU survey asked about incidents involving either the use of force or inability to consent because the victim was asleep, passed out, or incapacitated by drugs or alcohol. Suppose, for example, that two lovers fall asleep next to each other. The woman wakes up first in the morning and kisses her lover on the cheek while he sleeps. That is a "sexual assault". One hopes that most respondents would not report such events, but they technically meet the definition.[191]

Some surveys, by the way, use even broader definitions, wherein threatening to break up with someone if they won't have sex with you, expressing displeasure at someone's refusal to have sex, repeatedly pestering someone for sexual favors, or trying to get sex by making false promises all count as "sexual assault" or "attempted rape".[192]

Unlike the "1 in 4" rape statistic, the "1 in 4" sexual assault statistic is plausible, perhaps even an *under*estimate, given how the term is used.

Why might it be an underestimate? As noted, 26% of all the women who responded to the survey reported at least one sexual assault experience during their entire time at the university. But if you just focus on *fourth-year* undergraduate women (who are close to the end of their college careers), the rate was 31.5%. And the true rate of sexual assault may be even higher than that due to underreporting. Some students may have declined to report sexual assault experiences because they forgot the experiences, did not consider them worth reporting, or found it too emotionally unpleasant to report them.

It is also possible that the 26% is an overestimate. Of the students who were invited to participate in the AAU survey, only 22% filled it out. Such a low response rate for a survey is in general a cause for concern. In this case, the low response rate may be due to how time-consuming the survey was; in the full report, the list of questions goes on for 49 pages, including 15 pages before it even gets to questions about particular experiences of sexual misconduct. Perhaps students with bad experiences to report were more likely to find the motivation to fill out the survey. This would skew the numbers upward.[193]

---

[191] See the definitions in Cantor et al. 2020, p. v.

[192] See University of Texas at Austin School of Social Work 2017, pp. 120-21, where all of these are listed as potential methods of raping someone.

[193] Cantor et al. (appendix 4) discuss reasons to think the AAU survey might have produced an overestimate, citing the fact that late-responders to the survey

Conclusion: A quarter of women are not raped in college; the number is probably between 1% and 5%. It is plausible that at least one in four women are *sexually assaulted* while in college. However, the definition of "sexual assault" is broader than most people probably realize, making this statistic less alarming than it sounds.

reported slightly lower rates of sexual assault than early-responders, plus the fact that schools with higher response rates reported slightly less sexual assault. They argue that this evidence only suggests a slight overestimate at most. But no evidence rules out the plausible general speculation that people with negative experiences are more likely to fill out a lengthy survey.

13 Women Don't Lie

Myth

Women don't lie about rape or sexual assault. Or they lie only very rarely, no more than 2–10% of the time. Therefore, one should #Believe Women about these things.

Background

Historically, women who come forward with sexual assault or rape allegations have often been unreasonably doubted. This led to a reaction, circa 2017, in which progressive activists popularized the slogan "#BelieveWomen" or "#BelieveAllWomen". They have sometimes cited statistics about the rarity of false accusations in support of this.

During the 2020 U.S. Presidential campaign, progressives faced a dilemma when Tara Reade came forward with sexual assault allegations against Democratic Presidential candidate Joe Biden. Many were torn between adhering to the "believe women" slogan and supporting their favored political candidate.

Examples

There is disagreement among progressives about the meaning of "believe women". Some say that it just means that one should take women's accusations seriously; others, that it literally means one should believe all women when they make accusations of this kind:

> Women Don't 'Cry Rape': Why it's so unlikely any woman would lie about being raped.
>
> —U.S. News & World Report Headline

Women Don't Lie About Sexual Assault, Why Are They Treated

Like They Do?

                                             —Jean Boler, lawyer

The prevalence of false reporting for sexual assault crimes is low—between two percent and 10 percent.

                         —National Sexual Violence Resource Center

Though "false rape accusations" make for a good bogeyman, they are both rare and, according to the best evidence we have, shockingly obvious.

                                     —Jude Doyle, feminist author

For a woman to come forward in the glaring lights of focus, nationally, you've got to start off with the presumption that at least the essence of what she's talking about is real—whether or not she forgets facts ...

                   —Joe Biden, commenting when Brett Kavanaugh
                                    was accused of sexual assault

From the very beginning, I've said believing women means taking the woman's claim seriously when she steps forward, and then vet it. Look into it.

                —Joe Biden, when Joe Biden was accused of sexual assault

"Believe all women" has never been a slogan for anti-rape advocates. [...] The phrase is "believe women"—meaning, don't assume women as a gender are especially deceptive or vindictive, and recognize that false allegations are less common than real ones.

                                                   —Jude Doyle

We stand with Dr. Christine Blasey Ford, Deborah Ramirez, & Julie Swetnick. #BelieveAllWomen

             —Tweet from U.S. Representative Carolyn B. Maloney (D-NY)

I shouldn't have to tell you how critical it is to believe women. [...] What also needs to be made clear is that when you believe women on principle, you believe all women. No exceptions.

                          —Jenny Hollander, senior editor, *Bustle*[194]

---

[194] Sources: Tanenbaum 2018 (originally titled "Women Don't Lie About Being Raped"); Boler 2018; NSVRC n.d.; Doyle 2017; Soave 2020; Brzezinski 2020, from 4:33; Doyle 2017; Maloney 2018; Hollander 2017 (originally titled "Why 'Believe

Reality

(1) The meaning of "believe women"

Pace Joe Biden, "believe *x*", in English, does not mean "look into it". (Admittedly, "Don't automatically disbelieve women" is a less catchy slogan than "Believe women".) One might as well claim that "Lock up Joe" means "Give Joe a fair trial." And, notwithstanding feminist protestations to the contrary, as evidenced above, some people really have said "believe all women" and made clear that they meant it literally.

(2) Do women lie?

One hardly need explain the foolishness of claiming that women don't lie or that all women are credible. Women are humans, not angels; as such, they are as capable of deception as men are. Consider the infamous Duke lacrosse case.[195] In 2006, a stripper named Crystal Mangum accused the men of the Duke University lacrosse team of raping her at a party where she had been hired to perform. Despite multiple inconsistencies and implausible aspects of Mangum's testimony and an almost complete lack of evidence, rape charges were filed against three lacrosse team members. The team members were white, while Mangum was black, so the case fed into progressive narratives about oppression by white males. Predictably, the Duke community rushed to judgment, with many professors and students assuming the players' guilt and seizing the opportunity to condemn the presumed racism and sexism rampant in our society. The remainder of the lacrosse season was cancelled, and the coach of the team was forced to resign.

It turned out that Mangum was lying, which the prosecutor in the case had good reason to know. She had been tested on the night of the alleged incident, and no DNA from any of the lacrosse team members was on her; she contradicted herself multiple times; the other stripper who was present at the party called her story a "crock"; etc. The prosecutor was guilty of such severe misconduct that he wound up being disbarred and spending a day in jail (an almost unheard-of sanction). In an unrelated case, by the way, Crystal Mangum was herself later sent to prison for murdering her boyfriend.

Women' Means Believing Women Without Exception").
[195] See K.C. Johnson's (n.d.) blog about the case.

One interesting aspect of the case is that, although Mangum's accusations were among the least credible in the annals of the American justice system, many in the media and the academy were completely taken in. One CNN commentator sarcastically opined, "I'm so glad they didn't miss a lacrosse game over a little thing like gang rape!" before rhetorically wondering, "Why would you go to a cop in an alleged gang rape case, say, and lie and give misleading information?"[196] On the Duke campus, flyers appeared with names and photos of 40 lacrosse team members, urging the team members to come forward with evidence against their rapist peers.[197] This illustrates, again, the foolishness of deciding whom to believe based purely on gender.

(3) Understanding the 2-10% statistic

Let us agree, then, that women *sometimes* lie. But how often? There have been numerous studies attempting to assess the frequency of false rape accusations in one or another sample of accusations. Philip Rumney (2006) reviewed 20 such studies, finding estimates of the prevalence of false allegations ranging from 1.5% to 90%. Many of these studies used vague, subjective, under-explained, or unreliable methods of determining whether an accusation was false (e.g., assuming that complainants who wait long after the event in question to report a rape are lying).

The "2-10%" figure, commonly cited by activists, derives mainly from David Lisak et al.'s (2010) article reviewing ten studies of false rape accusations. Lisak et al. reject as unreliable half of the studies reviewed in the earlier Rumney article. The remaining studies, which Lisak et al. consider to have sufficiently reliable methodology, give estimates ranging from 2.1% to 10.9%. Lisak et al. also report the results of their own study of rape allegations made to a particular university police department during a ten year period. Based on the case files of all 136 rape cases handled by the department in that period, Lisak et al. found 8 cases (5.9%) to be false reports. This agrees with the police department's own finding.

You should be puzzled at this point: How could researchers know what percentage of rape accusations are true and what percentage are false in a particular sample? Wouldn't that require having some sort of crystal ball to see what really happened in each one of these cases?

---

[196] Grace 2006.
[197] Ruibal 2006. For more, see Wikipedia, "Reactions to the Duke lacrosse case".

Suppose a woman accuses a man of rape, and the man denies it. There are no other witnesses and no physical evidence. How would scholars figure out whether this was a true accusation or a false one?

The key lies in redefining the word "false". In Lisak et al.'s article, "false report" does not mean "report that isn't true". It means roughly, "report that was *proven* not to be true". That is, a "false report" is one such that the accuser admitted that she was lying, or other similarly clear evidence showed that the events she reported definitely did not happen.[198] If it was never determined whether the events happened, the report is *not* "false". So the sort of "he said, she said" case described in the preceding paragraph would be deemed non-false. That covers a large portion, perhaps half or more, of all cases.

So here is what Lisak et al. found in their sample: Of 136 cases, 8 accusations (6%) were shown to be false; in another 61 cases (45%), the police found insufficient evidence to pursue the case further; in 48 cases (35%), there was enough evidence for the case to proceed; and in 19 cases (14%), the case file had insufficient information to classify the case. That is all that Lisak et al. report. There was no attempt in their study to estimate how many accusations were actually true or false, except that the false accusations were almost certainly *at least* 8. All the other studies they cite are like this, because Lisak et al. treated it as an adequacy condition on a study that the study authors use the same definition of "false accusation".

In fairness, Lisak et al. did not invent this definition on their own; this is the criterion of "false report" used by the FBI and the International Association of Chiefs of Police.

(4) The correct use of "false"

What's wrong with using "false" to mean "shown to be false"? After all, we shouldn't label somebody's claim as false unless there is strong evidence that it's false, should we?

No, but by the same token, we shouldn't label somebody's claim as *true* unless there is strong evidence that it's true, should we? Suppose we adopted a parallel definition of "true report", where a "true report" is one such that the accused admitted to the rape, or other similarly strong evidence established that he definitely did it. In that case, we could claim that rape accusations are "true" only a minority of the time. We

---

[198] Lisak et al. 2010, pp. 1319-20.

could then start drawing lessons about how you should be skeptical of rape reports because fewer than half of them are true. Obviously, this would be radically misleading.

The parallel use of "false" to mean "proven false" is similarly misleading, and it is clear that those who quote the "false rape accusation" statistics have in fact been misled. The contexts make clear that the authors *think* they are quoting statistics for how often the events described in a complaint *did not happen*, and that the *rest* of the time the complaint is *true*. For instance, feminist activists say that you should believe women *because only 2% of their accusations are false*. This makes sense if the statistic means that 98% of the accusations are true. It does not make sense if the situation is that 2% of the time the accusation is proven to be false, while most of the time it is never discovered whether the accusation was true or false.

What is the actual rate of false rape accusations, then? No one knows. It is *at least* 2-10%, but it may be much more. In Lisak et al.'s study, police found insufficient evidence to proceed with the case 45% of the time. There is no way of knowing how many of these were in fact false accusations. In another 35% of cases, the police proceeded with the case, which probably means that most of these were true accusations. Finally, there were another 14% of cases about which we can say nothing because the case file was incomplete. So we can say with confidence that the false accusation rate was somewhere between 6% and 80%.[199]

(5) Generalizing from Police Reports

Even if the 2-10% figure actually measured false reports, there is another problem with the way these statistics are commonly used. The studies of "false reports of rape" are generally studies of *police reports*. Yet they are often used to draw lessons about very different contexts, such as university tribunals or accusations made against public officials in the media. E.g., when accusations of sexual assault were raised against Supreme Court nominee Brett Kavanaugh in 2018, or against Presidential candidate Joe Biden in 2020, some people said that since women very rarely lie about these things, Kavanaugh and/or Biden was

---

[199] 6% of allegations were proven false in Lisak et al.'s study. Of the 35% of cases that went forward, probably most were true allegations, plus at least some of the allegations from the 45% that had insufficient evidence. So it's reasonable to assume at least, say, 20% of all allegations were true.

almost surely guilty.

Let's first consider the university context. American universities have their own offices (separate from the police) for investigating accusations of sexual harassment, sexual assault, or other sexual misconduct. The investigators in these offices widely believe that, per the "2–10%" statistic, women rarely lie about these sorts of things. But the university context differs from the police context in five crucial ways:

   i. Reports to university offices are all made by people at the university (usually students), who are not a representative sample of the population as a whole. It is unknown whether college students are more or less prone to lying than the general population.

   ii. If you bring a complaint to the police, the police know that a conviction would require *proof beyond a reasonable doubt*; as a result, they will attempt to conduct a relatively rigorous investigation. In the university context, investigators only look for a *preponderance of the evidence* (meaning anything over a 50% chance that someone is guilty). So people are more likely to bring weak cases to university officials.

   iii. If you make a false rape accusation to the police, you may get someone sent to prison for many years. If you make a false complaint to a university office, then you could at most get someone kicked out of the university.

   iv. If you make a complaint to the police, you can expect to go through a lengthy process, which will involve going over your story many times, facing the accused, and being cross-examined by his lawyer in public. If you make a complaint to a university office, you will go through a much shorter process, wherein you need never face the accused or his lawyer.

   v. Universities have ideological orientations *much* more sympathetic to feminism and narratives about oppression by white males than one would expect to find in a typical police department.

   vi. Finally, filing a false police report is a crime; filing a false complaint with a university office is not (though you could be sued for it).

The effect of the first difference is unknown. The other five all point in the direction of making false reports more likely in university settings (though they would also tend to make actual victims more likely to report crimes).

Now turn to the case of accusations appearing in the media against public figures. These again differ from police reports in six ways:

i. The targets are all famous people, who are not representative of the population as a whole.
ii. Media investigations are less rigorous than police investigations.
iii. There is usually a salient possible political motive for making accusations against public figures.
iv. A false allegation in the media is likely meant to embarrass someone or make them lose an election, not get them sent to prison.
v. Journalists tend to be more sympathetic to accusations of sexual misconduct, especially if they play into narratives about white male oppression, than police departments.
vi. Making a false accusation in the media is not a crime.

Again, the last five of these all point in the direction of making people more likely to make false reports.

Objections

(1) Why would any woman lie about being raped or sexually assaulted?

Reply: Women lie for the same sorts of reasons that human beings in general lie, usually out of self-interest.[200] If you cannot imagine any cases in which someone would tell a false story about sexual victimization, then you probably don't have much experience with human beings.

Sociologist Eugene Kanin studied rape allegations in a small city during a nine-year period. Out of the 109 rape allegations reported to the police during that period, 45 (41%) were found to be false. In each case, the accuser admitted to having lied; no cases were classified as false without a recantation. In most cases, these recantations occurred easily and early in the process, and in no case did a complainant try to retract her recantation, despite being notified that she would be charged with filing a false complaint.

Complainants gave three main reasons for having made the false accusation.[201] The most common reason was to avoid getting in trouble with other people or having one's reputation damaged. In one case, for example, a woman was cheating on her husband while the husband was

---

[200] Kanin 1994; Zepezauer 1994; De Zutter 2018.
[201] Kanin 1994. De Zutter et al. (2018) add material gain, disturbed mental state, relabeling, and regret to the list of motives.

overseas. She feared that she had become pregnant by her lover, so she claimed to have been raped in order to hide the infidelity. In another case, a teenager feared that she had become pregnant by her boyfriend. She told a hospital that she had been raped in the hopes of getting something to abort the pregnancy. In a third case, a woman got a black eye and a cut lip during a drunken brawl. She claimed to have been raped in order to explain her injuries in a way that would not jeopardize an upcoming child custody hearing.

The second most common reason for a false accusation was to get revenge against a particular man. In one case, a young woman was sleeping with a boarder in her mother's house. When the mother discovered this, she expelled the boarder. The young woman went to the boarder while he was packing and told him she would be ready to leave with him in an hour. He replied, "Who the hell wants you?" She later got even with him by accusing him of rape. In another case, a teenager discovered that her boyfriend was cheating on her; she got even, again, by accusing him of rape.

A third reason for false allegations was to gain sympathy or attention. One teenager invented a story about being raped by a stranger to gain sympathy and attention from her friends. The friends took it upon themselves to report the incident to the police. She went along with this to avoid admitting to her friends that she had lied. Another woman who was undergoing counseling fabricated a rape story in order to gain sympathy from her counselor, whom she had feelings for. The counselor insisted on reporting the incident to the police; again, she went along with this to avoid admitting to him that she had lied.

Despite the incredulity with which some writers greet the idea of false accusations, none of the above are particularly surprising stories. There are plenty of human beings with the sort of motives and character traits displayed in those stories, and there are plenty of people in the sort of situations described. Given, for example, that people periodically cheat on their partners, that this can result in unwanted pregnancy, and that other people tend to have extremely negative reactions to infidelity, it would be shocking if women *didn't* sometimes claim to have been raped to cover up sexual infidelity. As Kanin notes, if men could get pregnant from illicit affairs, they too would periodically make false rape accusations.

(2) In Kanin's study, the police offered polygraph ("lie detector") tests to the

complainants.

This is considered bad practice and is strongly discouraged by the International Association of Chiefs of Police, as it is said to intimidate rape victims.[202]

Reply: Bear in mind that the relevant question is not whether the police department's practice was overall good. The relevant question for us is whether *it led to a drastic overestimate of false rape charges.* It is unclear why that would be the case. If, upon being offered a polygraph, or upon taking and failing a polygraph test, a complainant recants her complaint, what is the most likely explanation? It *could* be that taking a polygraph is so intimidating or unpleasant that it induces rape victims to falsely declare that they were not raped after all. It could also be that they persist in this even after being notified that they will be charged with filing a false complaint, because polygraphs are more intimidating than criminal charges. But the simpler explanation seems to be that the complainants recant because they were in fact lying and they believe they either have just been found out or are about to be found out.

Second, whatever you think of that, Kanin reports further evidence from two university police departments, *neither of which used polygraphs.*[203] These departments together handled 64 forcible rape complaints over a three-year period, which were all investigated by a female police officer. Again, no complaint was labelled false without a recantation by the complainant. Exactly half of the complaints were found to be false. Again, the most common reason for filing a false complaint was to provide some kind of alibi, with revenge as the second most common reason.

(3) I can't imagine lying about that sort of thing, and I don't know anyone who would.

This may be why many find the idea of widespread false rape charges incredible. We think about ourselves and the people we know, realize that, in our opinion, no one we know would do such a thing, then conclude that it must be very rare. Notice that this is parallel to the following reasoning: I would never rape someone, nor, I believe, do I know anyone who would; therefore, rape must be very rare.

Indeed, few people would do *either* of these things—either rape

---

[202] Lisak et al., pp. 1323-24.
[203] Kanin, p. 90.

someone or lie about being raped. Most people avoid such socially deviant behaviors. But a look at the crime statistics should convince you that there are people who do such things, even if you don't personally know any of them. Women are just as capable of immorality as men are, and false rape accusations are in fact *less* socially deviant and less harshly punished than rape itself. Therefore, on reflection, it would not be terribly surprising if false rape allegations occurred with comparable or greater frequency than actual rapes.

(4) Rape is drastically under-reported, not over-reported.

Objection: According to NCVS data, at least 80% of rape victims fail to report the crime.[204] One reason for this is that victims are afraid that they won't be believed. By promoting the idea of frequent false accusations, you are contributing to skepticism about rape charges, which contributes to the problem of under-reporting!

Reply: To begin with, note that the over-reporting of rape is completely consistent with the well-known *under*-reporting of rape. That is, the fact that women who *were* raped usually *do not* report it is entirely compatible with the hypothesis that women who *were not* raped often report that they *were*.

In fact, the under-reporting problem is part of *why* false accusations likely form a significant portion of the total. To illustrate, consider the extreme scenario in which 0% of actual rape victims report the crime. In that case, *100%* of the rape reports would have to be false reports. The qualitative point holds in less extreme cases: Holding the population of deceptive reporters fixed, the more reluctant actual victims are to make reports, the larger the *proportion* of reports that will be false. So the "objection" is not an objection at all.

The under-reporting, by the way, is completely understandable, as reporting sexual victimization generally entails being forced to relive the most humiliating and terrifying experience of one's life, repeatedly, in front of strangers, along with being cross-examined and having your credibility attacked by the perpetrator's lawyer. That, rather than the existence of scholars who tell the truth about false reports, is probably the main reason for under-reporting.

Having said that, the feminists are not wrong in thinking that a society in which women are invariably believed is a society in which

---

[204] Thompson and Tapp, p. 5.

more victims will come forward. Would that be better?

Here are two reasons for thinking it might not be. First, in jurisprudence, it is generally thought that it is much worse to punish an innocent person than to fail to punish a guilty person. Hence, it is said that it is better to let ten guilty people go free than to punish a single innocent person. If false rape accusations are common, then giving much more credence to rape accusations in general is likely to lead to many more innocent people being punished.

Second, even if you think false accusations are *currently* rare, their numbers would multiply if it were much easier for accusations to be believed. If it becomes widely known that society has adopted the #BelieveAllWomen philosophy, then potential false accusers who are *presently* deterred by fear of being found out will start to come forward. If, for example, an unproven allegation of sexual misconduct were sufficient to derail any political campaign, then accusers could probably be found for every important male politician.

Be that as it may, I do not regard my task as that of trying to influence victim responses. My task is simply to tell the truth.

Part IV: Gender Myths

In this part, we discuss myths about the nature of gender and the transgender phenomenon.

14 What Is Gender?

Myth

Gender is a social construct.

Examples

One progressive view of gender is that it is purely a social construct:

> *Gender* refers to the socially constructed roles, behaviors, activities, and attributes that a given society considers appropriate for boys and men or girls and women.
>
> —The American Psychological Association

This contrasts with an extreme conservative view in which gender either doesn't exist or is just another name for sex:

> I think gender is an arbitrary and useless concept invented by left-wing perverts in the mid-twentieth century in order to smuggle their degeneracy into the culture. I think we don't need gender because we have biological sex, and it accurately and completely describes the binary system.
>
> —Matt Walsh, anti-trans activist

I have mentioned both extreme views in this case because both need to be corrected if we are to understand reality.[205]

Reality

(1) Gender is cross-cultural.

If your gender is a social role, then societies that have *different social roles* must thereby have *different genders*. The cultures of, for example, Somalia,

---

[205] Sources: American Psychological Association 2011; Walsh 2021.

Japan, and Sweden assign different social roles to females. Therefore, on the APA's account of gender, women from these different societies *do not share a gender*, i.e., they could not all be "women" in the same sense.[206] To avoid this implausible conclusion, we must reject the identification of gender with a social role.

(2) The case of David Reimer

David Reimer was born in 1965 as one of a pair of identical twin boys. After his penis was damaged during a botched circumcision, his parents sought advice from Professor John Money, a leading psychologist and sex researcher. Dr. Money recommended that David undergo surgery to give him a vagina, then be raised as a girl. Because gender is purely socially constructed, Dr. Money assured them, the child would grow up as a perfectly psychologically normal girl, as long as everyone treated "her" as such and never told her of her history. The parents went along with this and named the child "Brenda". In subsequent years, Money reported the case as a great success—that Brenda was developing as a normal girl, thus confirming Money's theories about the social construction of gender.

In fact, Money was lying; the experiment was an abject failure. The child never accepted his assigned identity as a girl. The first time he wore a dress, he tried to rip it off; he preferred his brother's toys to his own; he insisted on peeing standing up; he got into physical fights in school; and so on. When he eventually found out what had happened to him, Reimer changed his name to "David" and began living as a man. Ultimately, he wound up committing suicide at the age of 38, an outcome that may have been influenced by the trauma he had suffered due to John Money's influence.[207]

Why did the child reject the female identity assigned to him? Why did he insist on acting like a boy? Everyone was telling him he was a girl, he had a vagina rather than a penis, and he had no way of knowing that he had ever been a boy. Seemingly the only explanation is that he had an innate sense, hard wired into his brain, of the sex he was supposed to have. If that is so, then probably most people have a similar sense; we simply do not normally notice this because our internal sense aligns with our external evidence. It is only when there is

---

[206] For more on this objection, see Bach 2012.
[207] For more on the case, see Walker 2004.

a clash that the existence of the internal sense becomes apparent.[208]

(3) Intersex individuals

Consider the case of infants born with ambiguous genitals, neither clearly male nor clearly female. The infant might, e.g., have a vaginal canal in addition to an organ that looks like a small penis or a very large clitoris. This is a rare but perfectly real phenomenon, which is considered a subset of "intersex" conditions.[209] In such cases, the child's *sex* is ambiguous. What happens with their gender?

It used to be thought that doctors could simply assign the baby to one gender or the other, perform a surgery to leave the baby with genitals appearing appropriate to the chosen gender, and then have the parents *raise* the child *as* the chosen gender. This is increasingly being recognized as a tragic mistake, possibly even a human rights violation, due in part to the high risk that the child will turn out not to have the gender chosen by the doctors.[210] In 2017, a lawsuit was settled for $440,000 over such a surgery. Doctors had operated on an intersex baby to "make him female". From the age of seven, however, the child firmly identified as a boy, rejecting the gender he had been assigned by the doctors. The child's foster parents sued the doctors for causing irreparable harm through their surgery.[211]

Individuals with ambiguous sex *sometimes* but *not always* have ambiguous gender. Sometimes, they firmly identify as boys and wind up behaving like normal boys. This can happen regardless of how the family raises them, even if the family attempts to raise them as girls. Others firmly identify as girls, even if the family attempts to raise them as boys.[212]

What explains this? Again, the natural explanation is that most human beings are endowed with an innate sense of the sex that their bodies are supposed to have, independent of what other people tell them and even independent of what they see with their eyes.

---

[208] Cf. Fileva 2019, p. 190.

[209] Cases of genital ambiguity are estimated to comprise between 1 in 2,000 and 1 in 4,500 people (Witchel 2018).

[210] Intersex Society of North America 2008; Human Rights Watch 2017.

[211] Ghorayshi 2017.

[212] Jacobson and Joel 2021; Human Rights Watch 2017.

(4) Transgender individuals

Here is where two progressive ideas contradict each other: The social construction theory clashes with accepting transgenderism. If gender is purely a social construct, then a person who is raised as a girl and treated as a girl *is ipso facto* a girl, and a person raised as a boy is a boy. Furthermore, there would be no explanation for how anyone could come to reject the gender that they were raised to accept, since there would be no source of gender identity other than society.

Yet there are such people; they are known as "transgender". They often experience severe distress about the clash between their inward sense of gender and the gender they outwardly appear to have; this distress is known as "gender dysphoria". It is sometimes successfully treated by surgery to alter the body's outward appearance.

Once again, these individuals appear to have an internal sense of their own gender that is independent of their outward appearance and of what the rest of society tells them.

(5) A theory of gender

I'm going to depart from reporting empirical facts now to engage in some anthropological theorizing because I think we need to understand gender better if we are to think clearly about the progressive gender myths.

Biological sex, in my view, is determined by one's inborn, reproduction-related physiological characteristics. Males normally have penises and testes; females normally have vaginas, ovaries, and wombs. If a person has overwhelmingly male-typical physiology, that person is a biological male; if one has overwhelmingly female-typical physiology, one is a biological female. Over 99.9% of people fall clearly into one of those two categories. If one has some combination of male and female features, or something in between the male-typical and the female-typical physiology, then one is intersex.

Evolution designed male and female bodies to be different from each other in a variety of respects in addition to the differences in our reproductive systems. For instance, male humans tend to have greater height and more upper body strength (though these are not *essential* to maleness; a short, weak male is still a male). There are at least *some* average physical differences between males and females in just about every organ of the body. Some of these differences are subtle and undetectable to the naked eye. For example, AI systems can be trained to distinguish male from female *retinas* with 87% accuracy, even though human observers see no differences between male and female retinas.[213]

It is thus unsurprising that there are average differences between male and female brains.[214] Some of these differences have been measured; others probably remain to be discovered and may be (like the retinal differences) invisible to human observers. Some (if not all) of these brain differences lead to psychological differences between typical males and typical females. Furthermore, at least *some* of these differences are probably *adaptations*—they exist because certain psychological traits better promoted survival and reproduction for males in our evolutionary history, while others better promoted survival and reproduction for females.

So here is my theory of gender: Gender is a set of psychological traits that evolution designed to go with a particular sex. The masculine gender is the set of traits designed for biological males; the feminine gender is the set of traits designed for biological females. To qualify as overall masculine-gendered, one need not have *all* the male-typical psychological traits; one need only have *enough* of them. For this purpose, the traits that are most strongly correlated with sex are the most important. This makes gender in principle vague; nevertheless, most people fall clearly on either the masculine or the feminine side.

Among the most robust psychological differences between typical males and typical females are these: (a) males are comfortable (only) in bodies with male-typical characteristics, whereas females are comfortable (only) in bodies with female-typical characteristics; (b) males show more affinity for other males (e.g., boys prefer to play with other boys, have male role models, and more easily understand other boys), while females show more affinity for other females; (c) males tend to prefer to look like and be treated like other males, while females prefer to look like and be treated like other females.[215] These traits are so strongly correlated with sex and so consistent across cultures as to make it very plausible that they have a biological basis.

---

[213] Korot et al. 2021.

[214] This is well-documented, though most of the differences are small and technical. See Goldman 2017; Wikipedia, "Neuroscience of Sex Differences".

[215] This list is derived from Fileva's (2019, p. 190) excellent account of gender, with small modification. Fileva does not, however, advance the evolutionary account given above in the text.

Undoubtedly there are many more psychological traits that are correlated with sex, but those are three of the traits most important to gender. Thus, if a person with a male body feels severe discomfort with that body's sexual characteristics, would strongly prefer to have female-typical physiology, shows greater affinity for girls than boys from a young age, and prefers to look like and be treated like a girl, then that person has feminine gender, despite their male sex. This explains at least part of the transgender phenomenon, as we will discuss in the next chapter.

15 Transgenderism

Myth

All transwomen are women. Transgender people are simply people who were born in the wrong body, i.e., their gender fails to match their biological sex. They are never or almost never mistaken about their gender, and they never or almost never change their minds. Anyone who disagrees with this is a bigot.

Background

Transgender people are people who identify with a gender that contrasts with the sex they were born with. Transwomen are people who were born male but identify as women (they feel that they were meant to be women, wish to be treated as women, etc.). Transmen are people who were born female but identify as men. Transgender identification is rare, affecting under 1% of the population, though the prevalence has greatly increased, especially among young people, in recent years.[216]

A popular progressive view of gender is that people are whatever gender they say they are, presumably because a person can tell their gender by direct introspection. This trumps other characteristics normally associated with masculinity or femininity, i.e., if a person identifies with women, then that person has feminine gender, regardless of whether they have other traits typical of women. Furthermore, the terms "man" and "woman" are tied to *gender*, rather than *sex*; therefore, transwomen are genuinely, literally *women*, and transmen are literally men.

Many conservatives take the opposite view. They say that transgender people are either lying or mistaken about their gender and that the terms "man" and "woman" refer to one's biological sex, which

---

[216] Ghorayshi 2022.

cannot diverge from one's gender.

Examples

First, some examples of the progressive view:

> *[G]ender* is different from *sex: Gender* is the sense of and expression of where one lies on the gender spectrum, whereas *sex* relates to biological anatomy.
>
> —University of San Francisco information page

> Be careful not to tell others how you think they should or shouldn't label their gender. Gender is a personal experience. There is no right or wrong way to define your gender.
>
> —The Trevor Project, trans activist group

> All cis-women are women (if they choose to identify that way, of course), all transwomen are women, no matter how anyone looks.
>
> —Hannah McKnight, trans activist

> Trans women are women. ... They have a right to have their identity respected without conforming to perceived sex and gender identity standards.
>
> —National Organization for Women

> [O]nce someone realizes they are different from the gender they were assigned at birth, they don't tend to flip flop or change their mind.
>
> —Martie Sirois, transgender rights activist

> To focus on "desisters"—people who experience gender dysphoria and then ultimately decide not to transition—is to focus on the rarest of cases, and to ignore the vastly more common experience of trans teens: that of being second-guessed.
>
> —Tey Meadow, sociologist, Columbia University

> Trans Women Are Women. This Isn't a Debate ... Trans women are a type of woman, just as women of color, disabled women and Christian women are types of women. Just as you would be bigoted to deny these women their womanhood, so would you be to deny trans women of [*sic*] theirs.
>
> —Raquel Willis, trans activist

Trans women are women. We will always stand up to this hate—whenever and wherever it occurs.

—Justin Trudeau, Prime Minister of Canada[217]

Now contrast the conservative view:

But "transgender women," that is, men who pose as women, are not *real* women. They are men wishing they were women, perhaps putting on effeminate affectations, but still not women.

—Christopher Tremoglie, conservative commentator

A woman is an adult female human.

—Wikipedia[218]

Reality

(1) This is a debate.

Pace Raquel Willis, there is actually disagreement about transgenderism. It cannot be eliminated merely by declaring that there is no debate.

(2) Early-onset gender dysphoria

Given the understanding of gender described in the previous chapter, there are indeed some people whose gender fails to match their biological sex. Gender dysphoria has traditionally been very rare, occurring in fewer than 1 in 10,000 people.[219] Traditionally, most cases have occurred in natal males (people who were born male). Gender dysphoria comes in at least two kinds: early-onset and late-onset.

In the early-onset case, children begin to behave like the opposite sex and experience gender dysphoria starting between 2 and 4 years old—the first time that children show gender-specific behaviors. According to the DSM (the standard reference work for psychiatrists), in *most* of these cases, gender dysphoria resolves on its own. However, in many cases it persists through puberty, in which case it almost

---

[217] Sources: Hager n.d.; Trevor Project n.d.; McKnight n.d.; National Organization for Women 2021; Sirois 2017; Meadow 2018; Willis 2017; Trudeau 2023.

[218] Sources: Tremoglie 2022; Wikipedia, "Woman". The Wikipedia page was presumably not intended to express a conservative view; it was undoubtedly written before pro-trans ideas became popular.

[219] My description in the text is based on the DSM-V (American Psychiatric Association 2013, pp. 451-9). For some compelling stories, see PBS 2015; Green 1987.

certainly will not resolve on its own. The dysphoria is then usually treated through transitioning to living as the opposite sex. In almost all of these cases, the patient is sexually attracted to members of their natal sex (men if they were born a boy, women if they were born a girl). This is just what one would expect on the theory that these patients have *brains* typical of one sex in *bodies* typical of the other sex, since most male brains are attracted to females and most female brains are attracted to males.

Further evidence comes from studies of brain physiology and function. As noted in the last chapter, male and female brains differ in measurable ways (these tend to be small differences that mean nothing to a non-scientist, such as one area being thicker or having more of one kind of cell in one sex). The brains of transgender people prior to receiving hormone treatments are not quite like the brains of cisgender people of either sex; they generally fall in between the average for their birth sex and the sex they identify with.[220]

These cases—people with early onset gender dysphoria that persists through puberty—are the clearest cases of people "born in the wrong body", i.e., with the gender corresponding to the opposite sex. It is hard to see any other description of the situation. It would be difficult to maintain that these people are merely *pretending* to be of the opposite gender—e.g., that a 2-year-old boy somehow decided to pretend to be a girl, then kept up that pretense throughout childhood—wearing dresses, playing with dolls, mimicking female mannerisms, etc.—and all the way into adulthood.

Whether or not such individuals are "really men" or "really women" is a semantic question. We could use the terms "man" and "woman" to describe a person's biological sex, or we could use them to describe a person's gender. Ordinary usage does not clearly settle the matter, since ordinary usage was created to describe common cases. Throughout history, sex and gender have coincided in 99.99% of cases, so that most people probably never met a single transgender person in their lives. We therefore never developed clear linguistic distinctions between sex and gender categories. In some contexts (e.g., medical contexts),

---

[220] See Mueller et al. 2021, but note that this study did not distinguish transgender people by sexual orientation or age of onset of dysphoria. Previous studies have reported that transgender brains simply resemble those of the gender they identify with (Russo 2016), but Mueller et al. show this to be an oversimplification.

biological sex might be more relevant, while in others (most social contexts), gender might be more relevant.

(3) Desistance and detransitioning

What I outlined above is, as I say, the clearest case of people with a sex/gender mismatch. But not all people who identify as transgender are like that.

Desistance is the phenomenon in which people who had gender dysphoria at one time come to identify with their natal sex at a later time. Detransitioning is a more specific phenomenon, in which someone transitions to living as the opposite sex, then later transitions back to living as their natal sex.

The frequency of desistance and detransitioning is uncertain. One can find estimates ranging from 7% to 98%. Figures in the neighborhood of 80% for desistance are most commonly quoted, though these have been disputed.[221] Desistance, however, appears to be much more common than *detransitioning*; that is, once a person goes as far as transitioning to living as the other sex, they are much less likely to later identify with their natal sex. This may be because those who transition are those who had more severe gender dysphoria to begin with, or because transitioning causes one to more firmly identify with the new sex, or for some other reason.

Whatever their frequency, desistance and detransitioning are real phenomena, and they show that people can, in fact, be mistaken about their own gender. They also show that not all transwomen are women: The transwomen who are later going to desist or detransition (and who will then say that they were never women) are presumably not women. Similarly for the transmen who will later desist or detransition.

How could a person be mistaken about their own gender? Very easily. Your gender, per the previous chapter, is a set of psychological traits that are biological adaptions for a particular sex. This set of traits is complex, and many of them consist of psychological *dispositions* rather than occurrent, introspectable feelings. Young people may be uncertain of what the gender-constituting traits *are*, let alone whether they have a sufficient number of them to qualify as of a given gender. Consider that young people are sometimes initially uncertain as to their own sexual

---

[221] 7%: Olson et al. 2022. 98%: Green 1987. 80%: Kaltiala-Heino et al. 2018, p. 33. For criticism of the 80% figure, see Temple Newhook 2018.

orientation, and then reflect on how much more complex and slippery the notion of gender is. (Cf. subsection 5 below.)

(4) Autogynephilia

In recent years, increasing numbers of people report gender dysphoria beginning in puberty or later (late-onset dysphoria).[222] This has been spreading particularly among teenagers. However, some people come out as trans, especially transwomen, even in middle age, after half a lifetime living as seemingly normally masculine males.

Among natal males with late onset dysphoria, most are gynephilic (sexually attracted to women). This is surprising if they are of feminine gender, because the overwhelming majority of women are androphilic (sexually attracted to men), not gynephilic.

Some psychologists have advanced the theory of "autogynephilia" to explain the prevalence of late-onset transwomen who are attracted to women.[223] The theory is that some males are sexually aroused by imagining themselves as women, and this motivates a desire to transition. This theory is supported by reports *from transwomen themselves:* In studies, most gynephilic transwomen themselves report autogynephilic feelings, while most androphilic transwomen do not. Some psychologists say that autogynephilia is a sexual orientation, that it encompasses broader romantic feelings (not only lust), and that it can lead to gender dysphoria.

Brain imaging studies find no evidence that the brains of gynephilic transwomen are more feminine than cisgender male brains; that is, unlike androphilic transwomen, their brains do not differ from typical male brains along the dimensions in which female brains tend to differ from male brains.[224] There is thus little reason to think that these individuals in general are literally women, regardless of whether we use "woman" to denote biological sex or to denote gender.

Many transgender activists are outraged by the autogynephilia theory, claiming that it "invalidates" transwomen and/or supports a right-wing political agenda.[225] This points to the main problem with recent discourse on gender: Discussion has been hijacked by histrionic

---

[222] Ghorayshi 2022.

[223] For a review of the theory and controversy surrounding it, see Lawrence 2017, from which most of my account here derives.

[224] Cantor 2011; Guillamon et al. 2016.

[225] Serano 2009; Veale et al. 2011.

ideologues who don't care about the truth; they only care about what makes them feel good or supports their political agenda. They often state this more or less explicitly, as in the example of people objecting to a scientific theory on the ground that it hurts people's feelings. These activists then try to silence dissent or intimidate scholars and journalists into agreeing with them. Consider, for example, how trans activists got Ryan Anderson's best-selling book, *When Harry Became Sally*, banned from Amazon,[226] or how they drove Professor Kathleen Stock out of the University of Sussex using threats of violence.[227] This sort of thing has the side effect of making it impossible to trust any expert claims in support of progressive views about gender: We can't know what the expert consensus would be if people were able to speak freely.

In any case, my goal isn't to either validate or invalidate anybody; my goal is to tell the truth. The argument, "I would benefit from being called a woman; therefore, I am a woman" is invalid. I therefore have no use for it.

Almost no one disputes the *existence* of autogynephilia. Most criticisms instead address how large of a causal influence it has, whether transwomen can be divided neatly into only two categories, and/or whether the theory of autogynephilia is harmful to transwomen.

But at least some transwomen report that the theory of autogynephilia applies to themselves.[228] Indeed, one of the leading proponents of the theory, Anne Lawrence, is a self-identified autogynephilic transwoman. It is hard to see why these individuals would say this if it were not true. It is plausible that many more transwomen would avow autogynephilia if not for the concerns about the emotional or political effects of the theory. So it is highly probable that at least some transgender identification is caused by autogynephilia. As one leading critic of the autogynephilia theory concedes, "No one disputes that autogynephilia exists or that it can explain the motivation of *some* MTF's [male-to-female transsexuals]."[229]

(5) Rapid onset gender dysphoria

The last decade has seen an explosion of trans identification. In 2013, the DSM cited estimates of the prevalence of gender dysphoria in the

---

[226] Fung 2021. The book is still available from Barnes & Noble.
[227] See Carr 2021, describing this and other cases of trans activist intimidation.
[228] Veale et al. 2011.
[229] Moser 2010, p. 791.

neighborhood of 0.01% of the population or less.[230] A 2022 report, however, found 0.6% of Americans identifying as trans. Among people aged 13-17, 1.4% now identify as trans (doubled from just five years earlier). The prevalence varies across states; among youths in New York, the rate is up to *3%*, or 300 times greater than the general prevalence in society in 2013.[231]

Gender dysphoria used to affect mostly natal males. After the recent increase, it now affects mostly natal females. There has been a particular increase among adolescents with no previous signs of gender dysphoria (what some call "rapid onset gender dysphoria").

Upon noticing this, medical researcher Lisa Littman decided to try to learn more about the phenomenon. She surveyed 256 parents whose children had undergone rapid onset gender dysphoria.[232] The survey revealed several striking patterns:

· Trans identification runs in friend groups. In 37% of friendship groups that parents described, more than half of the group came out as trans. In one case, four girls were taking group lessons with a popular coach. The coach came out as trans, and within a year, all four students announced that they were also trans. The probability of this happening by chance is about 1 in 26 million.[233]

· In 87% of cases, shortly before coming out as trans, the youth either had a recent increase in social media use or had one or more friends come out as trans.

· In 80% of cases, the teen had had zero symptoms of gender dysphoria in childhood.

· 48% of the teens had experienced a traumatic or stressful event shortly before becoming trans.

· 69% suffered from social anxiety.

· In 69% of cases, the parents thought that the teen, when coming out as trans, was using language taken from the internet. Many parents found websites containing verbatim matches to the words their child had used. As one parent put it, "it was like hearing someone who

---

[230] American Psychiatric Association 2013, p. 454.

[231] Herman et al. 2022; 2017. One recent survey found that 3% of Americans aged 18-25 identify as transgender (Brown 2022).

[232] Littman 2018. The survey only covered people whose children had rapid onset gender dysphoria; other forms of transgenderism were not represented.

[233] Assuming a prevalence of 1.4% for youths. $(0.014)^4 = 3.8 \times 10^{-8}$.

had memorized a lot of definitions for a vocabulary test."

- 61% of parents said that their child became more popular as a result of coming out as trans.
- 60% reported that their child's friend group mocked non-LGBT people.

You might wonder whether Littman's respondents were perhaps just prejudiced against trans people and were misdescribing their children's condition as a result. However, there was no evidence of this. For instance, 86% of respondents supported gay marriage, and 88% said that trans people deserve the same rights and protections as everyone else; these figures are similar to those for the wider society.[234]

All of this suggests that the rise in transgender identification among teenagers is not simply due to better diagnosis. It is not merely, for example, that with increasing social acceptance, we are now becoming aware of cases of gender dysphoria that people would previously have hidden. Rather, it appears that some teens are misdiagnosing themselves, due in part to peer influence and in part to other emotional disturbances which they have been encouraged to interpret as signs of gender dysphoria.

Littman lists examples of internet posts encouraging transgender identification. Some advise youths to lie to clinicians in order to get puberty blockers and hormones, e.g., to look up the symptoms of gender dysphoria from the DSM and pretend to have them. Others list vague, common adolescent experiences as symptoms of gender dysphoria; for example:

> Signs of indirect gender dysphoria: 1. Continual difficulty with simply getting through the day. 2. A sense of misalignment, disconnect, or estrangement from your own emotions. 3. A feeling of just going through the motions of everyday life, as if you're always reading from a script. 4. A seeming pointlessness to your life, and no sense of any real meaning or ultimate purpose. 5. Knowing you're somehow different from everyone else, and wishing you could be normal like them ...[235]

Can people really be so easily fooled about their own gender? Given

---

[234] Littman 2018, p. 11.
[235] Littman 2018, p. 6, citing <http://transgenderteensurvivalguide.com/post/62036014416/that-was-dysphoria-8-signs-and-symptoms-of>.

the difficulty of gender transitioning, is this really something that people would undertake as a result of peer pressure, persuasive internet content, or general malaise?

Yes, it is. We have seen similar phenomena in the past. It is well-documented that peer influence and social contagion play a major role in the spread of anorexia nervosa, particularly among adolescent females.[236] If girls who are literally starving can become convinced that they are fat, it is not such a stretch to believe that they can become convinced that they have a different gender from their actual gender.

Conclusion: It is possible to be mistaken about your gender. Not everyone who identifies as a man is a man, and not everyone who identifies as a woman is a woman.

Questions and Objections

(1) People should be free to live however they want and identify however they want. It's their own lives!

Reply: Yes, they should, with two qualifications: (a) Minors should not necessarily be allowed to do whatever they want; adults may need to stop minors from harming themselves. (b) Individuals may do what they want as long as their choices do not risk causing harm, or reasonably appear to risk causing harm, to others. So, as long as we're just talking about adults modifying their own bodies, clothing, and appearance, I agree that they should be free to do as they wish, regardless of whether they are correct or mistaken about their gender.

(2) Aren't you promoting hate against trans people?

Reply: No. No one should be hated because of their gender identification. To say that some people are mistaken about their gender is not to advocate hate or abuse toward those people. People who suffer gender dysphoria or gender confusion deserve our compassion, whatever the cause of the dysphoria.

(3) Then why won't you affirm everyone's chosen gender identities?!

Reply: Note first that individuals only have a right to live *their own lives* as they wish; this does not entail a right to require *other people* to express agreement with your beliefs (even beliefs about yourself). Second, it

---

[236] Allison et al. 2014.

isn't necessarily compassionate to fake agreement with someone's beliefs. If someone holds deep, mistaken beliefs about themselves, the compassionate thing may be to tell them the truth.

More generally, lies are usually harmful, and the truth is almost always more important than short-term emotional comfort. Society needs to make decisions about gender-related issues, racial issues, and so on, and making the right decisions almost certainly requires knowing the actual truth about these subjects. For example, covering up the facts about desistance and detransitioning will not help society make the right policy regarding gender transitioning for minors. The people advocating for such coverups are the real enemies of trans people.

People who lie to avoid causing offense are not your friends. They are selfish individuals who put their own emotional comfort and social status ahead of the good of others.

Part V: Economic Myths

Contemporary progressivism tends to support more economic regulation, higher taxes, more government social welfare spending, and more wealth redistribution from the rich to the poor. This is motivated largely by the sense that society is rigged in favor of the rich and that the rich do not deserve their wealth. The myths in this part of the book all concern those ideas.

16 Generational Wealth

Myth

Most wealth is due to inheritance, family connections, and luck. Once you are born poor, it is difficult or impossible to move up the income ladder.

Examples

> Strong liberals say the top drivers of wealth are family connections (48%), inheritance (40%), and getting lucky (31%).
> —Cato Institute survey report

> Just how deep does the myth that millionaires' wealth simply fell into their laps go? We found out that 74% of millennials believe millionaires inherited their money and more than half (52%) of baby boomers think the same thing.
> —Ramsey Solutions survey report

> On average, the wealthiest one percent has inherited just under $5 million in current dollars. Although media coverage of the super-wealthy, e.g. Forbes 400, tend to emphasize entrepreneurs and other "self-made" scions. [*sic*] In reality, inheritance plays a huge role in determining who winds up at the top and bottom of our society.
> —People's Policy Project (left-wing think tank)[237]

Reality

(1) Few millionaires got rich from inheritance.

A survey of 10,000 millionaires conducted in 2017-2018 found that 79% of millionaires in the U.S. had received *no* inheritance. Only 3%

---

[237] Sources: Ekins 2019; Ramsey Solutions 2022; Lewis and Bruenig 2017.

had inherited over $1 million. Most reported that regular, consistent investing over a long period of time was the key to their success.[238]

Pace the People's Policy Project, even the richest 1% of Americans (each of whom has more than $10 million[239]) have not inherited $5 million. According to a recent survey conducted by the Federal Reserve, the richest 1% of Americans have in fact inherited an average of $719,000.[240]

(2) The U.S. has great income mobility.

It is not extremely difficult to move up the income ladder in America. A 2007 Treasury Department report tracked individuals from 1996 to 2005. It found that 58% of people who started out in the bottom quintile of income earners in 1996 had moved up to a higher quintile by 2005. (A "quintile" is a group of one fifth of the population; in the report, the population was divided into quintiles by income level.) Meanwhile, those who began in the top quintile had a 31% chance of having moved down. Overall, more people moved up than moved down, a reflection of the general phenomenon that people tend to enter the labor market near the bottom of the scale and increase their incomes over the course of their careers. (See Table 1.)[241]

A 2015 report using U.S. tax data looked at income mobility over two-year periods. It found that 44% of individuals had an income change of at least 25% (either up or down) over the course of two years. Those at the bottom were most likely to go up: The lowest quintile of individuals saw a mean income increase of 68% ($7200) for men and 79% ($6500) for women.[242]

---

[238] Ramsey Solutions 2022, pp. 3, 5.

[239] Kelly 2019.

[240] Bricker et al. 2020. The People's Policy Project blog cryptically notes that they got the ~$5 million figure (actually $4.8 million) after assuming "a 5% rate of return" (Lewis and Bruenig 2017). My interpretation is that they imagined that all of the inheritance was invested at a 5% rate of return, then calculated how much the investment would have grown to over the years since the inheritance, then called *that* figure the amount inherited. I do not deem this to be honest reporting.

[241] U.S. Department of the Treasury 2007, p. 7. To help you read the table: It indicates that people who started in the lowest quintile in 1996 had a 42.4% chance of still being there in 2005, a 28.6% chance of having instead moved up to the second quintile, etc. Note that the "top 10%", "top 5%" and "top 1%" groups are *included* in the top quintile ("Highest").

[242] Larrimore et al. 2015, p. 24.

Table 1: Income mobility in the United States, 1996–2005

1996 Income Group	2005 Income Group							
	Lowest	Second	Middle	Fourth	Highest	Top 10%	Top 5%	Top 1%
Lowest	42.4	28.6	13.9	9.9	5.3	2.3	1.3	0.2
Second	17.0	33.3	26.7	15.1	7.9	3.0	1.2	0.1
Middle	7.1	17.5	33.3	29.6	12.5	4.2	1.4	0.3
Fourth	4.1	7.3	18.3	40.2	30.2	8.6	2.7	0.3
Highest	2.6	3.2	7.1	17.8	69.4	43.4	22.5	4.4
Top 10%	2.6	2.2	4.9	11.8	78.6	61.1	37.6	8.3
Top 5%	2.6	1.8	3.9	8.6	83.1	71.6	54.4	15.2
Top 1%	3.2	1.3	2.2	4.9	88.4	82.7	75.0	42.6
All Groups	13.2	16.8	19.6	23.3	27.1	13.4	6.4	1.2

(3) Why does parental income affect children's income?

The more money your parents made, the more money *you* are likely to make. On average, a 10 percentile increase in parents' income correlates to a 3.4 percentile increase in children's income.[243] (Example: A baby trades in parents at the median income for parents at the 60th percentile, and his own expected future income jumps from the 50th to the 53rd percentile.)

This effect is hardly overwhelming, but it is significant. Does it indicate an unfair distribution of opportunity?

Not necessarily. *One* explanation for the correlation between parental income and child income is that wealthier parents tend to give their children better opportunities—for example, by sending them to better schools, paying for college, providing them with valuable contacts in the business world, and so on. You might deem this unfair, since not everyone gets the same opportunities. (This is open to philosophical debate; perhaps parents have a right to give extra benefits to their offspring, as long as they aren't actively interfering with other people's children. But let's leave the philosophical debate aside.)

But there are other explanations for the correlation between parents' and children's income. Perhaps there are differences in productive

---

[243] Chetty et al. 2014.

abilities and *character traits* which have a partly genetic basis. High-income parents tend to have higher ability and more beneficial traits of character, which they tend to pass on to their children. These tendencies are imperfect; hence, a variation in parental income predicts a smaller variation in child's income.

The latter explanation is the correct one. One way to test this is by looking at adoption studies: If the correlation between parents' income and children's income is due to genetics, it should disappear for genetically unrelated children (adoptees). If it is due to upbringing, then it should be equally strong for adoptees as for biological offspring. And if it is due to a combination of factors, then the correlation should remain present but with a smaller magnitude for adoptees as compared to biological offspring.

Economist Bruce Sacerdote followed over 1000 Korean children who had been adopted into American families in the 1970's. He tracked the adoptees' income, educational attainment, and several other variables once the children had grown up. He found that the parents' income during the child's upbringing had almost no effect on the adoptees' income in adulthood. In other words, statistically, children adopted into a poor family had about as good financial prospects in adulthood as those who had been adopted into a wealthy family.[244]

Other studies find small to zero effects of nurture on income.[245] For example, one study compared identical twins with fraternal twins in Finland. The incomes of siblings tend to be correlated with each other. If this correlation is mainly due to similar *genes*, then identical twins (who share 100% of their genes) will tend to be closer in income than merely fraternal twins (who share only 50% of their genes). If the correlation is due to similar *environments*, then identical twins raised in the same household should be about equally close in income as fraternal twins raised in the same household. The Finnish study confirmed the former alternative: The income correlation is almost all due to genes. The authors conclude, "Consistent with the prior epidemiological and behavioral genetics literature on the heritability of complex traits, the contribution of the shared environment is negligible."[246]

What this shows is that the way in which wealthy parents help their

---

[244] Sacerdote 2007.
[245] For a summary of the findings, see Caplan 2011, ch. 2.
[246] Hyytinen et al. 2019, p. 331.

children become wealthier is not chiefly by giving them better school-ing, a better upbringing, better contacts, or any other environmental factor. It is by giving them good genes. You might still consider this cosmically unfair, but it is not exactly something that society (or anyone else) could be blamed for.

17 The Tax Burden

Myth

The rich are not paying their fair share of taxes.

Examples

For too long we've had an economy that gives every break in the world to the folks who need it the least. ... I'm not anti-corporate. But it's about time they start paying their fair share.

—U.S. President Joe Biden

Last year my federal tax bill ... was $6,938,744. ... But what I paid was only 17.4 percent of my taxable income—and that's actually a lower percentage than was paid by any of the other 20 people in our office. Their tax burdens ranged from 33 percent to 41 percent and averaged 36 percent.

—Warren Buffett, billionaire investor

The Rich Are Not Remotely Paying Their Fair Share
    —Headline from Common Dreams (progressive news site)

Billionaires like Elon Musk and Jeff Bezos pay a "true tax rate" of just 3% or less while working people around the globe pay far more. Enough is enough. It's time for the ultra-rich to pay their fair share of taxes.

—Oxfam America

At least 55 of the largest corporations in America paid no federal corporate income taxes in their most recent fiscal year despite enjoying substantial pretax profits in the United States.

—Institute on Taxation and Economic Policy

This isn't rocket science: giant corporations that report billions in profit shouldn't be able to pay $0 in federal taxes.

—Senator Elizabeth Warren[247]

Reality

(1) Does Warren Buffett's secretary really pay a higher tax rate than Buffett himself?[248]

Not really. There is a way of making the calculations come out that way, but it is highly misleading. Here is how Buffett arrived at that conclusion.

First, when reporting on his secretary's taxes, Buffett included all payroll taxes (Social Security and Medicare), which, at the time he was speaking, amounted to about 15%. Legally, half of payroll taxes are paid by the employee and half by the employer, but Buffett apparently treated them *all* as paid by the employee.[249]

Second, most of Buffett's income consisted of *capital gains* (profits derived from financial assets, such as stocks, bonds, or real estate), as opposed to wages or salary. Capital gains were taxed at 15%, which was much lower than most people's tax rate on wage or salary income.

However, Buffett did not take account of *corporate* taxes. Buffett's capital gains come from his *stock holdings*, which represent (partial) ownership of a variety of companies. For most large companies, the corporate tax rate in 2007 was 35%. But the taxes "paid by a company" are properly understood as being paid by the *owners* of that company (the shareholders, in the case of publicly traded companies)—all of the company's assets and profits ultimately belong to them, so the taxes that it pays out of those profits are really paid by the owners. This is part of why the capital gains tax rate is so low—because it is a kind of double tax. A company's profits are first taxed at the corporate income tax rate, then they are taxed again if and when the company passes them on to its owners. Or, to remove the fiction that companies are inde-

---

[247] Sources: Gabbatt 2021; Buffett 2011; Collins and Lord 2021; Oxfam America 2023; Gardner and Wamhoff 2021; Warren 2021.

[248] In addition to his 2011 remarks quoted above, see his 2007 interview with Tom Brokaw (Crippen 2007).

[249] People sometimes say that the payroll tax is "really" all paid by the employee in the form of lower wages. This is not correct. The burden is split between the employee (who must take lower wages) and the employer (who must take lower profits); there is no basis for claiming only one of them bears a cost. The exact split cannot be determined without detailed empirical evidence (see Carloni 2021).

pendent agents: The *owners* first pay corporate income tax on the profits that they made using their company, then, if and when they transfer those profits to their bank accounts (perhaps by selling stocks whose value has increased due to those profits), they must pay individual income tax on those same profits.

The situation is complicated because company profits do not immediately translate into dollar-for-dollar increases in company stock value. Nevertheless, *on average in the long term*, we should expect profits to translate into equivalent increases in stock value. So, as a rough approximation, a person who derives income from capital gains would in general have indirectly (through the corporation) paid about 35% on that income, before paying the 15% capital gains tax.[250]

If we take all of the above into account, Buffett's real tax rate was probably about 45%, and his staff probably paid about 29%.[251]

(2) Are billionaires paying 3%?

Again, there is a way to make the calculations come out this way, but it is highly misleading.

America's wealthiest people hold most of their wealth in the form of stocks. Jeff Bezos, for example, does not have $200 billion sitting in a bank account. Rather, he owns a large stake in Amazon. When you read that Bezos is worth $200 billion, that is based on the current Amazon stock price and the portion of the company that he owns. So if the price rises on the stock market, then his estimated net worth will go up.

The "3%" statistic is based on that. Amazon's stock price soared in 2020; hence, Bezos' estimated net worth increased by billions of dollars. It's not that he took in billions in cash, nor did he acquire billions in new assets; it's just that the market price of his preexisting assets went up. You don't get taxed on the increase in the market price of your assets until you "realize" the gains by selling them. Since Bezos did not sell his Amazon stock in 2020, he didn't get taxed on the increase in the stock price. That is what the 3% statistic is complaining about—that

---

[250] That was as of 2007. During the Trump administration, the corporate tax rate was reduced to 21%, which would bring Buffett's total tax rate closer to 33%.

[251] To estimate Buffett's tax rate: Assume one of his companies makes a dollar in profit. It gets reduced to $0.65 by the corporate tax. Then the capital gains tax reduces that to $0.65×.85 = $0.55. So he pays $0.45 in taxes. To estimate his staff's tax rate: In his 2011 editorial, he reported it as an average of 36%. But half of the payroll tax, or 7%, is paid by the employer. So call it 29%.

Bezos' income tax in some year was only 3% as large as the increase in his estimated net worth. Incidentally, in 2022, Amazon's stock price collapsed down to pre-2020 levels. Bezos also did not get to write that off as a loss of billions of dollars on his taxes, nor did anyone complain that he had to pay income tax despite having a huge negative income.

This is not something special to billionaires. Anyone who owns anything will have a gain or loss on paper whenever the market price of that thing changes. They do not have to pay income tax, nor can they write off losses, unless and until they sell the asset. For example, whenever the real estate market rises, millions of homeowners have a gain in their net worth, often by thousands or tens of thousands of dollars in a single year. They do not have to report that as "income" on their income tax return, unless and until they sell their houses. If they did, many people would be unable to pay their income taxes using their ordinary wages and would be forced to sell their houses in order to afford the tax. Retired people in particular would be systematically expelled from their homes during real estate booms. No one thinks this is a good idea. In general, no one thinks that you should be required to report *unrealized* gains as income and pay tax on them. It is therefore deceptive to report that Jeff Bezos is only paying 3% in income taxes.

(3) Did 55 companies with large profits pay zero federal taxes in 2020?

Apparently so. However, this is not as alarming as it sounds. It *sounds* as though companies are evading taxes left and right through "tax loopholes", but this is not the case.

Note first that 55 is not a large number of companies. There are approximately 6 million companies in the United States. Of course, most of them are small. But if we just look at companies with over a thousand employees, there are still over ten thousand such companies.[252] Thus, the situation of 55 large companies does not tell us the overall situation of businesses, or even of large businesses, in America.

Second, the way these companies avoided tax liability was generally through taking advantage of provisions of tax law in the way those provisions were intended, not through some kind of underhanded manipulation.[253] For example, the government wants to encourage research into green energy, so it offers tax credits to businesses for

---

[252] Statista 2023c.
[253] For discussion, see Jacobson 2021.

conducting such research. If a company does the research and takes the tax credit, that isn't a *loophole*; that is the law functioning exactly as it was intended.

Another feature of the tax code is that losses in a given year can be used to offset profits in the following year, thus decreasing your income tax the next year. This applies to both individuals and corporations. E.g., if you have an income of -$1,000 one year and $50,000 the next year, you only need pay taxes on a total of $49,000 over the two years. Similarly, if a company loses $10 million in 2019, then makes $10 million in 2020, they might use the 2019 loss to offset the 2020 profit, thus paying zero tax for the two years. This is not a loophole; in this example, the company's total profit over the two years is zero, so it makes sense that they would have zero income tax. Nor is this a weird scenario; many companies have narrow profit margins and many have net incomes that fluctuate between negative and positive values from year to year.

(4) Do the wealthy pay lower taxes than the middle class?

It is widely believed that the wealthy get away with paying lower tax rates than the rest of us due to "tax loopholes" and that the burden mainly falls on the middle class. This is the opposite of the truth.

Table 2 is based on data from the Congressional Budget Office.[254] I break the population into five groups (quintiles) by income. For each group, the table shows their market income (income derived from non-government sources), government transfers (money and benefits they received through federal social programs), and federal taxes they paid

Table 2: Income and taxes by income group, United States, 2019

	Lowest quintile	Second quintile	Third quintile	Fourth quintile	Highest quintile
Market Income	$17,200	$39,600	$67,500	$108,700	$318,900
Government Transfers	$15,300	$7,200	$3,700	$1,900	$1,000
Federal Taxes	$100	$4,600	$10,600	$20,600	$81,100
Net Tax	−$15,200	−$2,600	$6,900	$18,700	$80,100
Net Tax Rate	−88.4%	−6.6%	10.2%	17.2%	25.1%
Net Tax Share	**−17.3%**	**−3.0%**	**7.8%**	**21.3%**	**91.1%**

[254] U.S. Congressional Budget Office 2022.

(including payroll and income taxes; state and local taxes are not included since they are not in the CBO report). All of these numbers are *averages* for the group (naturally, the numbers vary between individuals within each income group).

In the fourth row, "Net Tax", I show the taxes each group paid *minus* the money they received from the government. This is the relevant figure for assessing someone's tax burden. (If the government takes $3 from you but then gives you $1, that is equivalent to their just taking $2; it doesn't matter how many transactions they use to arrive at this net result.) In the fifth row, I show each group's net tax as a percentage of their market income. This is their true tax rate in the relevant sense. Finally, the bottom row shows each group's net tax as a percentage of the total net taxes paid by all groups.

Notice that the bottom two quintiles have *negative* net taxes, meaning that they receive more money from the federal government than they pay in. The middle group has a small positive net tax (8% of the total). The fourth quintile is the only one that intuitively appears to be paying just about its fair share: It comprises 20% of the population and pays 21% of the net tax burden. Finally, the top quintile makes all of this possible by shouldering 91% of the total burden.

In case you're wondering about the notorious top 1% of income earners, I include their data in table 3. Despite comprising only 1% of the population, they shoulder a third of the entire net tax burden.

Table 3: Income & taxes of the top 1%, U.S., 2019

	Top 1%
Market Income	$1,983,700
Government Transfers	$800
Federal Taxes	$600,300
Net Tax	$599,500
Net Tax Rate	30.2%
Net Tax Share	34.1%

Does all this add up to the rich paying their fair share? Well, there is no consensus on what one's "fair share" is, so one can always say that the rich are paying less than their fair share no matter how much they pay. The option of increasing transfers from the rich to the poor raises the possibility of assigning to the rich a "fair share" even greater than 100%. But let's look at a common sense example.

Suppose you go out for dinner with four friends. At the end of the meal, the waitress brings the five of you a bill for $100. (That includes tip and taxes; it's a very affordable restaurant.) A conversation about how to divide the bill ensues. Two of your friends declare that they would like to pay nothing, as they are a bit strapped for cash. In fact, they would like the other three of you to give them some cash back, say, $20 to split between them. A third friend volunteers to pay just $8. Your fourth friend generously offers $21. Finally, your four friends all look at you. Given what the others are paying, there is now a $91 shortfall, which it falls upon *you* to pay. As you reluctantly get out your wallet, howls of outrage emerge from the other four about how *little* you are paying. They demand to know when you are going to start paying your fair share for meals.

That, in a nutshell, is the current situation with the distribution of federal taxes in the U.S.

Objections

(1) The poor help the rich to earn their money.

Nobody becomes rich through solitary activity. It generally requires the cooperation of many people throughout society. It is not only the Amazon employees who helped make Jeff Bezos rich; it is also Amazon's customers, their suppliers, the suppliers of their suppliers, and so on. This is unlike the restaurant example, in which, one assumes, each party brought money to the table that they obtained completely independently of the other diners.

Reply: This point is easily overstated. Not everyone is helping the rich or society in general. Unemployed people on government assistance are not helping; they are making things harder for the rest of us.

Nevertheless, let us modify the hypothetical to take account of this point. Assume that the five diners are all coworkers in the same company. Their collective activity enables the company to take in money, out of which all five people's salaries are paid. *Now* does it seem fair for one person to pay $91 so that two of the other diners can pay a much smaller amount and another two can get rebates? This still does not strike me as fair.

(2) The rich are overpaid to begin with.

Perhaps the progressive argument assumes that the wealthy are in general overpaid in the first place. (In what sense? I am not sure. Perhaps progressives would say that the wealthy are paid out of proportion to the true value of their contributions to total economic productivity? I don't consider this claim well-founded, but we can't discuss that here.) Perhaps the idea is that tax policy is an opportunity to partially rectify this pre-existing injustice.

Reply: To represent this, imagine that the diners—again, all working for the same company—are earning different amounts from that company. Each has negotiated a pay rate with the company, and each is being paid at the rate they agreed to. Of the five people at the dinner table, you are the one being paid the most. Some of your co-workers feel that you are overpaid; they do not see how your contributions to the company are worth the amount of money you are receiving. You, of course, disagree. But your co-workers want you to pay $91 to partially rectify the injustice consisting of your having too much money.

True or false: "Your co-workers are just asking you to pay your fair share for the meal." That still strikes me as obviously false.

(3) The government helps the wealthy to earn their money.

Without government, some people argue, social order would collapse, at which point none of the rich would have any of the wealth they currently have. Therefore, the government has the right to take a large portion of that wealth, perhaps as much as it wants.

Reply: There are other professions that are very important to society. For instance, without farmers, none of us would have any of the wealth we currently have, since we would die of starvation. Yet it does not follow that farmers have the right to seize a quarter of the income of rich people in order to give rebates to the poor. Nor would their doing so count as their merely "asking the rich to pay their fair share for food".

But let's modify the dinner scenario once again. Suppose one of the five diners is the company security guard. Suppose the diners know that the security guard once deterred a robbery of the company which would have resulted in the company going out of business and all five being unemployed.

True or false:

a. "The security guard now has the right to take as much money as he wants from the other company employees."

b. "If the security guard forces you to pay $91 for the dinner, he is just asking you to pay your fair share."

Both of these seem obviously false.

(4) The wealthy get greater benefits from the government.

A large part of what the government does is protect property rights. Without government, most things of value would quickly be stolen. Wealthy people have more property to protect than poor people do; therefore, wealthy people are receiving a greater benefit from the government than poor people are. Thus, it is fair for them to pay more for government services.

Reply: Judgments about fair distribution of costs are usually more tied to the *cost* that each person incurred than to the amount of *benefit* that they received. Thus, suppose that at the dinner, you ordered $10 worth of food, yet you clearly enjoyed the food so much that you got as much benefit from the meal as the other four diners combined. In this case, you incurred 10% of the total cost incurred by the group, yet you received 50% of the total benefit. What is your fair share of the bill?

Intuitively, your fair share of the bill is $10 (the amount that you added to that bill), not half of the total bill.

Now suppose that there was an item that was shared by the group— say, a $20 appetizer that everyone shared equally. In that case, your fair share, intuitively, is one fifth the cost of the common item, plus the cost of the items you ordered for yourself. In this example, your fair share is now up to $10 + $20/5 = $14.

Applying this to taxation, the fair distribution of taxes should turn on how much money each group is costing the government. It would be fair that each group pay an equal share of the cost of certain public goods that benefit everyone (e.g., national defense), plus the cost that that group adds to the government budget.

By this standard, the rich should have *lower* taxes than the poor. Poor neighborhoods have much higher crime rates than wealthy neighborhoods, which means that it costs more money to protect them from crime (including the costs of police officers, courts, and prisons) than it does to protect wealthy neighborhoods. Very wealthy people also tend to send their children to private schools, thus costing the government much less money for education. So the fair share for the rich to pay would probably be a *lower absolute dollar amount* than the fair share for the poor.

But even if you think that fair shares depend on how much *benefit* each taxpayer enjoys, there still is no rationale for the bottom two quintiles to have a *negative* share of the tax burden, unless they somehow are getting net harms from the government.

It is also unclear why the wealthy would pay a higher tax *rate* than the poor. If we wanted to make tax payments proportional to benefits received, then perhaps people would pay taxes proportional to their income. But the wealthy are in fact paying much more than that; they are paying a higher *proportion* of their income than the rest of society, often drastically higher.

18 Regulation

Myth

Regulations mainly protect consumers from rapacious businesses. That's why businesses oppose regulation and favor laissez-faire capitalism. The total benefits of regulation far outweigh the costs.

Examples

> [P]eriodically, as Americans experienced unacceptable harms from market practices, they have insisted that public authorities override protests from profit-seekers and step in to secure the public interest. … For many years, the U.S. Office of Management and Budget has systematically studied the costs of regulation. Looking at more than 100 major regulations over the ten-year period ending in 2010, it found that benefits were three to ten times greater than costs. For every regulatory agency considered, benefits exceeded costs.
>
> —Scholars Strategy Network

> A majority of the public (58%) says that government regulation of business is necessary to protect the public interest; fewer (41%) say government regulation of business usually does more harm than good. … 75% of Democrats say government regulation of business is necessary to protect the public interest, while 61% of Republicans say it usually does more harm than good.
>
> —Pew Research Center[255]

Reality

Obviously, some regulations are beneficial. A good example is the regulations concerning chlorofluorocarbons, a type of chemical that

---

[255] Sources: Lipsky 2016; Pew Research Center 2019.

used to be used in aerosol spray cans and refrigerators. In the 1970's, scientists discovered that these chemicals were damaging the Earth's ozone layer, which protects all of us from harmful ultraviolent radiation from the sun. Countries around the world then wisely banned the production of CFC's. No one that I know of disagrees with this outcome. More generally, regulations can be used to address cases in which businesses or individuals would impose significant harms on other people without those others' consent.

Nevertheless, many other regulations are harmful to society. Among these are many that are *supported* by the regulated industry for the purpose of limiting competition, increasing prices, and exploiting consumers. Supporters normally proclaim some superficially public-spirited rationale for regulations that are really designed to transfer money from consumers to influential industry players. Members of the public, lacking knowledge of economics, regularly swallow these rationalizations whole.

There are tens of thousands of regulations of many different kinds[256] (no one knows exactly how many), and it is not possible to discuss any significant fraction of them. It is thus extremely difficult to estimate what proportion of regulations are harmful. But harmful or exploitative regulations are a significant fraction of the total, probably a large majority. Many regulations of this kind are quite popular. Let's look at a couple of examples.

(1) Licensing laws hurt you.

Among the most popular types of regulation is occupational licensing. These are laws that require people to obtain a license to sell particular services. The requirements to obtain the license range from the modest to the extremely onerous. The most famous examples are medical and legal licensing, but many other occupations require a license in one state or another, such as teachers, electricians, funeral attendants, interior designers, travel agents, cosmetologists, and florists.[257] Licensing requirements have ballooned since the mid-twentieth century, going from 1 in 20 jobs requiring a license to about 1 in 4.[258]

This type of regulation is usually prompted *by the industry*.[259] Why?

---

[256] U.S. Office of the Federal Register 2023.
[257] McKenna 2023.
[258] McLaughlin et al. 2017; NCSL 2022.
[259] Larkin 2015, pp. 226-7.

Industry members say that they just want to protect consumers. Without licensing laws, who knows what kind of low-quality make-up and flower arrangements consumers might be saddled with?

Perhaps producers in many industries are really concerned about consumers ... or perhaps they are concerned about their own profits. When the government creates additional hurdles to enter a given profession, fewer people will enter that profession. The people already in the profession then face less competition from newcomers and can charge higher prices. This dynamic is well-known and undisputed in economics. A report from President Obama's economic advisors in 2015 put the point thus: "The evidence on licensing's effects on prices is unequivocal: many studies find that more restrictive licensing laws lead to higher prices for consumers."[260] The more onerous the licensing requirements are, the higher prices will go. This is one reason why medical and legal services in America are so outrageously expensive.

This also means that fewer people will receive the service in question. If you expel the bottom half of doctors from the profession, that doesn't mean that everyone gets treated by the top half of doctors. It means that there is roughly half as much medical care, so roughly half as many people receive care.[261]

Does licensing at least increase average quality? Not necessarily. Remember, licensing *reduces competition*. But competition tends to increase quality. Intuitively, if there is a chronic shortage of providers in a given industry, then providers can more easily get away with selling low quality services.

It *could* also be that licensing increases average quality by preventing low-quality providers from entering the industry. This is what advocates say. But the incentives are not aligned to make this happen. The licensing requirements are normally designed and overseen by industry insiders. For instance, medical licensing boards are staffed by doctors; bar associations are staffed by lawyers. That seems to make sense, as they would know what the job requires. But they also have a conflict of interests: It is in their interests to reduce competition with themselves. It is not particularly in their interests to try to insure high average quality for consumers. Indeed, what would *most* serve the economic interests of existing doctors or lawyers would be to prevent new *high-*

---

[260] U.S. Department of the Treasury et al. 2015, p. 14.
[261] This point derives from Friedman 2014, p. 41.

quality doctors or lawyers from entering the field, since those would be the most serious competitors to themselves. I am not suggesting that licensing boards expressly eliminate high-quality providers (after all, they probably have some conscience). But they probably do not take great pains to ensure quality either, since it isn't in their interests to do so.

Empirical studies align with this. The Obama administration report mentioned above concluded that "most research does not find that licensing improves quality or public health and safety."[262] A survey of nineteen studies of licensing requirements reported that just three studies found overall positive effects on quality, four found overall negative effects, and the rest found unclear, mixed, or neutral effects.[263]

(2) Red tape favors big business over small business.

At the end of his Presidency, Bill Clinton proposed a new Food and Drug Administration (FDA) regulation that would have required companies producing new genetically modified foods to submit information about the products to the FDA 120 days before bringing them to the market. It was anticipated that this would require an average of 209 man-hours of bureaucratic work for the company each time.[264]

Though the rule was not ultimately adopted, it is interesting to look at who supported it. It *wasn't* supported by anti-GMO activists; they wanted much stronger regulations. It *was* supported by Monsanto, the largest producer of genetically modified seeds in the U.S. They wrote to the FDA, "Monsanto supports the FDA's initiative to require a Premarket Biotechnology Notice (PBN) notice [*sic*] at least 120 days prior to the commercial distribution of a food or feed produced through biotechnology." It was also supported by the Biotechnology Industry Organization (BIO), an industry lobbying group. They wrote: "BIO strongly endorses a mandatory premarket notification process that will ensure review by the Food and Drug Administration ... of all food and feed products produced using biotechnology."

That's weird. Why would the industry want to be regulated more? Were they concerned about unsafe products that would harm consumers?

---

[262] U.S. Department of the Treasury et al. 2015, p. 13; cf. p. 58, table 1.
[263] McLaughlin et al. 2014.
[264] My account of this case derives from Carney 2006, pp. 120-25.

Hardly. The National Academy of Sciences, the American Dietetic Association, and the American Medical Association have all agreed that GMO's do not pose any special health risks. (By the way, humans have been selectively breeding animals and plants for thousands of years. That is just a low-tech form of genetic modification.)

What the companies said was that they wanted the new regulation because it would increase consumer confidence in genetically modified foods. I'm not sure this was their true reason, but it is in any case doubtful whether increasing consumer confidence is the FDA's job.

Another plausible motive is that the regulation would impose costs that would make it hard for smaller companies to compete with the large companies. This point applies to most regulations: There is usually a *fixed cost* to compliance. You have to hire lawyers to figure out how to comply with the regulation, and you have to hire employees to fill out paperwork or do other compliance-related tasks. These are *fixed* costs in the sense that the absolute cost is roughly the same regardless of the size of your company. In this case, a small company wouldn't require less time to fill out the paperwork; they would still need 209 hours of bureaucratic work.

But a fixed cost has a larger impact on a small company than a large company, because for the small company, the fixed cost is a larger *proportion* of their total revenues; therefore, the small company would be forced to raise prices more in order to cover the fixed cost. Thus, by imposing high bureaucratic costs on all businesses in a given industry, regulation can drive small companies out and let the large ones dominate.

(3) Big business captures regulatory agencies.

Why would government agencies make regulations that serve the interests of big business? Aren't they supposed to be serving the public?

Well, yes. But as it turns out, government behavior is not very well predicted by asking what they are *supposed* to do. It is better predicted by asking about the process by which government agents are selected and the *incentives* they face. The bureaucrats who make regulations generally have no incentive to protect the public, apart from the warm feeling inside that goes along with doing what one is supposed to do. If they make a regulation that causes prices to rise while having no effect or a slight negative effect on quality, nothing will happen to them. They won't lose money, they won't lose their jobs, and most members of the public will never even realize that they did that. If members of the public even hear about the regulation, most will assume that the agency had to do it to protect the public.

Why don't members of the public carefully monitor the government's regulatory activity? Because they have no incentive to do so, and they have their own lives to lead. The Code of Federal Regulations has 188,000 pages, detailing the tens of thousands of regulations the government has made. It would take many lifetimes to understand the effects of all of them. Any one of these regulations might realistically be indirectly costing you (and everyone else) a few dollars to a few dozen dollars a year, but it isn't worth it to try to figure out which ones are doing this. It isn't worth it for you to hire a lobbyist to go to Washington, or try to rally voters to go to a protest about this regulation that they never heard of before, just to try to save yourself a few dollars a year.

Everyone else in the country is in the same situation as you ... *except* the leaders of the big corporations in the industry that this regulation applies to. *They* face an entirely different situation. They have millions of dollars at their disposal, and they stand to make or lose millions depending on what regulations get made. For them, it is both feasible and rational to spend the time and money to influence the regulations in their industry.

Many observers have noticed the close relationships between regulators and the industries they regulate.[265] Regulatory agencies are often staffed by people who have worked in the industry, and regulators often go on to work in the industry after working in government. This makes sense, since the experts on a given industry are generally people who have worked in that industry. It does, however, make room for bias and undue influence due to personal connections between regulators and industry.

(4) Many studies find regulations harmful.

Did the Office of Management and Budget really report that most regulations produce benefits much greater than the costs?

Yes, sort of. The OMB issues regular reports to Congress on the costs and benefits of new regulations made by government agencies. However, the cost and benefit figures given by the OMB are not

---

[265] See Carney 2006; Dal Bo 2006.

established facts; they are simply taken from the estimates that *the regulatory agencies themselves* gave of the expected costs and benefits of the regulations they were about to impose. None of these estimates involve looking back at what actually happened with regulations that were imposed previously, nor are any produced by independent, non-government assessors.[266] It is not surprising that government agencies, when they impose a regulation, usually *say* that the regulation is going to produce greater benefits than costs. What else are they going to say?

What would be more interesting is what conclusions are drawn by independent economists looking at regulations that have been in effect for many years. The answer is that they almost always find the regulations to have been overall harmful. The Nobel laureate economist Ronald Coase was editor for 18 years of the *Journal of Law and Economics*. In 1997, he was interviewed about (among other things) his view of regulation:

> COASE: When I was editor of *The Journal of Law and Economics*, we published a whole series of studies of regulation and its effects. Almost all the studies—perhaps all the studies—suggested that the results of regulation had been bad, that the prices were higher, that the product was worse adapted to the needs of consumers, than it otherwise would have been. ... Regulation of transport, regulation of agriculture—agriculture is a, zoning is z. You know, you go from a to z, they are all bad. There were so many studies, and the result was quite universal: The effects were bad.[267]

(5) Regulation slows growth.

The biggest impact of regulation may be on the overall growth rate of the economy. Regulation slows economic growth because it makes it more difficult for new individuals or firms to enter an industry and more difficult for small firms to compete with large firms, as discussed above.

One 2013 study looked at the correlation between the economic growth rate and the overall amount of regulation (as measured by the growth of the Code of Federal Regulations).[268] The authors estimated that on average, the regulations added in the U.S. since 1949 have

---

[266] U.S. Office of Management and Budget 2021, p. 3.
[267] Hazlett 1997.
[268] Dawson and Seater 2013.

reduced economic growth by about 2 percentage points per year. As they note, this estimate is generally in line with or smaller than the estimates of regulation's impact found in earlier economic studies using a variety of different methods. Yet the total impact of 2 percentage points of growth over the course of several decades is enormous. The authors conclude:

> Federal regulations added over the past 50 years have reduced real output growth by about 2 percentage points on average over the period 1949–2005. That reduction in the growth rate has led to an accumulated reduction in GDP of about $38.8 trillion as of the end of 2011. That is, GDP at the end of 2011 would have been $53.9 trillion instead of $15.1 trillion if regulation had remained at its 1949 level.[269]

---

[269] In fairness, this estimate seems implausibly high. Perhaps as GDP grew to much higher levels, it would have plateaued; in other words, perhaps the "2 percentage point" estimate ceases to be valid for societies with extremely high productivity.

Part VI: Science Myths

In recent years, the idea of "trusting science"—or trusting what we are told about science—has become something of a progressive cause, with many conservatives being more skeptical of what science is said to support. The idea has been invoked especially in discussions of human-caused climate change, vaccine safety and effectiveness, and the efficacy of masks in protecting from viruses. The idea has initial appeal because science is, for the questions that it applies to, the most reliable way we have of discovering the truth. However, as we will see in this part, trusting *science* is often quite different from trusting *what activists and media sources tell you about science*.

19 The Global Warming Consensus

Myth

Almost all scientists agree that humans are the main cause of global warming.

Examples

Of the 4,014 abstracts that expressed a position on the issue of human-induced climate change, Cook et al. (2013) found that over 97% endorsed the view that the Earth is warming up and human emissions of greenhouse gases are the main cause.
— Daniel Bedford and John Cook, academic researchers

Scientists Reach 100% Consensus on Anthropogenic Global Warming
— Recent academic article title

Case Closed: The Debate about Global Warming Is Over
— Brookings Institution article title[270]

The Relevance of Consensus

Before addressing the above claims, let's first ask: Why should we care about the scientific consensus? As the famous novelist and climate skeptic Michael Crichton put it:

[T]he work of science has nothing whatever to do with consensus. Consensus is the business of politics. Science, on the contrary, requires only one investigator who happens to be right, which means

---

[270] Sources: Bedford and Cook 2013, p. 2021; Powell 2019; Easterbrook 2006.

that he or she has results that are verifiable by reference to the real world. In science consensus is irrelevant.[271]

In reply, Michael Crichton is partly right and partly wrong. The correct part: The ultimate justification for a scientific theory—the reason why scientists should adopt the theory to begin with—must lie in the external evidence for the theory, not in facts about who believes it. Thus, the original journal articles that argue for the theory of global warming had better cite some *physical evidence* that the theory explains (which they do). When scientists evaluate those articles, they should set aside whatever they know about other scientists' opinions so that they can make an independent assessment of the evidence. Only in this way can scientific opinion be reliable.

The wrong part: Crichton treats it as a straightforward matter to determine who happens to be right, overlooking the fact that many scientific issues require extensive background knowledge and expertise, which is not feasible for lay people to acquire. Without such expertise, we cannot evaluate the evidence; we could not even understand what the main arguments for the global warming theory are. The same is true, by the way, of all well-developed areas of human inquiry. One cannot, just from a few days of browsing on the internet, acquire the knowledge that people learn during a five-year PhD program. Yet, in a democratic society, voters still need to make some sort of assessment of climatological claims when public policies are being proposed to address the climate.

That is why lay people need to consult the opinions of climate experts. If one is not competent to assess the arguments regarding global warming, the best one can do is listen to people who are. This is fallible, as Crichton points out. So is everything that we humans do. Nevertheless, it seems better than either ignoring the issue or relying on the guesses of people who can't understand the scientific arguments (including oneself), which seem to be the only alternatives.

I shall therefore assume that the scientific consensus matters. But what is the actual scientific consensus?

Reality

(1) Is the Earth warming?

---

[271] Crichton 2003.

Yes. I'm no scientist, but it is very plausible to me that scientists would be able to tell if temperatures were going up. The overwhelming majority of scientists think that the Earth is warming, so that is probably correct. Recent estimates are that global average temperatures have gone up by about 1.1°C (2°F) since the start of the Industrial Revolution.[272]

(2) Are humans part of the cause?

Probably. This is what the famous 97% statistic refers to. The origin of the statistic is a 2013 paper by John Cook and others, reporting the results of a survey of scientific articles relevant to climate change.[273] The authors found 11,944 papers in the scientific literature that matched the keywords "global climate change" or "global warming". They reviewed the abstracts of these papers to try to discern their authors' position on man-made global warming. 66% of the abstracts expressed no discernible position on that. 33% either stated or implied that human activity had *at least some role* in causing global warming. 1% either rejected or expressed doubt about man-made global warming.

Suppose we ignore the abstracts that expressed no position on man-made global warming. Then 97% *of the remainder* express support for some human causal role in global warming. This led to the claim, often reported in the media, that 97% of climate scientists agree that humans are causing (or are "the cause" or "the main cause") of global warming. But that is not in fact what the study found.

First, the study surveyed *papers*, not *people*. Not every scientist necessarily publishes papers expressing their opinions about global warming. There could, for example, be scientists who are privately skeptical without publishing papers on the subject, while other scientists might publish multiple papers expressing their views. To determine the actual distribution of opinion, a better approach would have been to directly survey a large number of scientists (more on that later).

Second, more importantly, the 97% is only the percentage *among those papers that expressed a position on the question*. The majority of papers expressed no position, and we don't know how many of those authors would turn out to be skeptics.

---

[272] IPCC 2023a, p. 4.
[273] Cook et al. 2013. See also the survey by Doran and Zimmerman (2009); for critique, see Cofnas 2017.

Some argue that perhaps most papers do not express a position on the theory of man-made global warming because this theory is so well-established that there is no need to even state it.[274] This is possible. It is also possible that most papers do not express a position on the theory of man-made global warming because the authors *do not know* whether the phenomenon is real. Or perhaps the topic is too politically charged and researchers are afraid to anger climate activists. Note that *if* there were to be many scientists who were unsure whether global warming was man-made, then you would expect many papers that refrain from taking a stance. Since there *are* many such papers, we cannot rule out that many scientists are unsure.

The point is that the "97%" figure is deceptive. It purports to be established by the data. But, just from Cook et al.'s data, we have no way of knowing how many climate scientists agree with man-made global warming, except that it is very probably over 33%.

(3) Are humans the main cause?

Here we come to the biggest problem with the 97% figure as it is often reported. Bedford and Cook (yes, that's the same Cook who worked on the original study) later glossed Cook et al.'s result as showing that "over 97% [of scientists] endorsed the view that the Earth is warming up and human emissions of greenhouse gases are *the main cause*" (emphasis mine).[275]

But that is a mischaracterization.[276] The 97% referred to scientists who thought that human activity was causing *at least some* of the global warming, not scientists who thought that humans were *the main* cause. That is what Cook and his co-authors themselves said in their original study. By their own account, they actually collected data on how many abstracts said that humans were *the primary* cause of global warming (or, caused more than 50% of the warming), but they for some reason *do not report* that number. Instead, "to simplify the analysis", they only report a number for the combination of all abstracts that either say or imply that humans are causing *at least some* of the warming.[277] Why would they do that? Maybe because that makes for a better-sounding statistic for political purposes?

---

[274] Cook et al. 2013, p. 5.
[275] Bedford and Cook 2013, p. 2021, summarizing Cook et al. 2013.
[276] See David Friedman's (2023b) discussion, which accuses Cook of lying.
[277] Cook et al. 2013, p. 3.

Internet commenter Mark Bahner obtained the raw data that was omitted from Cook et al.'s paper.[278] Using that data, it turns out that just *1.6%* (64 out of 3,974) of the abstracts that expressed a view about man-made global warming actually said that humans were the *primary* cause of global warming. That is very different from 97%. Most of the abstracts did not make any attempt to quantify how much of the warming was due to human activity. So, just from Cook et al.'s data, we cannot infer how many scientists would have said human activity was *the main cause*, except that the number would be between 1.6% and 99%.

But wait. It turns out that, around the same time Cook et al. did their study, someone actually directly asked the members of the American Meteorological Society for their views on climate change. If you're wondering why you've never heard of this survey, it might be because it didn't have the outcome that political activists wanted.

It turned out that just 52% of the meteorologists agreed that global warming was both real and mostly human-caused, though members who specialized in climate science in particular were more likely to blame humans for most of the warming (71%; see Table 4).[279]

Table 4: Opinions of AMS members on global warming

Q: Is GW happening? If so, what is its cause?	Climate specialists	All respondents
Yes; mostly human	71%	52%
Yes; equally human and natural	9%	10%
Yes; mostly natural	3%	5%
Yes; insufficient evidence	11%	20%
Yes; don't know cause	1%	1%
Don't know if GW is happening	2%	7%
GW is not happening	1%	4%

From the standpoint of a non-expert, this is still pretty good reason

---

[278] See Henderson 2014 and Bahner's first comment thereon. The data had been posted on the internet, but it appears to have since been taken down (the link Bahner provides is dead). The full data, per Bahner: 64 abstracts explicitly endorsed and quantified AGW (anthropogenic global warming) as 50+%; 922 explicitly endorsed but did not quantify or minimize AGW; 2,910 implicitly endorsed AGW without minimizing it; 7,970 took no position; 54 implicitly minimized/rejected AGW; 15 explicitly minimized/rejected AGW but did not quantify; and 9 explicitly minimized/rejected AGW as less than 50%.
[279] Stenhouse et al. 2013, p. 1034, Table 1.

to think humans are the main cause of global warming. It is, however, a far cry from the 97% (or even 100%!) consensus that one hears bandied about in popular media.

A later (2021) survey found 91% of geoscientists agreeing that humans are the major cause of global warming.[280] Why the discrepancy between the two surveys? There may be a difference between the opinions of geoscientists and those of meteorologists. In addition, opinion may have shifted in the several years between the two surveys. Another possibility is that the issue has become increasingly politicized, so that more scientists have become afraid to express dissent. Finally, one or both surveys may be inaccurate since both had response rates near one quarter (meaning three quarters of people declined to fill out the survey).

(4) Is scientific opinion objective?

Another interesting result emerged from the American Meteorological Society survey. Participants' belief in human-caused warming was correlated with their degree of expertise in climate science, with more expertise predicting greater belief. However, it was even more strongly correlated with (a) perception of consensus (members who thought that there was a consensus were more likely to endorse that presumed consensus) and (b) political ideology (members who self-described as liberal were more likely to endorse human-caused warming).

(a) is understandable but nevertheless of concern because it suggests that scientists' judgments may not be independent. If many experts *independently* evaluate the evidence and conclude that global warming is man-made, that is strong reason for lay people to believe that global warming is indeed man-made. If, however, most scientists are forming their opinions based on what they think *other* scientists believe, then that consensus is much less reliable. That is how one can wind up with large numbers of people all being wrong in the same way.

(b) is of concern because it suggests that scientific opinion may be influenced by scientists' political views. Political beliefs are notoriously unreliable and awful guides to scientific truth. This led the study authors to conclude:

> At least for the measure of expertise that we used, climate science expertise may be a less important influence on global warming views

---

[280] Myers et al. 2021.

than political ideology or social consensus norms. More than any other result of the study, this would be strong evidence against the idea that expert scientists' views on politically controversial topics can be completely objective.[281]

(5) The lessons of Climategate

In 2009, unknown hackers broke into the server of the Climatic Research Unit (CRU) at the University of East Anglia in England, which is one of the world's leading academic groups studying global warming. The hackers stole some of CRU's internal emails and data and released them on the internet. Climate skeptics then seized on some of the emails to suggest that global warming is a hoax. Of course, nothing in the emails suggests that global warming is a hoax. But the emails *did* reveal strenuous efforts by CRU members to withhold data from critics. Referring to two climate skeptics who were trying to get a hold of CRU's data, no doubt for purposes of finding ways to poke holes in it, the head of CRU wrote in one internal email:

> The two MMs have been after the CRU station data for years. If they ever hear there is a Freedom of Information Act now in the UK, I think I'll delete the file rather than send to anyone.

This would be both illegal and contrary to scientific norms. In another message, a scientist responded to a skeptic's request for data by asking, "Why should I make the data available to you, when your aim is to try and find something wrong with it?"[282]

Other emails suggested that CRU members sought to silence academic criticism of the theory of man-made global warming. In one message, a professor bragged of using his role as a peer reviewer to stop criticism from being published, saying he had "recently rejected two papers from people saying CRU has it wrong over Siberia. Went to town in both reviews, hopefully successfully."

In another email, a journal editor directed a peer reviewer to recommend rejection of a paper: "I have to nag you about that review. Confidentially I now need a hard and if required extensive case for rejecting [an unnamed paper] … as soon as you can. Please." This is

---

[281] Stenhouse et al. 2013, p. 1036.
[282] Pearce 2010, pp. 144, 150. In another episode, a scientist directs another to delete emails to prevent them from being disclosed per a freedom-of-information-act request (p. 147).

odd (not to mention fraudulent); the purpose of peer review is for the editor to *find out* whether a paper is publication-worthy. The purpose is defeated if the editor tells the reviewer what verdict to give.

In a third message, a peer reviewer asks another professor for help in finding reasons to reject a paper that he (the reviewer) disagrees with: "If published as is, this paper could really do some damage. It won't be easy to dismiss out of hand as the math appears to be correct theoretically, but it suffers from the classic problem of pointing out theoretical deficiencies, without showing that their improved method is actually better in a practical sense."

In another message, a scientist discussed the idea of organizing a boycott of the journal *Climate Research* because the journal had published some papers skeptical of mainstream views on global warming. Another told a journal that he would have nothing to do with them until they got rid of the editor who was accepting papers by climate skeptics.

In another message, the head of CRU, who was one of the authors of the next IPCC report, spoke of wanting to prevent two climate skeptics' papers from being mentioned in the IPCC report: "I can't see either of these papers being in the next IPCC report. Kevin and I will keep them out somehow—even if we have to redefine what the peer review literature is!" (Those papers ultimately did in fact get cited in the IPCC report.)[283]

Maybe the scientists in these cases were merely trying to prevent scientifically unsound work from being published. Or maybe they wanted to stop their pet theories from being subject to critical scrutiny. From a lay person's perspective, both explanations are plausible. The expressed concern about a skeptical paper "doing damage" suggests a political motive: Climate hawks believe that climate skeptics are harming society by sowing doubts about the mainstream climate theories and hence delaying political action on climate issues. (The skeptics no doubt believe, similarly, that the climate hawks are harming society.)

My point here is not to scold the scientists involved in Climategate. It doesn't matter whether they are good or bad people. What matters is what Climategate tells us about the *intellectual culture* of climatology. Different areas of academic inquiry have different cultures, and these cultures are important to the reliability of those fields. The consensus in

---

[283] See Pearce 2010, ch. 11. The preceding quotes in the text are from pp. 127, 129, 129-30, 138.

a given field matters only if that field has an intellectual culture that makes it trustworthy. For example, if someone tells me that the consensus view in Gender Studies is x, this will not incline me to accept x, because, to put it mildly, I believe the culture of Gender Studies is insufficiently truth-oriented.

There are at least three key values that make for a truth-directed intellectual culture: (i) transparency, (ii) openness to criticism, and (iii) freedom from political bias. The Climategate scandal suggests that climate science has less of those features than one might have hoped. The hacked emails suggest that climate scientists may be influenced by their policy preferences, that they accept the idea of using peer review to suppress papers that criticize one's own views, and that they endorse hiding one's data from people who would critically scrutinize that data. It is understandable why this might be the case, since some people believe that the future of our planet is at stake and that skeptics are causing untold harm. Nevertheless, if that is indeed an accurate snapshot of climatology culture, it is easy to see how we could end up with a seemingly strong consensus in the literature on something that was not in fact true.

This may also explain why the apparent consensus derived from reviews of the *literature* is so much stronger than the consensus found in direct surveys of scientists' opinions: The majority is using its power to minimize expressions of dissent.

Conclusion

I am not concluding that global warming is bogus, or even that it isn't man-made. Despite what I have said above, the majority are still more likely to be right than the minority. This is not, however, *overwhelmingly* likely; for the reasons discussed above, it would not be shocking if the majority turned out to be wrong.

I thus find the climate hawks' insistence that "the debate about global warming is over" (and similar remarks) to be dogmatic. Indeed, I consider them a troubling attempt to short-circuit the norms of rational inquiry, which is precisely the sort of thing that should shake our confidence in the reliability of the consensus.

20 Existential Climate Risk

Myth

Scientists say that global warming is likely to destroy civilization if we don't take drastic action very soon.

Examples

> The world is going to end in 12 years if we don't address climate change, and your biggest issue is how are we gonna pay for it?
> —Congresswoman Alexandria Ocasio-Cortez (D-NY)

> New Report Suggests 'High Likelihood of Human Civilization Coming to an End' Starting in 2050
> —Vice News headline

> We live in a strange world, where all the united science tells us that we are about eleven years away from setting off an irreversible chain reaction, way beyond human control, that will probably be the end of our civilization as we know it.
> —Greta Thunberg, leading climate activist

> Climate change is literally an existential threat to our nation and to the world.
> —U.S. President Joe Biden

The above sorts of pronouncements seem to be having an effect: A 2019 survey found that 38% of Americans think that climate change is likely to cause the extinction of the human race. In 2022, an OECD survey found that in high-income countries, 59% of people think climate change is likely to kill all of us. [284]

---

[284] Sources: Ocasio-Cortez 2019, 53:37-50; Ahmed 2019; Thunberg 2019, "A Strange World"; Biden 2022; YouGov 2019, p. 7; Dechezleprêtre et al. 2022, p. 60.

Reality

(1) Is the world coming to an end in 12 years?

No, that's ridiculous. Thunberg and Ocasio-Cortez confused the expert consensus that climate change *is real* with the fringe activist claim that climate change *means the end of the world.*

If there is one source that best represents the mainstream scientific consensus on global warming, it is the Intergovernmental Panel on Climate Change (IPCC). The IPCC is an international panel of experts established by the United Nations in 1988 for the purpose of assessing and spreading scientific knowledge about climate change. Their reports are widely cited by environmental activists, scientists, and policy experts. They are the source of the "12 years" (or 11 years) figure cited by Alexandria Ocasio-Cortez and Greta Thunberg.[285]

But the IPCC did not say what Thunberg and Ocasio-Cortez claim. James Skea, co-chairman of the report, told the Associated Press that the panel "did not say we have 12 years left to save the world" and "the hotter it gets, the worse it gets, but there is no cliff edge."[286]

The report *did* say, in 2018, that we had to drastically cut carbon emissions by 2030 (then 12 years in the future) *if we wanted to keep global warming under 1.5°C.* We would also need to reach zero net carbon emissions by 2050 (again, *if* we were to keep global warming under 1.5°C relative to pre-industrial times). But they nowhere claimed that failure to do so would destroy our civilization, either in 12 years or ever. No IPCC projection, regardless of the level of warming, has ever anticipated the end of human civilization from global warming.

Other mainstream scientists agree. Adam Schlosser, the Deputy Director of the MIT Joint Program on the Science and Policy of Global Change, says, "If I had to rate odds, I would say the chances of climate change driving us to the point of human extinction are very low, if not zero."[287] Climatologist Michael Mann, one of the world's leading climate alarmists, says, "There is no evidence of climate change scenarios that would render human beings extinct."[288]

---

[285] See IPCC 2018; Watts 2018. Thunberg updated the figure to 11 years in 2019, while Ocasio-Cortez left it at 12.
[286] Woodward et al. 2019.
[287] Kroll 2023.
[288] Pester 2021.

What sort of consequences do mainstream scientists expect from global warming? Ocean levels are expected to rise by 0.4-0.8 meters by the year 2100. This will not submerge New York City (as some alarmists in the media imagine); it will, however, slightly increase the risk of flooding in coastal cities.

The IPCC projects that an excess 250,000 people will die annually worldwide due to climate change by mid-century due to increased heat, undernutrition, and disease. That will be out of an expected total of 92 million deaths per year from all causes by that time, so global warming will account for about a quarter of a percent of the death rate. A more pessimistic study suggests that excess deaths due to global warming could increase to 2 million per year for the second half of the century. Among the more alarming projections is one claiming that, if left completely unchecked, global warming could cause as many as 73 deaths per 100,000 population per year by 2100, which would make it comparable to the current death rate for infectious diseases. (For an expected population of 10 billion by 2100, that would mean 7.3 million deaths per year.) Economist William Nordhaus, a leading expert on the impacts of climate change, estimates that global warming will have costs on the order of 2.5% of total world GDP by the end of the century.[289]

I mention these projections, not to claim that these things are in fact going to happen, but to give you a sense of the order of magnitude of the harms that scientists are concerned about. I stress that these are not *skeptics'* projections; these are the sort of projections made by mainstream scientists who are worried about global warming. Skeptics are far more optimistic, with some arguing that the benefits of global warming may outweigh the costs.[290]

Admittedly, one can find scientists who worry about global catastrophe.[291] But these are outliers, comparable to the outliers who deny that global warming exists at all, but on the other end of the spectrum.

---

[289] Sources: Ocean levels: IPCC 2023c. 250k deaths: IPCC 2023b, p. 1. 92 million deaths: Our World in Data n.d. 2 million deaths: Rom 2018. 73 per 100k: Carleton et al. 2022. 2.5%: Nordhaus 2008, p. 6.

[290] Economist David Friedman (2023a) argues that mainstream estimates neglect most of the benefits of climate change and that it is unclear whether global warming is overall good or bad. Note, e.g., that cold kills far more people every year than heat.

[291] Kemp et al. 2022. Even these authors do not claim that human extinction is likely; they merely argue that we should prepare for the worst.

(2) The history of doom

When I was a child growing up in California, I was repeatedly warned that we were overdue for a huge earthquake. When the Big One came, the streets of Los Angeles would be buried a foot deep in shattered glass. We did disaster drills in school, where we were taught how to hide under our desks and cover our necks.

At the time, I accepted these warnings and many others at face value. Decades later, I'm still waiting. The Big One never came, nor did any of the other disasters I was told to worry about.

At the end of the 1990's, we were told to worry about the "Y2k bug", a computer programming error that would supposedly cause computers around the country to go crazy at the turn of the millennium.[292] You see, in the early days of computing, many people had written programs in which the current year would be represented with two digits, making the programs unable to distinguish the year 2000 from the year 1900. People worried about the unpredictable consequences that would ensue when the actual year changed to 2000. Some were stocking up on canned goods, water, and ammo in case of a breakdown of society. In the event, nothing happened.

No one seems to learn anything from these events. In my decades on this planet, I have repeatedly heard dire warnings of one disaster or another. Every disaster that was supposed to happen in my lifetime thus far has failed to materialize. When the disasters fail to appear, you just stop hearing about them, and the media and the intellectuals simply move on unselfconsciously to the next disaster.

That is to explain why, when I heard Greta Thunberg's dire warnings of climate catastrophe, I did not take them seriously. Experiences like the above convinced me long ago that human beings, especially journalists and activists, have a bias toward the dramatic, the titillating, and especially the frightening. Whenever you hear a new disaster prediction, your first assumption should be that it is probably a product of this bias.

Here are some of the dire warnings that we have been treated to over the years:[293]

1966   Geologist predicts that the U.S. will run out of oil in 10 years.

---

[292] See Wikipedia, "Year 2000 Problem".
[293] This list is taken (with some omissions) from Ebell and Milloy (2019) and Perry (2019), who provide further details.

1967   Stanford University biologist Paul Ehrlich predicts worldwide famine by 1975 due to overpopulation.

1969   Ehrlich predicts that "unless we are extremely lucky, everybody will disappear in a cloud of blue steam in 20 years."

1970   Ehrlich predicts that the oceans will be dead in 10 years.

1970   Harvard biologist and environmental activist George Wald warns that civilization will end within 15-30 years unless immediate action is taken against the problems facing mankind.

1970s   Scientists predict a new ice age in the early 21st century due to air pollution.

1976   Climatologist Stephen Schneider publishes *The Genesis Strategy*, which reports the consensus of climate scientists that an ice age is coming. (Schneider later became a leading advocate for the theory of global warming.)

1988   Scientists warn that the Maldives (a group of islands in the Indian Ocean) may be completely submerged in 30 years.

1989   A UN official warns that entire nations could be wiped off the face of the Earth if global warming isn't stopped by the year 2000.

1989   Climate expert Jim Hansen predicts that the West Side Highway in New York City will be underwater in 20 years.

2000   Climatic Research Unit scientist David Viner predicts that within a few years, winter snowfall will be very rare, and "children just aren't going to know what snow is."

2004   A Pentagon report predicts that by 2020, Britain will have a "Siberian" climate, and there will be nuclear conflict, megadroughts, and widespread rioting across the world.

2005   The UN warns that global warming could create 50 million environmental refugees by the end of the decade.

2008   Former Vice President Al Gore predicts that the entire north polar ice cap will likely be ice free during the summer by 2013.

2009   Prince Charles warns that we have just 8 years left to avoid "irretrievable climate and ecosystem collapse".

2013   A U.S. Department of Energy research project predicts that the Arctic could be ice free during the summer by 2016.

Just in case you missed the theme here: None of those things happened.

(3) Is global warming our top priority?

Okay, so global warming isn't a civilization-ending catastrophe. But it's still a top priority for humanity, right?

Maybe not. The harms that are anticipated from global warming over the next century are comparable to many other global problems, such as the problems of malnutrition, malaria, tuberculosis, war, and poor sanitation. It is not immediately obvious, without doing serious study, that mitigating global warming should be one of our top priorities.

To figure this out, the Danish environmentalist and political scientist Bjørn Lomborg started the Copenhagen Consensus project. He brought together leading experts on a variety of proposed solutions to global problems and had them write research papers on the expected costs and benefits of these solutions. For example, malaria is one of the world's major problems. One (partial) solution to it is to provide insecticide-treated bed nets to people in the developing world. This costs some money but provides large benefits by reducing the spread of malaria by mosquitos.

Lomborg then convened a panel of eminent economists to prioritize the solutions. The economists were asked to assess, based on cost-benefit analysis, which proposed solutions should be adopted first, given that we have limited resources. As Lomborg stresses, the idea is not to prioritize *problems* but to prioritize *solutions*.[294] In other words, the question is not "What are the worst problems?" but "What are the most cost-effective interventions we can make to help the world?" It makes sense to ask this because governments and philanthropists have limited funds and cannot realistically address all problems.

The Copenhagen Consensus held major conferences three times, in 2004, 2008, and 2012, each time devising a list of the top priorities for improving the world.[295] Micronutrient supplementation programs (to address malnutrition) came out as the top priority the last two times. Other top priorities included deworming (to deal with intestinal worms), increased vaccination, and programs to alleviate malaria and tuberculosis. All three times, solutions to global warming came out as a low priority (not in the top 10). I stress that these conclusions were not driven by climate skepticism. The Copenhagen Consensus assumed the

---

[294] Lomborg 2007.
[295] Lomborg 2004; 2009; 2013.

mainstream views about global warming as given in the IPCC reports—
in particular, that global warming is real, is mostly man-made, and will
impose serious costs on future generations. Nonetheless, when experts
perform a cost-benefit analysis, they tend to agree that global warming
interventions are relatively cost-ineffective.

How can this be? There are a few key points that environmentalists
tend to underappreciate. First, the other problems that I mentioned
above—malnutrition, malaria, tuberculosis, and intestinal worms—are
huge problems. *Millions* die from these causes *every year*, and many more
suffer greatly reduced quality of life. These problems don't appear on
the radar screen of most activists and journalists because they are less
entertaining to talk about and less politically charged than global
warming or racism. You don't get to express your political orientation
by talking about malaria, as you do by talking about racism or global
warming. But that doesn't mean that they aren't in fact among the
world's greatest preventable problems.

Second, there are excellent interventions available for each of these
problems—interventions that can make a huge difference to the
problems, with relatively little cost.

Third, all of these are immediate problems—they are killing many
people *right now*, just as they have for many years in the past and will
continue to do for many years in the future if we don't do something
about them.

Global warming also threatens to impose large costs on society, as
discussed earlier. But most of these costs are expected to fall on future
generations, when people will, in all probability, be vastly richer than
today. (No one knows how much richer, but, for example, economists
Angus Hooke and Lauren Alati project a *seventeenfold* increase in world
GDP by 2100, when the population will be only 40% larger.[296]) Therefore, the people impacted by climate change will, for the most part, be
much better able to afford to adapt than the poor people today are able
to adapt to malaria, tuberculosis, and the like. Finally, plans to mitigate
the harms of global warming are generally extremely expensive, for a
relatively small impact. Lomborg notes that to achieve net zero carbon
emissions by 2050—as many climate alarmists are now advocating—
would cost about $25 trillion a year, which is more than the total tax
revenues of all governments in the world combined.

---

[296] Hooke and Alati 2022.

Objections

(1) The Precautionary Principle

Granted, climate alarmism is probably mistaken. But given that there are at least *some* scientists who think that global warming might extinguish the human species, shouldn't we assign some non-negligible credence to that view? And if there is even a chance that global warming will extinguish the human species, then shouldn't we take drastic measures now to avert that risk?

Reply: I don't think so, because there simply are too many things that people (even scientists) claim are likely to cause some major disaster. That is part of why I listed sixteen false warnings of disaster above. All of those were sufficiently serious that they would have justified undertaking major costs to avert the alleged impending disaster. There are warnings of that kind coming *all the time*. If we regularly responded to them based on the reasoning in the present objection, our society would be bankrupted by its responses to all the false warnings.

Given the human bias toward doomsday predictions, the fact that a few scientists say global warming might extinguish the human species is really next to zero evidence that that outcome has any non-negligible probability.

(2) Pragmatic reasons for exaggerating

Okay, many of the climate activists are exaggerating the threat of global warming. But maybe that's a good thing. If we portray the dangers accurately, people will ignore them. To get the public and the government to take reasonable measures against a real problem, we have to scare them.

Reply: The above is, I suspect, the true reason for much of the reckless exaggeration in this area. I don't think it's a good idea, though. First, we might be misled into adopting climate solutions that do more harm than good. If you think that the world is coming to an end unless we stop climate change, then you might be willing, say, to spend 25 trillion dollars fighting it. In the end, though, the benefit of your programs might be much less than the cost because you drastically overstated the problem.

Second, the exaggeration of this issue may crowd out other issues. Governments and philanthropists might decide to spend more resources fighting climate change and less fighting other problems for which they could have done a lot more good, such as malnutrition and disease.

Third, extreme pessimism could lead to a sense of hopelessness, such that some people give up even trying to improve the world.

Fourth, there is one core problem that purveyors of misleading propaganda on all kinds of issues regularly ignore: What happens when people find out the truth? It's not as if the public has no way of finding out. When 2030 comes, everyone is going to look around and notice that they are still alive. Some of those people are then going to draw the following inference: "The scientists said the world was coming to an end. But that's ridiculously false. So I guess we can't trust scientists." As I've been emphasizing, the scientists, in general, *didn't* say that. The *political activists* said that the scientists said that. But most lay people won't know that, so they will blame the scientists. It will then become harder to get people to take real threats seriously in the future.

Conclusion

Global warming is happening, and human activity is likely the main cause. But it isn't going to end civilization, destroy all life on Earth, or anything remotely like that. It will probably become a moderately serious global problem (as global problems go) in the next few generations. However, the most drastic solutions people are proposing, such as reducing our carbon emissions to net zero, are wildly infeasible and cost-ineffective. Global warming has captured the imagination of journalists and activists, but there are many other global problems that are more deserving of our attention.

21 Mask Science

Myth

Science shows that face masks are highly effective protection against respiratory viruses such as Covid-19.

Background

During the Covid-19 pandemic of 2020 to 2022, about 7 million people worldwide died from the disease.[297] Many medical experts, journalists, and political leaders at the time gave advice/commands regarding how to reduce the spread of the disease.

One fraught topic was the use of face masks covering the nose and mouth. At the start of the pandemic, there was a shortage of face masks in the U.S., as individuals quickly bought up available supplies. At this time, both the U.S. Surgeon General and the U.S. Centers for Disease Control (CDC) advised citizens *not* to buy face masks, claiming that such masks were only useful for medical professionals. Several weeks later, they changed their minds and told everyone to start wearing face masks, which became the received wisdom for the rest of the pandemic. Some people concluded that public health officials had simply lied about the effectiveness of masks at the beginning in order to preserve masks for health care workers, then told the truth when the mask shortage ended. Many locations around the U.S.—hospitals, stores, universities, airlines, and so on—*mandated* the use of these masks.[298]

Due in part to President Trump's conspicuous refusal to mask, the issue quickly became politicized: left-wing individuals tended to be fervent mask champions, while right-wing individuals tended to be mask skeptics.

---

[297] Alcantara et al. 2020.
[298] On the government's changing mask guidelines, see Netburn 2021.

One could also observe odd phenomena that future generations will find hard to believe, such as people driving down the street, alone in their cars, wearing face masks. There were restaurants where you had to wear a mask to enter, but you could take it off as soon as you sat down. One could be forgiven for questioning how much protection these measures provided.

Examples

> There should be universal wearing of masks.
>> —Dr. Anthony Fauci, Director, National Institute
>> of Allergy and Infectious Diseases (August 2020)

> These face masks are the most important, powerful public health tool we have … I might even go so far as to say that this face mask is more guaranteed to protect me against COVID than when I take a COVID vaccine.
>> —CDC Director Robert Redfield (September 2020)

> Huge, gold-standard study shows unequivocally that surgical masks work to reduce coronavirus spread. … The results … should "end any scientific debate" on whether masks are effective in battling the spread of COVID-19, Jason Abaluck, an economist at Yale and one of the authors who helped lead the study, told *The Washington Post.*
>> —Live Science (2021)[299]

Reality

There have been numerous studies of the effectiveness of masks against respiratory viruses, most of them done before the Covid-19 pandemic. Some find small benefits, some find no benefit, and some find net *harms* (that is, masks might *increase* the spread of disease). Overall, the case for masking is very weak, and that is what you would have been told before the issue became politicized. Indeed, that is what we *were* told by some of the same official sources who would later become ardent masko-philes:

> Seriously people — STOP BUYING MASKS! They are NOT effective in preventing general public from catching #Coronavirus, but if healthcare providers can't get them to care for sick patients, it puts

[299] Sources: Castillejo and Yang 2020; Redfield 2020; Saplakoglu 2021.

them and our communities at risk!

—U.S. Surgeon General Jerome Adams (February 2020)

Right now in the United States, people should not be walking around with masks…. There's no reason to be walking around with a mask.

—Dr. Anthony Fauci (March 2020)

During normal day-to-day activities facemasks do not provide protection from respiratory viruses, such as COVID-19 and do not need to be worn by staff…

—Public Health England (official U.K. health agency) (February 2020)

[T]here is no specific evidence to suggest that the wearing of masks by the mass population has any particular benefit. In fact there's some evidence to suggest the opposite…

—Dr. Michael Ryan, Executive Director, Health Emergencies Programme, World Health Organization (March 2020)[300]

Now you might wonder: How could masking possibly *increase* the spread of disease? There are a couple of ways. For one thing, people commonly touch the front of their mask with their hands, then touch other parts of their face. As Anthony Fauci put it (before he and the rest of the government shifted their position), "Often, there are unintended consequences [of wearing masks]. People keep fiddling with the mask, and they keep touching their face."[301] Most people also wear the same mask repeatedly for many days, so pathogens may accumulate in the mask. This is a particular problem with cloth masks, which many people wore during the pandemic; indeed, one study found that cloth masks caused a nearly *sevenfold increase* in the risk of influenza-like illness, compared to wearing no mask.[302] Masks may become saturated with saliva from extended use, which helps viruses to survive in the material. Finally, it is possible that people engage in relatively riskier behavior due to their (mistaken) belief that they are well protected by a face mask.[303]

---

[300] Sources: Netburn 2021; Fauci and LaPook 2020; Public Health England 2020; World Health Organization 2020, p. 7.

[301] Fauci 2020. Michael Ryan raises the same concern (World Health Organization 2020, p. 7).

[302] MacIntyre et al. 2015.

[303] Jefferson et al. (2023, p. 34) mention all of these possibilities.

In 2023, a team of medical researchers (Jefferson et al.) published a meta-analysis reviewing 78 RCT's (randomized, controlled trials, the best kind of scientific study) of various interventions designed to reduce the spread of respiratory viruses such as Covid-19. This included 12 RCT's specifically about the usefulness of surgical masks compared to no masking. The authors concluded:

> The pooled results of RCTs did not show a clear reduction in respiratory viral infection with the use of medical/surgical masks.

Some of the studies focused on your risk of developing influenza-like symptoms. These showed an average 5% reduction in risk as a result of wearing a mask; however, this result was not statistically significant, and the evidence failed to rule out the possibility that masks actually increase the risk of disease.[304] Other studies focused more specifically on your risk of testing positive for a respiratory virus in a laboratory test. These found an expected 1% *increase* in risk from wearing masks, also not statistically significant.[305]

What about the amazing "gold standard" study that we heard about above that should "end any scientific debate" about the effectiveness of masks? This was a study conducted in rural Bangladesh (Abaluck et al. 2022) that compared villages in which there was a program to promote mask usage to villages in which there was no such program. This was a "gold standard" study simply in the sense that it was a randomized, controlled trial; that is, they randomly assigned villages to either get or not get the pro-mask intervention. After several weeks, in the places with no intervention, 8.6% of people showed Covid symptoms. In the places that got the mask-promotion program, only 7.6% of people showed Covid symptoms.

The Bangladesh study was included in the Jefferson et al. meta-analysis that I referred to above. All the other studies in that meta-analysis were also RCT's. Again, results vary across studies; sometimes,

---

[304] Jefferson et al. 2023, p. 2: "Wearing masks in the community probably makes little or no difference to the outcome of influenza-like illness (ILI)/COVID-19 like illness compared to not wearing masks (risk ratio (RR) 0.95, 95% confidence interval (CI) 0.84 to 1.09; 9 trials, 276,917 participants; moderate-certainty evidence)."

[305] Ibid.: "Wearing masks in the community probably makes little or no difference to the outcome of laboratory-confirmed influenza/SARS-CoV-2 compared to not wearing masks (RR 1.01, 95% CI 0.72 to 1.42; 6 trials, 13,919 participants; moderate-certainty evidence)."

masks seem to have a small positive effect, sometimes not. This, by the way, is common in statistical research; different studies often show conflicting results. This could be due to chance, differing study design, slightly different research questions, or differing sources of bias in the data that could not be completely controlled for (the Jefferson review mentions several possible sources of bias for various studies, including the Bangladesh study). It is possible, for example, that rural Bangladesh differs in some (perhaps unknown) relevant ways from other locations in the world. This is why it is best to look for meta-analyses that pool the results of many studies, like the Jefferson et al. paper.

Conclusion

My conclusion is not that masks have *no* effect. It is that they probably have only small benefits, and it is not out of the question that they might be overall harmful, especially given the bad habits of most users. If I had to guess, I'd say cloth masks are overall harmful, and surgical masks probably produce a tiny net benefit. In any case, Robert Redfield was foolish to claim that masks were our "most powerful public health tool" or that they were more effective than vaccines. Given the small and uncertain benefits, nationwide mask mandates were ill-justified.

What should we make of public health experts' changing position on masks? I think their *original* statements were basically correct and sincere. They knew that the payoff of masking for average citizens was minimal at best and could be negative. Masks were more important for health care workers, however, because (a) those workers would come into contact with many more people, including many sick people, and (b) health care workers would be more likely to practice correct hygiene, e.g., disposing of the mask after each use and not touching the mask's surface. So the *original* advice from the Surgeon General and Dr. Fauci was good advice.

Later, public health officials decided that they wanted to make everyone wear masks. I suspect that this was partly out of a desire to look as if they were *doing something*, given the widespread (if mistaken) public belief that masks are effective. And, once mask mandates were common around the world, U.S. officials didn't want to stand out by adopting different policies. In addition, again, the issue became politicized because President Trump downplayed the pandemic and refused to wear a mask. This caused Democrats in the U.S. (which probably included most public health officials and the overwhelming majority of journalists) to become pandemic alarmists and mask fanatics.

Once they had decided that the official, politically correct position was pro-mask, people started wildly exaggerating both the certainty and the magnitude of the benefits—hence the ridiculous remarks of Robert Redfield quoted above. In doing so, public health officials burned a good deal of their credibility.

Part VII: Analysis

Up till now, I have mainly tried to recount the empirical facts regarding particular myths of progressivism. In this final part of the book, I will say what I make of all this: Why do we have all these progressive myths, what is bad about them, and what should we do about the situation? These will be my personal guesses, not established facts, but you may find them interesting.

22 The Roots of Wokism

I named this book "Progressive Myths" because "progressive" seemed like the best brief name for a perspective that includes all the myths in the previous chapters. I didn't call it "Woke Myths" because that leaves out the myths of Parts V–VI.[306] Nevertheless, most of our myths have been woke myths. So it is interesting to ask where woke ideology came from.

A. Origins of the Civil Rights Movement

In 1960's America, there were two looming political issues that concerned liberal people: the war in Vietnam and civil rights.[307] Many faculty and especially students on college campuses were strongly opposed to the Vietnam War. More importantly for our story, they were strongly opposed to the rampant racism in American society.

The civil rights leaders were not worried about microaggressions or unconscious biases; indeed, they would surely have laughed at the sort of concerns raised by contemporary progressives. Before the Civil Rights Movement, no one needed academic training or special sensitivity to find racism; it was fully explicit and utterly shameless. A few examples:

> All marriages between a white person and a negro, or between a white person and a person of negro descent to the fourth generation, inclusive, are hereby forever prohibited.
>
> —Florida constitution of 1885

> The following persons shall not be witnesses: ... Indians, or persons

---

[306] I also rejected the term "liberal" because the people who propound the above myths are often extremely illiberal (e.g., they favor silencing critics of their political views). Admittedly, "progressive" could also be misleading, as contemporary progressivism bears little resemblance to earlier "progressive" movements.

[307] Much of my understanding of this period derives from Searle (1971).

having one-half or more of indian blood, and negroes, or persons having one-half or more of negro blood, in an action or proceeding to which a white person is a party.

—California Practice Act (1854)

It shall be unlawful for a Negro and a white person to play together or in company with each other in any game of cards, dice, dominoes, checkers, baseball, softball, football, basketball or similar games.

—General Code of the City of Birmingham, AL
(as amended in 1950)[308]

At one time, nearly everyone was a racist of (what we today would call) the most extreme kind. Try to guess who gave the following white supremacist tirade:

I am not, nor ever have been, in favor of making voters or jurors of negroes, nor of qualifying them to hold office, nor to intermarry with white people ... [T]here is a physical difference between the white and black races which I believe will forever forbid the two races living together on terms of social and political equality. ... [T]here must be the position of superior and inferior, and I as much as any other man am in favor of the superior position assigned to the white race.

Those were the words of the Great Emancipator, Abraham Lincoln, in an 1858 Presidential debate.[309] He was the *less* racist candidate in that election.

Even after slavery was abolished in America, the white majority spent a century refusing to recognize blacks as equals. For example, there were laws explicitly prohibiting whites and blacks from intermarrying, eating in the same restaurant, or attending the same schools, while other laws tried to stop blacks from voting.

In 1963, Alabama governor George Wallace stood in the spot where Jefferson Davis had once been sworn in as President of the Confederate States of America during the American Civil War, and declared:

---

[308] Sources: (i) Art. XVI, §24 (http://library.law.fsu.edu/Digital-Collections/CRC/CRC-1998/conhist/1885con.html); (ii) Title XI, ch. 1, §394 (Labatt 1860, p. 220; by "indians", they meant Native Americans); (iii) §597 (https://shec.ashp.cuny.edu/items/show/866).

[309] Opening speech, fourth debate, Charleston, IL, September 18, 1878 (Nicolay and Hay 1920, pp. 369-70).

Today I have stood, where once Jefferson Davis stood, and took an oath to my people. It is very appropriate then that from this Cradle of the Confederacy, this very Heart of the Great Anglo-Saxon Southland, that today we sound the drum for freedom as have our generations of forebears before us done ... In the name of the greatest people that have ever trod this earth, I draw the line in the dust and toss the gauntlet before the feet of tyranny, and I say: segregation now, segregation tomorrow, segregation forever.[310]

That was the sort of rank bigotry that the Civil Rights Movement was founded to combat.

The movement was particularly successful with intellectuals, particularly on college campuses, due to the actual serious injustices it opposed. The movement quickly brought enormous progress toward equality and respect for the rights of all individuals in America. Segregation was repealed, and racial discrimination (along with discrimination based on sex, nationality, and religion) was banned by the Civil Rights Act of 1964. Over the next few decades, attitudes of average Americans shifted radically away from racism. Even George Wallace eventually admitted that he was wrong.

B. The Drive to Keep the Movement Alive

Overall, the success of the Civil Rights Movement was an enormous win for American values. But a side effect of the movement was the politicization of college campuses, where many of the protests against racism and the Vietnam War had occurred. That established in people's minds the idea that activism and taking stances on current political issues were major parts of the business of a college student or professor. Many of the left-wing student activists of the 1960's would become professors by the 1970's.

It is also crucial to understand the emotional significance of these movements for their participants. Human beings have a powerful need for a sense of *meaning* and a sense of *community*, both of which have eroded in modern times. Religion has historically provided those things, but religion has been on the wane for decades. Political ideology has arisen as a secular substitute for religion.[311] Participation in a movement

---

[310] Wallace 1963.

[311] Indeed, John McWhorter (2021) makes a strong case that woke ideology literally *is* a religion.

for social justice feels deeply meaningful, and it gives one a community centered around a common goal. An ideology may also give one a satisfyingly simple way of dividing the world into "good" people and "bad" people. Thus, the protestors of the 1960's were not merely improving society; they were also satisfying profound needs of their own psyches.

Suppose that what I have said is true, and imagine for a moment that the political movements in question were to succeed. What if they actually changed society in exactly the ways they wanted to? If they were to *recognize* that that had happened, they would presumably have to end the movement. Given the importance of the movement in their lives, all the incentives would be for them *not* to recognize that. So as the supply of injustices dwindles, the demand for "injustices" grows increasingly desperate.

In the case of the Vietnam War, it would be pretty hard to refuse to recognize that the war is over. But the case of racism is another story. Racism did not end decisively at a discrete time, as the Vietnam War did. There were landmark events, such as the passage of the Civil Rights Act, but they left behind some racism that one could reasonably continue to oppose. The racism in American attitudes only gradually declined over a period of decades. This gave activists and theorists on the left plenty of time to adjust.

What they did was to gradually move the goalposts. They ramped up their demands, and they developed increasingly sensitive racism detectors and increasingly sophisticated accounts of how one facet or another of American life that seemed innocuous to the *hoi polloi* was really a form of "white supremacy" or other bigotry. After working on this project for the last half century, academics have arrived at positions unrecognizable to the original civil rights protestors. No longer content with ending discrimination against women and blacks, for example, they now demand increasingly extreme discrimination *in favor* of women and blacks. Not content with saying that blacks are equal to whites and women equal to men, they now argue in essence that blacks are morally *better* than whites and women morally better than men.

Aside: If you talk to a woke person, they will no doubt deny that they are anti-white or anti-male. Here is a thought experiment to gauge how you should receive that denial. Imagine you have a professor whose lessons always seem to have something to do with wrongs committed by *Jews*. The historical events he is interested in all seem to be times that

Jews exploited or oppressed gentiles. His take on any contemporary issue always seems to somehow connect it to evils committed by Jews. Yet he swears, hand on his heart, that he is no anti-Semite; he is just very committed to protecting the rights of gentiles. What would you think of this?

I hope you would agree that the guy is an obvious anti-Semite; he's only denying it because he knows that it is socially bad to be labeled an "anti-Semite", and he's hoping that a bare denial will fool you.

If the anti-Semite's denial wouldn't fool you, you shouldn't be fooled by woke ideologues either. They are obviously anti-white, anti-male, anti-American, etc., bigots. Everything about their ideology telegraphs this constantly, and everyone but them can see it.

In 2018, by the way, a group of academics was able to get a paper titled "Our Struggle Is My Struggle" accepted for publication in the feminist social work journal *Affilia*. The paper contained a rewritten version of a 3600-word passage from Adolf Hitler's *Mein Kampf*, with modifications to make the passage about "feminism" and "privilege" instead of "National Socialism" and "Jews". With these changes, it apparently fit right into the woke academic discourse.[312]

C. How the Academy Works

(1) The importance of peer approval

The academy is the original source of the ideas of wokism. To understand how the movement for civil rights evolved into wokism, one must understand a few things about how the academic world works. In the academy, the humanities and social sciences are filled with high-IQ people who are accountable mainly to *each other*, not to objective reality. That is, their success depends almost entirely on their ability to impress each other with their complex ideas, verbal gymnastics, and displays of loyalty, not on their ability to achieve practical results in the outside world. This is the ideal sort of person to devise rationalizations to keep a political movement alive. If you have decades to work on it and you put thousands of people with PhD's on the task, you can come up with a way that anything is racist—especially if you're ready to play fast and loose with empirical facts.

Aside: Why are the natural sciences different from the humanities

---

[312] Lindsay et al. 2018; Wikipedia, "Affilia".

and social sciences? Mainly because the natural sciences have more decisive ways of finding things out; practitioners' reputations are thus influenced more by whether they actually get things right. The humanities and social sciences have *some* ways of figuring things out, but they are less reliable and more dependent on subjective judgment, making it relatively more important to know how to impress people and less important to be objectively correct. In addition, the natural sciences deal far less often with politically charged questions; thus, there is less opportunity for political bias to influence decisions (though as we have seen in the last few chapters, there are times when natural science becomes politicized, to its detriment).

So the left-wing professors after the 1960's have kept the movement for "social justice" alive. Each generation of professors teaches the next generation the current theories of how America is horrifyingly oppressive. The new crop of academics then compete with each other to take the radical theorizing to greater extremes. Though academics like to style ourselves as bold innovators always open to new ideas, the truth is that our profession rewards timid people who swallow their field's intellectual orthodoxy so completely that the only sort of "challenge" they can contemplate is to take the orthodoxy's assumptions to an even greater extreme.

One reason why this is true is the sheer amount of peer evaluation involved in being an academic. Whenever one tries to publish a paper (which one must do periodically to keep one's job as an academic researcher), that paper will be reviewed by one or two peer reviewers in addition to the editor. Because journals get *a lot* more submissions than they have space to publish, the editor is *looking* for a reason to reject your paper. If a reviewer disagrees with your viewpoint, that is very likely to lead to some negative comments from the reviewer, which will lead to a rejection. Knowing this, you have every incentive to try to conform to your field's orthodoxy, to the extent that it has one. The *theory* behind peer review is that it maintains intellectual quality, and that is indeed *part* of what it does—certain kinds of incompetence are screened out. But it also helps to enforce intellectual orthodoxy.

This dynamic does not just operate in academic publishing. Virtually all advancement for a young academic requires getting recommendations from established academics—and hence requires young academics to curry favor with the old guard. Every time an academic is reviewed for tenure, their school will solicit evaluations from several well-known academics in their field (at my school, a minimum of six letters from outside reviewers are required, and we usually have more). If the field has an orthodoxy, these well-known academics will typically be among the developers and advocates of that orthodoxy. Therefore, again, it behooves a young academic to conform.

The same process occurs whenever an academic is considered for a prize, for a promotion, or for a job at another university (all things to which many academics aspire).

(2) Data on ideological discrimination

But surely, well-established academics can put aside their personal opinions in order to evaluate someone's work objectively, right?

Sometimes, yes. But sometimes not. We don't have many hard data on the prevalence of political discrimination, but in one survey of social psychologists, large majorities admitted to having at least some bias against conservatives in an academic context. That is, they admitted that they would be at least a little bit less likely to hire a conservative than an equally qualified liberal for a job, a little less likely to recommend publication of a paper with a conservative viewpoint, a little less likely to approve a grant proposal with a conservative viewpoint, and a little less likely to invite a conservative to participate in a symposium. On a scale of 1 ("not at all") to 7 ("very much"), the academic psychologists on average rated their willingness to discriminate between 2.1 and 2.9, depending on the context.[313] Bear in mind that it is common for people, in surveys, to downplay their socially undesirable traits; therefore, the psychologists were probably more biased than they admitted.

Controlled experiments have verified this discriminatory tendency. In one experiment, research psychologists were asked to evaluate the publishability of a manuscript reporting results of a fictitious psychological study. In one condition, the study was said to show that left-wing activists were psychologically *healthier* than non-activists. In another condition, the study, with the identical design, was said to show that left-wing activists were *less* psychologically healthy. The former version of the study was rated more publishable. In another experiment, it was found that studies investigating discrimination against minorities were

---

[313] Inbar and Lammers 2012; Duarte et al. 2015, p. 11. The willingness to discriminate was 2.1 for a symposium invitation, 2.4 for a paper review, 2.5 for a grant review, and 2.9 for a hiring decision.

more likely to be approved by Internal Review Boards than otherwise identical studies investigating discrimination against white males.[314]

The above data concern the field of psychology. I do not have data on other academic fields; it appears that psychologists prefer to study themselves over other academics. But it would be surprising if other social science and humanities fields did not face similar problems.

(3) Anecdotes of ideological discrimination

Explicit attempts to silence academic work for ideological reasons seem to have proliferated in the last decade. Here are a few anecdotes:

a. In 2018, sociologist Noah Carl was awarded a prestigious three-year fellowship at St. Edmund's College at the University of Cambridge.[315] Then a group of progressive students and professors discovered that Carl had done research on, in their words, "the claimed relationship between 'race', 'criminality' and 'genetic intelligence'", in addition to having attended the London Conference on Intelligence, where they say racist work has been presented by others. They expressed concern that Carl's work was being used by right-wing extremists to support harmful political views. Over 500 professors and 800 students signed a petition expressing these concerns and demanding that the university publicly dissociate itself from Carl's research and launch an investigation into how Carl got hired.[316] They did not cite any specific papers by Carl, nor did they provide any quotations from his work, but they most likely had in mind Carl's article, "How Stifling Debate Around Race, Genes and IQ Can Do Harm", which argues that scholars should be permitted to freely debate questions about race, genes, and intelligence.[317]

The college capitulated, launching an investigation, which predictably concluded that Carl was a bad scholar and therefore academic freedom didn't apply to him.

Note: Carl is a graduate of Oxford University who has published many articles in respected academic journals. No one seemed to think he was a bad scholar until he was accused of supporting un-

---

[314] Duarte et al. 2015, pp. 10-11, citing Abramowitz et al. 1975 and Ceci et al. 1985.

[315] Wikipedia, "Noah Carl"; Quillette 2019.

[316] No to Racist Pseudoscience 2018.

[317] Carl 2018. For a list of Carl's papers, see https://scholar.google.com/citations ?user=CUywRJoAAAAJ.

woke views. Several highly respected scholars and newspapers came to Carl's defense, including Jonathan Haidt, Cass Sunstein, Peter Singer, *The Times of London*, and the *Daily Telegraph*. None of this was enough to save him. The college fired him in 2019, with apologies for the "hurt and offence" caused by hiring him.

Carl subsequently raised over $100,000 for a lawsuit against the college. The case was settled out of court by a confidential agreement between the parties.

b. In 2020, researchers published a study of the effects of female mentorship on scientists.[318] Briefly, the study found that women scientists do worse in their careers if they have female mentors, as compared to male mentors. This swiftly drew the ire of many academics, with over *7,600* signing an open letter attacking the article. The critics objected to the use of co-authorship as an indicator of mentorship as well as the use of citation counts as an indicator of academic success (these are the sort of objections that are common in academic contexts and do not normally engender howls of outrage or demands for retraction). The main concern was political: The critics argued that the study could harm female scholars by promoting sexist stereotypes.[319]

Bowing to the pressure, the study's authors swiftly agreed to retract their paper. In their retraction notice, they stood by "all the key findings of the paper with regards to co-authorship between junior and senior researchers" yet still agreed that it was best to retract the article. They concluded by affirming their "unwavering commitment to gender equity", expressing their solidarity with women scientists, and apologizing for the "pain" that their research had caused.[320]

c. In 2024, the philosophy journal *The New Bioethics* accepted for publication an article by philosopher Perry Hendricks titled "Abortion Restrictions Are Good for Black Women".[321] In brief, Hendricks argues that it is in one's interest to be prevented from committing moral wrongs, abortion is seriously wrong, and therefore abortion restrictions *benefit* women. Since black women tend to have more abortions than other women, abortion restrictions are especial-

---

[318] AlShebli et al. 2020a.
[319] TWAS Young Affiliates Network 2020.
[320] AlShebli et al. 2020b.
[321] Hendricks 2024b. The story is reported by Roberson 2024.

ly good for black women. (This is meant as a counter to the progressive claim that abortion restrictions are especially *bad* for black women.)

After the author posted a draft of this paper on the internet, a mob of Twitter users attacked him. The editor of the journal then wrote to Hendricks to say that he was *rescinding* the offer to publish. In his letter, the editor claimed to have not read the paper before it was accepted. Upon reading it, he developed concerns about "quality and rigour". He went on to cite Hendricks' race and sex, writing, "where white authors write about racial inequalities, or when male authors write about women's rights, this needs to be done with a considerable degree of circumspection, humility, and sensitivity. This manuscript falls short in that regard…"

d. In 2020, a group of five academic researchers (Clark et al.) published an article arguing that, as their title puts it, "declines in religiosity predict increases in violent crime—but not among countries with relatively high average IQ". In other words: Some countries have higher average IQ's than others. If you're in one of the low-IQ countries, then religion helps to decrease crime, but in the high-IQ countries, religion has no effect. At the end of the paper, the authors speculate that perhaps we should be wary of promoting modern, liberal values and undermining traditional religion in societies where the people are less intelligent.[322]

This paper provoked outrage online due to its "racial essentialism" and reliance on IQ figures for different nations.[323] Some argued that its data on IQ and crime were unreliable; the main concern, however, was ideological. As one of the article's leading critics admitted, "It's pretty clear that all this fuss is about the article's political content, not its data problems."[324] The authors bowed to the pressure and agreed to retract their paper.[325] The editor who had accepted the paper then apologized for failing "to think about the racial implications of the manuscript". Another editor then issued an apology for the "harm" caused by "publishing research without sufficient sensitivity". "As social scientists," she explained, "we have a respon-

---

[322] Clark et al. 2020.
[323] Gelman 2020; Marcus 2020.
[324] Gelman 2020.
[325] Bauer 2020.

sibility to be sensitive to the political, social, and cultural issues raised by our work."[326]

These anecdotes illustrate the current ethic of academia: Our responsibility is not simply to the truth; our responsibility is to be *sensitive to political issues*. More specifically, any evidence or arguments that might call certain cherished left-wing ideas into question or lead to right-wing political outcomes should be suppressed. I don't know how many academics believe this. I only know that shocking numbers are happy to sign petitions and open letters based on this premise.

By the way, the field of philosophy tends to show more intellectual integrity and less bias than other humanities and social science disciplines; philosophers tend to focus more on the quality of one's arguments rather than the political faction they might support. Nevertheless, there are still cases of rank cowardice and dishonesty in philosophy, like example (c) above.

(4) The pinnacle of discrimination: the diversity statement

The most blatant and shameless form of ideological discrimination in the academy has arisen in the last several years: Many colleges and universities now require all applicants to submit a "Diversity Statement" in order to be considered for an academic job. These are often used to eliminate applicants from consideration without regard to their research, teaching, or other job qualifications. In one job search at UC Berkeley, over *75%* of otherwise qualified applicants were rejected based on inadequate diversity statements.[327]

Diversity statements are essays in which the applicant explains how she will contribute to the DEI ("Diversity, Equity, and Inclusion") goals of the university. There are two keys to a good diversity statement. First, talk about your race, sex, or other "identity" characteristics that the university is legally prohibited from considering in the hiring process. Needless to say, you want the *right* identity group characteristics, e.g., black, female, disabled, gay, transgender. Second, talk about your past and future activism on behalf of left-wing, woke causes. Academics widely view the diversity statement as an ideological litmus test, and many nevertheless support it.[328] Universities do not care that

---

[326] Stephen Lindsay and Patricial Bauer, respectively, quoted in Oransky 2020.
[327] Brint and Frey 2023, p. 3.
[328] For discussion, see McBrayer 2022; Hendricks 2024a.

their hiring practices violate the Civil Rights Act, nor do the universities in California care that they are also violating Proposition 209, which was passed in California in 1996 to stop universities from using affirmative action.[329]

My main point here is not about the illegal racial and gender discrimination in the academy. My main point is about the aggressive exclusion of those who dissent from the ideological orthodoxy. *No* conservative could honestly write a statement that would get past the DEI screeners. Right-of-center thinkers are already a tiny minority of the academy, but in the next few decades, if woke administrators have their way, non-leftist voices will be completely eliminated from the academic world, and college "education" will consist of pure ideological brainwashing. This will not be an unintended *side effect* of programs to increase "diversity"; this is precisely what woke activists want. They want complete, unquestioning submission to every element of their ideology, from every single person in the academic world. Such is their commitment to diversity.

Sometimes, you can hear academics debating whether DEI statements might be a bit politically discriminatory. This is akin to debating whether Jim Crow laws were possibly a bit racist. No *clearer* example of discrimination could be imagined.

(5) A little discrimination goes a long way

Many other anecdotes could be told of ideological discrimination in the academy.[330] These stories have a dramatic impact on how professors do their jobs.

One reason for this is that the academic world is highly competitive. In my own department, for example, we have done a number of hires over the past two and a half decades that I have been an academic. When we advertise a job opening, we receive literally *hundreds* of applications, including applications from graduates of some of the world's top universities. Every time, there are going to be at least several candidates we are considering at the end who are all excellent and all very close to each other in qualifications. Given this, a young academic cannot afford to take on any gratuitous disadvantages. If there is one person on a hiring committee who is a little bit biased against you

---

[329] For discussion, see Huemer 2020.
[330] See Savolainen 2024; Duarte et al. 2015; Haidt 2011.

because of your political views, that could very easily be the reason you don't get a job. And that could make the difference between securing an excellent position for life and being driven out of the profession, having wasted the six years that you spent getting a PhD.

Academics, as a rule, are not the most courageous of people. Once they have secured a comfortable academic position, they do not want to risk career suicide just to speak their minds on some political issue. Academics also tend to be high in "agreeableness" (as they say in personality psychology). Thus, they are very uncomfortable with having many people publicly attacking them. So, even without any threat of losing their jobs, academics can be convinced to shut up or take back something they have said if they learn that many peers disagree with it.

All of this helps to explain how woke ideology maintains its strangle hold on the academic world and why academics have generally not repudiated the numerous errors propounded by woke ideologues. If a conservative or other non-leftist were inclined to become an academic, she would probably be deterred by the thought of spending her life working in a culture that holds such disdain for conservatives and conservative views as academia does. If she decided to enter academia anyway, it is likely that she would fail as an academic due to ideological discrimination. If she succeeded, it is likely that she would keep her political views to herself. And if she expressed those views, it is likely that she would then be pressured to retract what she had said.

(6) The failure of tenure

Isn't this the sort of thing that the institution of tenure is meant to avoid? Once a professor has tenure, he can say whatever he wants, right?

Indeed, the official rules of most universities will state or imply that you can't be fired for your political views, particularly if you have tenure. But that does not mean that you can't in fact be fired for your political views. It just means that *if you are*, then you have a good shot of winning a lawsuit against the university, assuming that you have tens of thousands of dollars to fund such a suit. But who wants to take the chance? And that is not to mention all the smaller disadvantages that you risk by expressing politically incorrect ideas—not getting your papers published, not being invited to conferences, and so on.

Moreover, the institution of tenure does little to prevent ideological discrimination because anyone who wants to discriminate can do so during the tenure review process. Anyone with conservative views and a habit of speaking her mind will probably out herself in one way or another during her first six years as a professor. If her school wants to discriminate, it will simply reject that person when she comes up for tenure in her seventh year. They may indeed be *more* likely to do this than to fire a *non*-tenure-track instructor, because the risk of tenuring a conservative professor is too high: if the school does not fire her during tenure review, they will be forced to keep her for life (again, on pain of lawsuits).

(7) Groupthink

There is one final dynamic that one must grasp to understand the ideological extremism of the academy: the dynamic of *groupthink*. This is a psychological phenomenon that often develops when a social group has overwhelming agreement on certain beliefs that are controversial outside the group. When this happens, the members of the group can start to confuse *loyalty to the group* with *loyalty to those beliefs*.[331] Anyone who questions the group's beliefs is seen as a traitor, someone who sides with outsiders against the group. Status in the group starts to depend on displays of commitment to the group's beliefs, and members start to compete with each other in displays of commitment, which devolves into embracing ever *more extreme* versions of the common ideas. Irrationality may even be treated as a virtue, for as one moves to ever more irrational extremes, one displays ever more thoroughgoing commitment to the group. After all, it takes an *extremely* loyal person to reject logic and evidence to defend the group's ideas.

To avoid the trap of groupthink, a group needs a certain amount of intellectual diversity. If the majority hold some ideological position, there should nevertheless be a substantial minority of dissenters. If there are no dissenters, or if the minority is too small to feel comfortable speaking, the group is in danger of falling into groupthink. Many academic departments and even whole disciplines have long since fallen into that trap.

---

[331] Janis 1972.

23 How Myths Thrive

In the last chapter, we saw some of why contemporary progressive ideology has the content that it has. Let us now try to understand why political myths are so widespread in modern times. Most of what I say here will apply to the myths spread by all political ideologies, not just progressivism.

A. Motivated Reasoning

When people think about politics, they are rarely just trying to figure out the truth. Rather, they have certain positions that they *want* to hold for various reasons that are independent of the truth of those positions.[332]

(1) Self-image construction

A key psychological function of political beliefs is self-image construction: You want to paint a certain image of yourself—both to yourself and to others—and only some political positions fit with that image. Progressives prefer to portray themselves as compassionate, broad-minded defenders of the downtrodden. Many also wish to be seen, and to see themselves, as victims, perhaps to draw sympathy, to lower the expectations placed on them, or to gain credibility with other leftists. This requires them to believe that oppression is widespread in their society; hence, they look for signs that this is the case.

Conservatives, on the other hand, would rather be seen and see themselves as strong, respectable, and tough-minded defenders of tradition. They thus tend to take uncompromising positions on violations of traditional norms, and they look for signs that their society and its traditions are good. Both sides look for signs that the other side is wrong.

---

[332] For discussion, see Huemer 2015.

(2) Tribal signaling

A second key function of political beliefs is *signaling*. Human beings are tribal animals; we are biologically predisposed to sort ourselves into groups, then promote our own group's interests at the expense of rival groups. In our history, this tendency has often led to outright war between neighboring societies. The tendency is so strong that in psychological experiments, assigning people to different groups *arbitrarily* is enough to make people discriminate in favor of their own group members and against others.[333] For most of the history of our species, the main groups in competition with each other were primitive tribes. In modern society, we lack literal tribes, so we divide ourselves along other lines, such as race, religion, and political ideology.

Given our tribal nature, human beings also want to know who belongs to which group. Each individual especially wants his own tribe to recognize him as a loyal member of the group. Hence, there is a natural desire to signal one's affiliation to other group members. One way to do this, when it comes to ideological tribes, is by loudly avowing beliefs appropriate to one's chosen tribe. This also creates psychological pressure for one to genuinely *believe* what other group members say, regardless of whether those beliefs correspond to reality.

Modern American progressives include some of the most incessant tribal signalers you could ever hope to meet. Many of them choose to signal their ideological affiliation in nearly every interaction they have. For example, many include "land acknowledgements" (statements about how some land they are using was stolen from natives) in their email signatures. Many introduce themselves with "I use he/him pronouns" or "My pronouns are she/her" whenever they meet a new person. This is a way of politicizing essentially all interactions and signaling one's devotion to the progressive tribe.[334] If progressives have their way, no one will be able to talk about anything without first identifying their stance with respect to progressive ideology.

Another popular form of signaling is to introduce vocabulary that your tribe prefers, with some ideological rationalization of why that vocabulary is better than the more common expressions used by the *hoi polloi*. One then changes the vocabulary periodically so that only those who are plugged in to your tribe's discussions will be able to use the

---

[333] Tajfel et al. 1971.
[334] For discussion, see Huemer 2023.

signal properly. E.g., progressives introduce terms such as "people of color" (for brown-skinned people, not to be confused with "colored people"!), "Latinx" (for Hispanics), and "the unhoused" (for homeless people), so that you can tell who belongs to the progressive tribe by how they speak. An added bonus is the pleasure of berating other people for not using your preferred words when they talk.

(3) Political beliefs are not normal beliefs

It is important to understand how political beliefs differ from most other beliefs that people deploy in their day-to-day lives. For *most* of your beliefs, you bear a personal cost if you are wrong. If you're wrong about the location of the supermarket, you'll have a hard time getting food. If you're wrong about what is the best career for you, you'll miss out on that career option. And so on.

Politics is different. In politics, a single, ordinary individual has next to zero chance of *ever* influencing *any* of the relevant events. So we anticipate almost zero chance of suffering any negative consequences from holding false beliefs. If you are wrong about who is the best Presidential candidate, for instance, that won't actually change which President you get, except in the vanishingly improbable event that the election turns on a single vote (or you are a high-ranking party insider, or you are a very wealthy campaign donor). You'll just get whatever candidate the majority votes for, regardless of what belief you personally adopt.

Most people are perfectly well aware of this, even if they won't admit it and even if they like to repeat slogans like "every vote matters" during election season. Since each of us knows that we are (almost certainly) never going to actually affect government policy, that frees us to adopt whatever beliefs we feel like having, without fear that we will suffer harms from being wrong.

I am not suggesting that people expressly choose false or unjustified beliefs as such; no one says to himself, "I think I'll adopt an irrational belief right now." What I suggest is that identifying the most rational beliefs about controversial subjects is difficult work, and most people will not exert the effort required, in part because they do not fear any significant costs from being wrong. When our beliefs are emotionally satisfying, and we do not fear personal costs of being wrong, we do not bother to examine those beliefs. Indeed, we may look for any excuse to hold the beliefs that we prefer.[335]

This account does not assume that we have the ability to choose to believe just *anything, at will*. Most people have some rationality constraint, some degree of irrationality that they are psychologically unable to exceed. If evidence is highly ambiguous, we can get ourselves to believe what we want, but if the evidence is completely clear and one-sided, most cannot simply believe what they want.[336] This is why it is *sometimes* possible to argue someone into something they don't want to believe. However, political ideologues tend to have high irrationality thresholds, making it extremely difficult to argue them out of anything.

(4) How to tell what activists really want

The preceding account implies that many or most political beliefs are held in bad faith. We *tell ourselves* that these things are true, but we do not really care if they are. We tell ourselves that we are motivated by the good of society, but we are really moved by our own private, emotional needs.

This is an uncomfortably cynical take on humans engaging in politics. Why not think, instead, that almost everyone who indulges in political discourse is sincerely trying their best to identify the truth and help society? Why not assume that any errors are due to our not being very good at identifying the truth, rather than our not caring?

If a person is sincerely trying to *improve society*, that would no doubt look very similar to a person who is just trying to *portray himself* as caring about society. These two people, you might think, would do the same things, since the best way of portraying yourself as caring about society is to help society.

But there are differences. The key point is that if you want to actually benefit society, then you need to have true beliefs about society's current situation and how to improve it. If you just want to *portray yourself* as caring about society, then you don't need that. If you want to convince other people that you care about society, you just need to do the things that other people in your social group *believe* are good for society. You don't have to check on whether their beliefs are correct. By the same token, if you want to make yourself *feel like* you are helping society, then you just need *strong beliefs* about what helps society,

---

[335] As Caplan (2007) puts it, people are often "rationally irrational".
[336] For elaboration, see Huemer 2024.

and you need to pursue the things that those beliefs identify. You don't have to check whether your beliefs are correct.

So we have a way of telling which political activists actually care about society and which are merely trying to portray themselves as caring: The ones who actually care will exert significant effort to make sure that their beliefs are correct. They won't form dogmatic beliefs about complex and difficult issues. They will try to take into account countervailing evidence. If a policy they supported appears not to be working, they will consider changing their position to avoid further wasted effort.

The people who are just trying to make themselves feel good will not do those things. They will avoid countervailing evidence, since it might undermine the strength of their convictions. For instance, they will avoid listening to news sources with a different political orientation. If you start to give them a logical argument, they will try to misunderstand it or to not hear it. If they accidentally acquire some evidence against their beliefs, they will immediately try to rationalize it away or simply distract themselves from it so that they can return to the happy state of complete conviction of their rightness. For instance, when confronted with a serious flaw of their preferred political candidate, they might immediately change the subject to some different flaw in the *other* candidate. These behaviors are the way to make yourself feel good; they are not the way to help society.

By this criterion, based on casual observation, I would say that most politically engaged people fall into the category of "trying to make themselves feel good" or "trying to portray themselves as caring", rather than "trying to actually help society". By the way, dear reader, just in case this wasn't clear: I am not telling you this simply so that you can have an excuse to dismiss the opinions of other people who disagree with you. I am hoping that this discussion will make you reflect on yourself. How much are *you* doing to check on the accuracy of your beliefs? Do you welcome objections and counter-evidence, or do you try to sweep them away?

B. The Role of the Internet

In the last section, we saw the fundamental reason why there is a demand for political myths. It is because people *want* to believe certain political claims, but there may not be enough evidence for those claims for us to be able to believe them straightaway. We therefore need someone to manufacture evidence for the things we want to believe. The manufacturer must of course claim that the evidence is genuine. We can then decline to look into matters further and just accept the evidence at face value.

All of that has been true for a long time. But the problem has worsened in recent years due to certain aspects of how the internet works.

(1) The free media business model

Since the advent of radio, much of our information about social and political issues has come from "free" media sources—first radio, then television, then an explosion of internet sources, including news web sites, blogs, and social media platforms such as Facebook and Twitter. All of these information sources require money to operate. How can they give away their product for free?

There's a saying, "If you're not paying for the product, *you're* the product." Modern media companies, from television stations to social media platforms, are not in the business of informing you of true and important facts. Still less are they in the business of helping democracy function. They are in the business of *capturing your attention*, so they can sell it to advertisers. That is how they get paid, so that is what they are competing with each other to do, and that is where they are developing expertise. All of their great innovations will be innovations in capturing attention. If one media company figures out how to ensure that its readers do not come away with mistaken impressions from its stories, while a second company figures out how to capture more people's attention and keep it for longer, then the first company may get a warm feeling inside, but it is the second company that will grow richer and larger.

Once you understand the incentive structure, you can understand the outcome. Our media system selects for the most attention-grabbing, emotion-stimulating content. It turns out that the best way to grab people's attention, to keep them reading, and to inspire them to share content with their friends, is not to provide the most accurate, sober analyses of the most objectively important issues. The best way is to create or promote content that confirms people's biases and that stokes fear, anger, or hate.[337] It does not matter to the media companies or their advertisers if this content makes the audience feel worse, if it damages their relationships with others, or if it tears the country apart.

This sort of content will rarely be a fair representation of reality— rarely does the world just happen to offer up the maximally entertaining or emotionally salient pattern of facts for us. Content providers who focus on factual accuracy and objective importance will therefore lose out in competition with less scrupulous providers.

(2) The internet exacerbates the problems of modern media

With the rise of the internet and especially social media, we have seen an explosion of content providers. Back in the television age, the news was dominated by three or four main providers. Today, there are thousands or millions of sources providing content about social and political issues. Anyone with an internet connection can start providing content that could reach thousands or millions of others. This exacerbates the problems with free media for four reasons.

First, it means a drop in the average intelligence, education, maturity, and sanity level of content providers. This is not to say that legacy media journalists were geniuses. But there were generally at least some filters on who could be a journalist and expect to get a large audience. A 14-year-old prankster, for example, could not make up a story and read it on the evening news. Today, a 14-year-old troll can easily transmit stories to people all over the world.

Second, due to the large number of content providers, reputation plays a smaller role than it used to. When there were only three major news networks, each one had to worry that if they were caught lying too badly, they would ruin their reputation. Today, there are so many content providers that most of them have no reputation with most viewers. Some content providers are not even real people. Twitter estimates that 16 million of its 368 million users are bots (computer programs); some observers put the number as much as four times higher.[338] In this environment, readers cannot be expected to know who is a reliable information source or even who is a real person. If we were perfectly rational, we would therefore view nearly all internet and social media content with suspicion. But in fact, most people have a

---

[337] Admittedly, one can also grab attention with cat videos and porn.
[338] Timothy 2022.

tendency to swallow whatever information they hear that fits their ideological biases, as long as they don't have proof that the source is unreliable.

Third, the large number of content providers means that it is possible to tailor the news to specific ideological predilections. For some products, this kind of customization is good—e.g., it's great that everyone can now listen to just the kind of music they like the most. But it's not so great that everyone can now get just the kind of news they like the most.

Fourth, we now have a vastly more efficient system for producing attention-grabbing content than the yellow journalists of the past could dream of. We have decentralized content-generation, delegating it to masses of users, while we have computer algorithms that systematically go through all the vast troves of content that are constantly being generated and select the most attention-grabbing gems to promote.

(3) Political myths win

In this system, political myths spread easily. There are thousands of people out there at any given time devising ideologically biased, outrage-promoting takes on current events or the general state of society. If, for example, a black person is shot by police, there is going to be someone (and likely many people) in the vast user base of social media ready to claim that it was a racist murder and further proof that American police departments are filled with Nazis. Because this message plays to a certain ideological orientation and provokes outrage, it will draw engagement from users—more views, comments, shares. The person who makes the claim (whether true or false) "benefits" from this, insofar as social media users crave attention. Users thus compete in generating this kind of content, which gets promoted by media platforms.

Of course, other people are free to debunk political myths. But doing so is a lot less entertaining (both for the debunker and for his audience) than spreading the myths. It takes a lot more time and effort to thoroughly debunk a myth than it does to spread it to a receptive audience. Most people who have consumed political myths are not particularly interested in having their beliefs corrected, so they are not going to read a book like this one.

C. Ideological Defense Systems

There is one more piece of the puzzle of how political myths thrive. Most political myths appeal to particular ideologies and are rejected by other ideologies. But people with conflicting ideologies often interact with each other. This interaction can force people to confront objections to their beliefs. How do ideologues ensure that they won't wind up being forced to change their political beliefs by people from rival tribes annoyingly citing contrary facts and evidence?

One "solution" is to develop an *ideological defense system*. This is a set of beliefs that, once incorporated into an ideology, make it extremely difficult for anyone to erode your ideology through evidence and reasoning.[339] Following are some examples.

1. "It is morally wrong to question this belief system."

   Modern progressives have taken a page from traditional religion, where apostasy and heresy have often been considered grave sins and faith has been deemed a key virtue. Though progressives do not use the same *terminology* as traditional religionists use, they use similar ideas, viewing disagreement with them as immoral. Those who disagree with progressives are commonly labeled "racists", "transphobes", etc., and their statements are labeled "hate speech", the modern version of heresy. Consider, e.g., when the conservative humor site The Babylon Bee was kicked off Twitter in 2022 for referring to transwoman Rachel Levine as a "man". Twitter claimed that this violated their policy against hate speech.[340]

   Once one accepts this idea, it becomes extremely difficult for one to correct errors in one's belief system, should any errors exist. As soon as any doubts start to creep in, or one starts to hear evidence counter to one's existing beliefs, one is meant to shut down the process for fear of falling into immorality. It is very hard to objectively evaluate an idea if you start out with the presumption that it is immoral to doubt it. This short-circuits reason by substituting *moral disapproval* for rational judgment.

   In some cases, the work is done, not so much by the *belief* that it is wrong to question this belief system but by the *feeling* that it is

---

[339] For discussion of belief system defenses in the context of Christianity, see Armstrong 2023, ch. 2.
[340] Klar 2022.

wrong; this can be more effective as an ideological defense, given that moral emotions are often recalcitrant to rational judgment.

2. "It is harmful to 'platform' people who contradict this ideology."

For example, it is said that anyone who denies that all transwomen are women is "causing harm" to transwomen. Sometimes, progressive activists will claim that words (that disagree with progressivism) are "violence". Sometimes, they simply appeal to the potential for free speech (by right-wing speakers) to lead to the wrong political results.

This idea also functions as a belief-system defense. If it's wrong to platform people you disagree with, then it is appropriate to shout them down or prevent them from coming to your university or other venue to speak. This guarantees that they won't give you any evidence against your beliefs. Since these are the people most likely to give you evidence against your beliefs, this is an effective way of maintaining your ideology.

Of course, you could simply *not go* to the event where a critic of your ideology is speaking. But that would not deal with the problem that other people might be persuaded. People who hold an ideology or religion are usually eager to police their fellow tribe-members' loyalty.

Aside: If the would-be speakers who disagree with you have bad arguments, then you could try verbally rebutting their arguments, which should expose the foolishness of their position. But if you secretly suspect that they have *good* arguments, which your side would be unable to rebut, then silencing them is the only defense. This is why people who are wrong, especially people who on some level *know* they are wrong, are the ones who most often call for speech restrictions.

The truth usually comes off better in open debate. So if your position is correct, you should probably want there to be an open debate; if your position is wrong, you should probably avoid open debate. Therefore, if you see a controversy in which one side is trying to stifle debate while the other welcomes open debate, you can make an inference about who is most likely right.

There are of course exceptions to this. E.g., if you know a particular individual is simply a better debater than you (or a better manipulator), you might avoid debating him, even if you are right. You also might avoid debate if you lack respect for the audience and thus think many of them will be persuaded by the worse arguments (which, in fairness, is sometimes true).

3. "Oppressed minorities have epistemic privilege. We should defer to their lived experience. Failing to believe them is an 'epistemic injustice'."

This idea is meant to silence anyone from the wrong group (particularly white men) who disagrees with your ideology. The claim is that only minorities know what it's like to be a minority, only they know the burden our society places on them, and therefore, one should simply accept assertions made by them about the oppression they have suffered. Of course, these same minorities are also the people who would have the greatest *interest* in claiming that minorities are oppressed, since this might justify giving them compensation, holding them to lower standards, and so on. But advocates of the "epistemic privilege" argument seldom take notice of this.

This is a useful belief-system defense because it enables one to dismiss the objections of anyone who isn't a minority member (which includes most people), without regard to the actual content of their objections, based solely on their identity. This is especially handy if you in fact would be unable to address the content of those objections.

4. "Minority members who deny that they are oppressed are (a) traitors, (b) shills for powerful interests, or (c) suffering from 'false consciousness' or 'internalized oppression'."

For instance, black conservatives, such as Supreme Court Justice Clarence Thomas, are sometimes called "Uncle Toms" and accused of being motivated by money or the favor of whites.[341] In Marxist ideology, poor people who don't acknowledge that they are being oppressed by the capitalists are said to suffer from "false consciousness", meaning that they have been hoodwinked by the ideology of the ruling class.

The upshot of this is that, notwithstanding point #3 above, one should *not* listen to minorities if they disagree with progressivism. The "Uncle Tom" (and similar) accusations are also designed to intimidate other minority members who might provide evidence against progressivism into silence. When ideas #3 and #4 are com-

---

[341] See Paoletta 2022; Blake 2023.

bined, the intended effect is to silence *any* criticism of progressivism from anyone, regardless of the evidence behind that criticism.

5. "White fragility perpetuates racism."

This idea is from Robin DiAngelo's famous "anti-racist" book, *White Fragility*.[342] When white people are accused of racism or taught progressive ideas about race, DiAngelo observes, they often engage in "defensive moves", including "display of emotions such as anger, fear, and guilt, and behaviors such as argumentation, silence, and leaving the stress-inducing situation".[343] These are examples of white fragility, which results from and tends to sustain the white supremacy culture of America.

Notice that white fragility, in DiAngelo's reckoning, includes virtually any response other than saying, "Yes, Robin DiAngelo, you are correct." If someone argues with DiAngelo, *or* remains silent, *or* declines to talk to her, all those indicate white fragility, which is bad because it perpetuates racism. So virtually the only way to not support racism is to agree with whatever DiAngelo says. It never occurs to her that the reason people react defensively to her could be that she is attacking them unfairly. Perhaps she is unable to entertain that possibility because of her own fragility.

6. "Rationality and objectivity are either impossible or bad."

Sometimes people say that objectivity is impossible; one can only ever view things from one's own, subjective viewpoint. Other times, people say that the ideal of objectivity is a Western, patriarchal, white value. One popular "anti-racist" training document contains a list of elements of "white supremacy culture" that people should watch out for, including such items as "perfectionism", "worship of the written word", and "objectivity".[344]

This sort of claim functions to discourage people from trying to think objectively—i.e., trying to avoid bias and consider all available evidence fairly. This enables one to maintain one's current ideology

---

[342] DiAngelo 2018. I use scare quotes because what progressives call "anti-racism" I consider a form of racism.

[343] DiAngelo 2011, p. 57.

[344] Okun 2020; Pan and Prescod 2021. Okun's complete list of elements of white supremacy culture: perfectionism; sense of urgency; defensiveness; quantity over quality; worship of the written word; only one right way; paternalism; either/or thinking; power hoarding; fear of open conflict; individualism; I'm the only one; progress is bigger, more; objectivity; right to comfort.

without regard to the truth. If one's ideology is in blatant conflict with reality, then the only way to protect the belief system is to reject objectivity.

Similarly for the idea that rationality is either impossible or undesirable: This is a ploy to avoid the inevitable refutation of one's belief system, given that one's belief system is irrational.

The embrace of these ideological defense mechanisms is part of why political myths are recalcitrant.

Of course, if a belief system is true, then it *should* be defended. The problem with the above belief system defenses is that they enable a belief system to be defended *regardless* of its truth. No matter how strong the evidence against one's belief system is, one can dismiss that evidence if one has adopted these sorts of defensive beliefs. Therefore, the fact that someone adopts such defenses is evidence that they do not want to know the truth, or they do not want *you* to know the truth. Let me tell you an allegory about this.

Detective Libby Holmes (Sherlock Holmes' granddaughter) is investigating a murder. She goes to interview her first suspect, Lucky Lefty, whereupon they have the following conversation.

Libby: Where were you on the night of January 16th?

Lefty: How dare you question me? I can have you fired for this!

Libby: Settle down, no one is accusing you. I just want to know where you were.

Lefty: I was at home.

Libby: Is there anyone who can corroborate that?

Lefty: Sure, ask my mom. If she says I was there, it would be immoral for you not to believe her. But if she denies I was there, don't listen to her.

Libby: Okay, we'll look into that. In the meantime, we've found some fingerprints at the crime scene. You wouldn't mind giving me your fingerprints, would you?

Lefty: Absolutely not! Fingerprinting causes harm. It would be immoral to even *look* at the fingerprints! Anyway, it's impossible to collect a perfect fingerprint; all fingerprint images are inherently flawed. And whatever you do, absolutely *do not* review the security camera footage!

Libby: Oh, okay. I guess you must be completely innocent then.

In this dialogue, Lefty tries to intimidate Libby into not investigating him, then tries to steer Libby toward easily biased evidence (his mom's testimony) and away from more objective evidence (fingerprints and security footage). What is the best explanation for Lefty's behavior? I suppose it *could* be that Lefty is innocent but he just happens to believe that seemingly objective evidence frequently implicates innocent people. But it hardly takes a master detective to deduce the more likely explanation: Lefty committed the murder. He knows that a review of the evidence would lead to that conclusion, so he is trying to prevent Libby from reviewing the evidence. Obviously.

That is how we should view the efforts of progressives to discourage objective thinking, silence unwoke speakers, and intimidate their critics. The simplest explanation for their behavior is that an open, objective review of the evidence would refute the progressive viewpoint, and deep down, the progressives know this.

24 The Dangers of Progressive Myths

A. Failed Policy

In this chapter, we discuss what is so bad about the prevalence of progressive myths. The most obvious harm of political myths of any kind is that they lead to failed policy. To solve any social problem, you need to understand the problem correctly. If you don't understand what the problem is, what causes it, and so on, then the solutions you come up with will probably be worthless at best. They will be like the treatments prescribed by a "doctor" who never attended medical school and does not know what disease the patient has. If the doctor prescribed treatment based on whatever diagnosis he found most entertaining and emotionally salient, the treatment would almost certainly do more harm than good.

For example, suppose you are concerned about police shootings, and you believe that there is an epidemic of racist police shooting peaceful, unarmed black men. To solve this alleged problem, you might try to defund the police, or give the police anti-racism training, or even prohibit police from carrying firearms.

But suppose, as is actually the case, that there is no such epidemic, that most police shootings are of dangerous criminals who are attacking the police at the time, and that police shootings show a bias against whites rather than against blacks. Then all your programs will fail. Defunding the police will result in more people getting killed by the criminals whom the police would otherwise have apprehended. Giving the police anti-racism training will have no effect on shootings. And disarming police will lead to more police being killed and more criminals escaping, which will harm all communities, especially black communities.

B. The Institution that Cried "Wolf"

The second harm of political myths is to undermine the transmission of correct information to the public. Perhaps if the myth-maker had total control of all information sources, this would not happen. But in our world, members of the public periodically *find out* that they have been deceived, whereupon they learn to distrust the sources who misled them. This distrust may easily spread to whole *categories* of information providers, e.g., all of academia, all public officials, all journalists.

For example, during the Covid-19 pandemic, members of the public first heard that face masks were ineffective against respiratory viruses. A few months later, they were told that masks were a crucial form of protection that everyone *must* wear. Lacking medical expertise, lay people didn't know *which* statement was a lie. But most probably realized they had been lied to, since the two statements contradicted each other (and most were not naïve enough to believe that the science had changed so radically). The rational inference is that *public health officials cannot be trusted*, since they will lie for political reasons. The long-term consequences of teaching that lesson may be far worse than the consequences of letting everyone walk around unmasked during the Covid-19 outbreak.

Many people, particularly Republicans, have acquired a general distrust of academics and academic research due to the well-known political bias of the academy. Suppose, for example, you hear that the entire black/white test score gap can be explained by Stereotype Threat. Later, you learn that that is false and was never supported by the research. You might then be tempted to distrust all reports that you hear about the results of academic research. If you look a little more closely and review a few more cases, you might notice a more specific pattern: Reports of academic research *that support left-wing ideas* frequently turn out to be false, exaggerated, or otherwise misleading. Then the rational conclusion is that *one cannot trust reports of academic research that seem to support left-wing ideas*. Add in a few stories about blatant ideological discrimination in the academy, and you have a simple debunking explanation for why academic research often supports left-wing ideas: It is because academics deliberately suppress evidence supporting right-wing ideas and promote or manufacture evidence for left-wing ideas.

Much the same is true of the relentless leftward bias of mainstream news media. Many of the myths we have discussed have been spread by mainstream media sources.

These sources, by the way, often appear to collude with each other in a way perfectly designed to play into the hands of conspiracy theorists. Sometimes, you can find multiple news sources not only giving the same take on a story but using *identical phrases* to express it. In 2017, many journalists predicted that President Trump was shortly going to be forced to resign due to the investigation then underway by special counsel Robert Mueller. Many different journalists all used the exact phrases "the walls closing in on him" and "the beginning of the end" to describe Trump's impending fate, thus showing that they had coordinated with each other. As many viewers soon noticed, the walls did not close in on Mr. Trump, and Mr. Trump in fact served out his full term. There have been many other cases in which multiple television news reporters have all said the same thing; I invite the reader to view some of these on the internet.[345]

The natural conclusion for viewers is that the mainstream news media cannot be trusted, particularly when they report on politically charged stories. They are biased toward reporting what they want to believe, and they are openly coordinating with each other.

And what is the problem with all this? The problem is like that of the boy who cried wolf. Suppose that one day, public officials, the academic world, and mainstream media have something *true* to tell us, something that we actually need to know. Inevitably, a significant fraction of the public will refuse to believe it.

This may be part of the story of vaccine hesitancy: Part of why many people refuse to take effective vaccines may be the distrust in mainstream information sources resulting from those sources' past deceptions. If, for example, public health officials would lie about masks for political reasons, who is to say that they aren't lying about vaccines in order to make money for big pharma?

You might think that this last hypothesis sounds like a crazy conspiracy theory. But *many* lay people in fact do not, on their own, have any way of assessing the plausibility of that theory. Their only way of assessing it would be to trust some expert. But once they know that experts sometimes lie, they have no way of knowing which experts can

---

[345] Gerald 2019, https://youtu.be/yshJn7lgVsY.

be trusted about which questions. They have no reason to assume that experts would only lie about masks but not about vaccines. Being told "that's a crazy conspiracy theory" does not help, since that could simply be part of the lie. Nor can lay people turn to journalists or academics to tell them when the government is lying, because journalists and academics often coordinate with each other and deliberately echo the positions of the government.

In some cases, society's elite institutions seem to be coordinating on things that lay people believe they can just see to be false, such as the idea that some people with penises and beards are women. Academics, journalists, major tech companies, and Democratic political leaders all seem to agree on that. The people working in these institutions *think* that they are thereby promoting the correct, tolerant, compassionate gender theory. What they are actually doing is burning through their institutions' credibility.

C. Polarization

The last two harms of political myths stand in contrast to each other: The "failed policy" problem depends on some people's *believing* the myths and then trying to enact policy on that basis. The "distrust" problem depends on people's *disbelieving* the myths.

The third harm caused by political myths turns on the fact that they are typically accepted by some people and rejected by others. Political myths are designed to play on the emotions and biases of partisans of a particular ideology, to strengthen those biases, and to solidify those people's political affiliation. People of opposing ideologies typically reject the myths, learn to distrust the sources that are propounding them, and may even retreat into separate bubbles with their own information sources. Thus, political myths *polarize* society: They push both sides further away from each other, strengthening their feelings of opposition to each other.

And what is wrong with polarization? One problem is that it may lead to civil unrest, as in the Charlottesville riot of 2017 or the BLM riots of 2020. Political *protests* are perfectly in order when one disagrees with government policy (as one often should). But when our culture is highly polarized, as it has become in the last decade, protests are likely to give way to actual violence between partisans of opposing sides.

Another problem is that polarization makes it harder for us as a society to get useful things done. When one side wants to do something, the other side is more likely to oppose it simply because the first side wants it. People may be driven to adopt perverse positions to spite the other party. For instance, some supporters of President Trump have been seen wearing T-shirts with the message, "I'd rather be a Russian than a Democrat", an attitude that would have been anathema to any earlier generation of Republicans.[346]

D. Harming Minorities

The above three problems apply to political myths in general. But there is a particular problem that I see with the *progressive* myths we have discussed: They harm the very minorities that progressives claim to help. They sow distrust of the majority and of the dominant institutions of society in the minds of minority members. For example, if blacks believe that police are racist killers, they will be reluctant to call on the police or to cooperate with police. This makes it easier for criminals to victimize black neighborhoods. If blacks believe (as some progressives teach) that all whites are racists, then they may distrust white doctors, white teachers, white bosses and coworkers. They may resist going to "white colleges" and learning "white culture". All of this causes little trouble for *white* people. A white doctor is not particularly harmed if her black patients do not listen to her medical advice; a white cop is not particularly harmed if he fails to catch criminals in black neighborhoods. Black distrust of whites is mainly a problem for *black* people.

During the Covid-19 pandemic, Dr. Anthony Fauci and D.C. Mayor Muriel Bowser went around Washington, D.C. trying to get people vaccinated. Some of their encounters were aired on public television. In one encounter, they speak to a black man in a predominantly black neighborhood. The man compares Covid-19 to the flu:

Man: Something like the common flu then, right? Basically.

Fauci: It's much more serious than the flu.

Man: Well, the flu kills a lot of people annually too.

Fauci: You know how many people died of the flu the last year? I mean not this year, virtually none. But the previous year, about 20 to 30,000. You know how many people have died from Covid-19 in the United States? 600,000 Americans.

---

[346] Evon 2018.

Man: Well, the number that you all given that died, that's, that's once again, that's you all's number.

Bowser: You gonna pass?

Man: Yeah, definitely. Because when you start talking about paying people to get vaccinated, when you start talking about incentivizing things, to get people vaccinated, there's something else going on with that. Something else, something going on with that.[347]

I do not know whether Dr. Fauci's whiteness played a role in this man's suspicion. But this illustrates the consequences of a general distrust of society and its dominant institutions. *Dr. Fauci* suffered no cost from the man's distrust; the man stood only to harm himself and those around him by refusing vaccination.

E. Keeping Racism Alive

It goes without saying that progressive myths promote anti-white racism. Perhaps less obvious is that they also help to keep traditional racism against minorities alive. One way they do this is by making race *salient*. The constant, obsessive discussion of race keeps racial categorizations in the front of everyone's minds.

A key feature of human psychology is that most humans have an instinctive sense of loyalty to their own group. How we identify "our group" can change, e.g., one may be able to shift from thinking of one's group as "white people" to thinking of one's group as "Americans", but however we identify it, we will tend to favor our group over other groups. So the insistence that *race* is the core of one's identity tends to make people more inclined to favor their *race* over other races.

Most people's loyalty to their group is stronger than their loyalty to abstract morality. Thus, if you succeed in convincing people that their group is inherently exploitative, they are more likely to decide that they are now in favor of exploitation, rather than to decide that they are opposed to their own group. (Why does this not happen to white progressives? Perhaps because they are more strongly identified with the "progressive" group than with the "white" group.)

Furthermore, most people resent being blamed for things they manifestly did not do—for example, being blamed for slavery or Jim

---

[347] PBS 2023, 5:43-6:25.

Crow. Today, resentment on the part of mainstream Americans against progressive ideologues is mounting, and far right political candidates are happy to take advantage of this. It is not hard to imagine some of that resentment spilling over to the minorities on behalf of whom progressives claim to be acting. How long can you expect to lecture people about how racist they are, how it is all their fault that black people are not succeeding, and how performance standards need to be lowered for black people, before they start to really resent black people?

You may say it is unjust or evil that human beings are prone to the sort of feelings of group loyalty and resentment that I have described. Certainly it is unfortunate. But it is a fact nonetheless, and as long as it is a fact, the way to combat racism is probably to *deemphasize race* in favor of some shared identity, rather than to emphasize racial identities and then attack the majority race.

But then, the goal of progressives may not be to combat racism after all. Perhaps their goal is rather to keep their own movement alive (see Chapter 22, §B).

F. Undermining America

Let us conclude with the most serious problem with progressive myths: They are almost perfectly calibrated to undermine social loyalty and trust. Before explaining why I say that, let me first say some words about what social trust and loyalty are and why they matter.

(1) The problem of social conflict

Human beings are *selfish social animals*. That is, we want to live together in large groups, but each of us cares a lot more about our own interests than about the interests of most other group members.[348] There are enormous benefits from living in a society; most people, indeed, would be unable to survive alone, and certainly would not have *good* lives even if they survived. However, our selfishness creates a standing problem for social cooperation. In social life, there are many opportunities for an individual to do things that would benefit himself at the expense of others. Often, the harm to others would be vastly out of proportion to

---

[348] People often form emotional bonds with others, particularly family and friends, which can lead to unselfish behavior toward these others. But modern societies contain far too many people for one to form emotional bonds with most other members of one's society.

the benefit to oneself. (Example: killing a person to steal their wallet.) So if human selfishness were not restrained, we would be unable to live together.

(2) The role of loyalty and trust

The solution adopted by every human society is in broad outlines the same: We have *laws* (socially accepted rules regarding how we may treat each other), and we have established *procedures and institutions* for enforcing the law and adjudicating disputes. For this solution to work, most people must have a certain amount of respect for the society's procedures and institutions, such that they are prepared to follow the procedures and defer to the institutions even when they do not get their way. For instance, when you have a dispute with someone, you submit the dispute to the courts (if it is sufficiently serious), then abide by the court's decision. Most people must do this voluntarily, because no society has the resources to enforce the law if most people are disobeying it. When, on occasion, someone violates the social norms, other people must also be willing to undertake some cost or effort to punish the violation. This punishment is necessary to deter the small number of people who have anti-social traits and would otherwise show no respect for social norms.

The emotional attitudes that move us to voluntarily respect the norms and punish violations are *loyalty* to the society and *trust* in its institutions. It is largely because Americans are loyal to America that, when we fail to get our way—when we lose an election, or a court case, or we don't get the laws we want—we accept our loss and continue to follow the procedures, rather than trying to undermine the institutions that failed to give us our way. This loyalty is also why, when we see someone who tries to undermine our institutions, we are disposed to punish that person.

Why does this require an emotion of loyalty? Theoretically, these same behaviors could be motivated by pure utilitarian calculation. People could have a general desire for the good and an enlightened understanding that maintaining respect for institutions is more important in the long run than getting our way about any given issue. The problem is simply that few people are so enlightened. Few people, if calculating purely instrumentally, would correctly assess the expected net benefit of violating established procedures in order to get the "correct" policy in a particular case. (One reason why people miscalculate, by the way, is that almost everyone ignores the very high chance that their political views are *incorrect*. They also tend to underweight small chances of long-term harms.) For this reason, society needs members with an *emotional* attachment to its norms and institutions.

(3) The foundation for loyalty and trust

Why would people feel trust and loyalty toward their society? This may have a partly biological basis. But biology is not enough; many societies have insufficient trust and loyalty and thus have widespread disorder. Society also needs to *teach* its members loyalty and trust.

How is this done? Some of it is done by emotional and aesthetic appeals, e.g., the display of patriotic art and symbols, the recounting of inspiring stories about the nation's past.[349] Some of it is also done rationally, by giving people good reasons why their institutions are beneficial and just.

I experienced some of this instruction myself when I was in primary school. I was taught about the courage of America's founding fathers, who risked their lives fighting for freedom against the world's most powerful nation. I learned of the honesty of George Washington and Abraham Lincoln. I learned that America stood for democracy, and freedom, and equality. I learned that we had a system of government designed with checks and balances and separation of powers to prevent the abuse of power. And that we had Constitutional guarantees of certain fundamental rights of the individual.

It wasn't all roses; my teachers covered slavery and Jim Crow, too. These things were, as far as I recall, represented as monstrous departures from our founding ideals, which tore the country apart and were finally eliminated.

I can't say for sure what effect all this instruction had on my generation. But I think it had something to do with my appreciation for America and desire to preserve its ideals.

(4) Undermining loyalty and trust

What if you wanted to *undermine* social loyalty and trust? Perhaps the first thing you would do is try to convince people that their society was evil to its core, that its institutions were thoroughly unjust, that its fundamental values were corrupt. On an emotional level, you might

---

[349] For elaboration, see Wingo 2003.

attack the society's heroes and dismantle its symbols.

Another tactic would be to weaken people's identification with the *nation* and strengthen their identification with particular *groups* within the nation—especially groups that have historically had tensions with each other. One could try to convince people that these groups are their *real* identity and that the interests of these different groups are at odds.

One might even go so far as to try to convince minority group members that the majority hates them, that it is unjustly oppressing them, and that all their problems are due to the majority group. This should have the effect of setting different groups within your society against each other. One could sow distrust of social institutions by arguing that the society's dominant institutions exist only to exploit and oppress certain groups.

All of that, it seems to me, is just about the most toxic propaganda program one could devise, the one best calculated to destroy your society, if anything could. And that is what contemporary progressive ideology is. The progressive myths we have discussed are not random errors. They are parts of an overall narrative designed to convince us that our society is fundamentally evil and unworthy of preservation. The feminist myths argue that our society hates women and oppresses them for the benefit of men. The racial myths argue that our society hates racial minorities and oppresses them for the benefit of whites. The economic myths argue that our society oppresses and exploits the poor for the benefit of the rich. Often, the accusations against America are the most incendiary imaginable—that our society supports rape and murder purely out of bigotry. We are told that cis-hetero white men are oppressing everyone else, and that all of society's institutions are nothing but a cover for their bigotry. This story is calibrated to fill the "oppressed" minorities with rage and the majority with shame and guilt. Why would anyone feel any loyalty to this society or trust in its institutions after being taught this story?

Progressives are not the only ones sowing distrust and division. Alt-right sources in recent years have promoted psychotic conspiracy theories about the U.S. being run by satanic pedophile rings and elections being stolen by Venezuelan voting machines. (No exaggeration.) Prominent Republicans have suggested that the 2020 election was stolen and that Democrats are inviting foreign murderers and rapists into the country to "replace" the current electorate. Both the extreme left and the extreme right are seemingly doing everything in their power to sabotage our society. For different reasons, both agree that our institutions are thoroughly untrustworthy and should be burned to the ground.

(5) Why not undermine society?

I suppose that some would argue that it is *good* to undermine social trust and loyalty, because our institutions are in fact untrustworthy and our society unworthy of loyalty. Perhaps we *should* tear down this society, so that we can remake it according to ideals of equity and justice. What is wrong with that line of thinking?

Briefly, I think the first thing that one needs is to get some sense of what human life has been like for almost everyone, almost everywhere, throughout history. Today, the average American is expected to live about 78 years.[350] In world history, the average life expectancy was around 24 years.[351] That simple number conceals vast, untold misery and pain. There is a reason why the first teaching of Buddhism is "Life is suffering". This isn't the Buddha being melodramatic; it was a banal observation for almost everyone in history. And the suffering was not that of hearing someone use the wrong word to refer to your group or asking you "Where are you from?" (two classic microaggressions). It was the suffering of starvation, plague, war, and the deaths of your children. People were not worried about the "violence" of offensive language; they were worried about the violence of getting stabbed to death. As political philosopher David Schmidtz puts it, poverty today means wondering "Can we afford a second car?"; a few centuries ago, poverty meant wondering, "Can we afford to bury our five-year-old child in his own shirt, or do we need to save his possibly plague-infested shirt for his younger brother?"[352]

Many of the horrors human beings of the past endured were deliberately inflicted by other human beings. Steven Pinker has detailed the many horrors that human beings used to inflict on each other that have been either abolished or greatly diminished, including war, slavery, gladiatorial combat, torture, and so on.[353] To take one example, people in the Middle Ages thought that a good way to identify witches was to

---

[350] Miniño and Xu, 2024.
[351] Statista 2006. This low figure is mainly due to infant and child mortality.
[352] Schmidtz 2023, p. 223.
[353] Pinker 2012; but see Thomson and Halstead 2022 for criticism of Pinker's figures for historical rates of death by violence.

torture a suspected witch until she confessed. The torture techniques are too depraved to detail here. Once the witch confessed, she could then be forced to name other witches that she knew, who would also be tortured to "confirm" their guilt. All the witches would then be burned alive.

So the *natural* state of human beings is not one of harmony, freedom, and equality. The natural state of human beings is one of strife, exploitation, oppression, and misery. The current state of American society is a historical fluke, marked by its extraordinarily *low* levels of exploitation, oppression, and injustice. Somehow, we have reached a metastable equilibrium of peace and prosperity that earlier generations could only dream of. The key sources of this happy state include such institutions as democracy, free markets, and modern science.

So what should we do now? No doubt, we can still make things even better; there are still some injustices to fight. But perhaps we should take a bit of advice from the Hippocratic oath: First, do no harm. If we undermine our current norms and institutions, the most likely result is not that we will be swept into a paradise of justice and sisterly love. The most likely result is that we will revert to something closer to the natural state of human beings, in which a small cadre of the powerful oppress, exploit, and commit violence against the majority.

This, by the way, is essentially what happened in the twentieth century when many societies around the world heeded the Marxists' call to tear down their institutions to build a new world of equality for all. This did not bring equality and justice for the workers. It brought oppression, poverty, and the deaths of tens of millions. Which should have been completely unsurprising to any observer of human history.

Progressive ideology will not destroy society immediately or on its own. And if there were just a few myths going around, there would be little cause for concern. But if there are *enough* incendiary, divisive ideas, being promoted by enough people, for long enough, they gradually dial up social tensions and weaken people's loyalty and trust. There is no way to know what the future holds for our society, but weakening the emotional attitudes that hold society together cannot be good. It is like weakening your body's immune system; you cannot predict what disease will next attack your body, but you know that things will not go better.

25 Avoiding Myths

A. Reverse the Presumption

What should we do to avoid the harms of political myths? My central advice is obvious, but I will say it anyway. The main thing we should do is to be a lot more skeptical. When you hear some politically relevant information, ask yourself whether this is the kind of information that plays to a particular ideological orientation. Would you expect this, say, to be shared only by conservatives, or only by progressives?

If the answer is "yes", you should immediately be skeptical. Do not presume that it is honest content; presume that it is deceptive until proven honest.

We all are born credulous, tending to accept content merely because it was asserted by someone. Fortunately, most assertions are true. "It's raining outside"; "Today is Tuesday"; "Sue recently got married"—if someone tells you any of these things, they are almost certainly correct. But there are particular kinds of assertions—especially political, religious, and philosophical assertions—that are *radically* less reliable than other assertions. This is something that it generally takes a person many years to appreciate, and many people never appreciate it because they never actually check up on the claims that they absorb.

This book is my attempt to accelerate the process for you. I cannot cover all political myths or even all progressive myths; however, the myths discussed above are, I believe, not atypical. Persuasive political content that is transmitted in the popular culture is almost always deceptive—oversimplified at the very least, often omitting crucial details that would reverse the conclusion you would naturally draw, and sometimes founded on outright lies.

This is not unique to progressives; all ideologies accumulate deceptive supporters. It is merely that at the present time, progressives seem to be the most skilled at producing and spreading this kind of content.

B. Don't Be Part of the Problem

Having adopted a skeptical attitude toward persuasive political content, you should refrain from amplifying that content until you have verified it. If you see some information on social media, you should not share it, like it, or comment in favor of it, unless and until you verify its accuracy. If someone tells you a bit of political information in conversation, you should not repeat it unless and until you verify it.

Verifying all of the persuasive content that you hear is a tall order. Most people do not have time to verify more than a small fraction of the claims they hear. So most people should simply refrain from promoting almost all political information.

This does not entail complete disengagement. It would be appropriate to engage in a questioning mode, e.g., to ask your source where they got their information from, to ask for further details, or to raise what initially seem to be problems for the assertion.

C. How to Verify

Suppose you really want to know whether a particular political claim is correct. How can you find out?

As the preceding chapters have shown, media reports are unreliable. Prominent government officials, especially politicians, are also unreliable. Even reports of academic research are frequently unreliable.

Nevertheless, I believe, there are some relatively reliable information sources. If you want to know about a court case, look up the court documents or trial proceedings. E.g., you can view actual footage from the Kyle Rittenhouse trial, or read the judge's sentencing decision in the Derek Chauvin/George Floyd case. Like all human institutions, courts sometimes make errors, but they will generally review all the available evidence in detail, and they will generally make a serious effort to render a decision based on that evidence and the applicable law, not based on the ideology of the judge or jury. (There may be exceptions when a case raises controversial philosophical issues and the law is ambiguous.)

Similarly useful are certain official government reports, particularly ones that are prepared to inform policymakers. For instance, if you want to know about the Michael Brown/Darren Wilson case, you can read the Justice Department's report on the federal investigation of the case, which is extremely illuminating. In the U.S., the government also publishes all kinds of useful data about the country. Thus, if you want to know something about the U.S. economy, you can probably get the data from the Federal Reserve (fred.stlouisfed.org). If you want to know something about crime in the U.S., you can probably get it from the Justice Department's Bureau of Justice Statistics (bjs.ojp.gov).

In an ideal world, journalists would do that research for you, then give objective, easily digestible summaries of what they learned. But that is not our world. In our world, as far as I can tell, most journalists do almost no research; most appear to consult only other journalists and social media. This is easier than doing real research, and viewers let them get away with it.

Another important information source is academic research. But note that some fields of academic research are more reliable than others. In my view, most of the humanities are extremely unreliable, to the point of uselessness. Natural sciences are more reliable but rarely relevant to social and political issues. So the research I have in mind here is mostly research in the social sciences plus social psychology.

Caveat: Even academics sometimes misdescribe their own research in their statements to the public. For this reason, one has to look up the original articles; academics are more circumspect and less ideological in their purely academic writings than in their statements to the public.

Bear in mind that many studies are contradicted by other studies. Thus, if you learn of an interesting research finding, try to find out whether later (or earlier) studies confirmed or contradicted it. Ideally, try to find a meta-analysis, an article that collects together the results of multiple studies of the same issue (these generally try to cover all the relevant studies up to that point).

D. Listen to Critics

Any persuasive political content on a controversial issue will almost certainly have critics. Before accepting any such content, find out what the other side says. If you don't know the other side of the issue, then you don't know anything.

Sometimes, the other side will bluster and change the subject. Example: Say a politician is accused of wrongdoing. You should listen to his response to the charges. If his main response is to attack the character of his accuser, or to attack some politician from the other party, that tells you something: If that is his strongest response, he probably did the thing he is accused of.

Other times, the other side will point out key facts that your first source ignored that completely alter the picture. Example: You hear that women get paid 80 cents for every dollar that men earn. If you look up conservative responses to this, you learn that if you control for occupation, the 80 cents goes up to something like 99 cents.

A main reason why political myths are so prevalent is simply that most people who consume them never make the small effort to find out what the other side says about them.

E. Identify Reliable Individuals

Another aid to acquiring true beliefs is to find public intellectuals who are reliable and who have already taken the time to research the topics you are interested in. For this purpose, the author's general intelligence matters (stupid people tend to be unreliable); however, once you get above a certain level (which the great majority of public intellectuals in fact exceed), objectivity and fair-mindedness are much more important than raw intelligence. This is because a biased person with a high IQ can use their intelligence to rationalize what they want to believe, rather than using it as a tool to get to the truth. With that in mind, here are some signs of reliability:

1. Reliable thinkers tend to *give non-circular arguments* for their views, rather than simply assuming a controversial ideological viewpoint. That is, they will cite evidence that a neutral party could reasonably be expected to agree with and could see to be evidence for their view without having already accepted their ideology.
2. Reliable thinkers *qualify claims*. They will say that something is *probably* the case, or *almost* always true, rather than definitely always true. Authors who make too many absolute statements are likely to be oversimplifying and may not be thoughtful enough to notice exceptions. (But there are exceptions even to this; *some* things, such as mathematical truths, are really definitely always true.)
3. Reliable authors tend to *acknowledge reasons pointing in different directions,* particularly about controversial matters. If smart people disagree about some policy, then there usually are both costs and benefits to the policy. If an author does not acknowledge this, the author is probably not fair-minded. (Again, there are exceptions; some ideas really are just dumb. Use your judgment in each case.)
4. Relatedly, reliable authors tend to *discuss objections* to their arguments.

Authors who never address objections either have never thought about objections (in which case their thought process is unreliable) or have thought of objections but decided not to mention them (in which case they may not be entirely forthcoming).

5. Reliable thinkers *do not always agree with one of the standard political orientations.* It is highly unlikely that either the Democrats or the Republicans are wrong about everything; probably each side is sometimes right and sometimes wrong. If someone believes one side is virtually always right and the other side virtually always wrong, that person is probably forming beliefs based on a tribal identity rather than objective examination of the issues.

6. Reliable thinkers are *not overly emotional.* Now, you might wonder: "Why shouldn't I be emotional? Political issues are important! The future of the nation is at stake!" Well, perhaps so. Nevertheless, a person's emotions can interfere with objective judgment. If someone is unable to control his emotions for purposes of public discourse, he probably also cannot control them for purposes of making objective judgments.

7. Reliable thinkers provide *serious discussion of the evidence.* They might cite academic studies, government reports, court documents, and so on. They do not simply opine based on armchair guesses about the empirical facts.

8. Reliable thinkers *make sense.* When you read their work, it will lead you through logical lines of thought. It will not simply assert things, or appeal to emotionally charged language, or give you vague impressions.

9. Reliable thinkers are *clear.* My general sense is that, if an author is very hard to follow, that is probably because either (i) the author himself is confused or (ii) the author is trying to persuade you by non-rational means, which is a red flag (being rationally persuaded generally requires a clear understanding).

F. Question Ideology

I did not write this book only to persuade you to reject the specific myths listed in the previous chapters. I wrote this book to undermine progressive ideology as a whole. Let me make my intended argument explicit.

The controversial parts of progressive ideology are mainly *empirical* claims, i.e., they depend on evidence from observation. Conservatives and progressives generally do not disagree about value judgments such as "Racism is bad" or "Men and women deserve equal rights." They disagree about claims like "Racism and sexism are pervasive in America", "The poor in America lack the opportunity to succeed", and "American blacks are primarily held back by white racism." These are mainly empirical claims, and progressives believe them based in large part on "testimony", that is, information they have taken on trust from other people.

Aside: Some may claim to know these sorts of things from their own experience. But no individual can know, from personal experience, any generalization about society. One can directly know one's own life, but one cannot make a cogent generalization based on only a single case. By the way, we may not even understand *our own experience* in way that is independent of testimony. We often *interpret* our experiences using ideas that we learned from other people. For instance, if someone tells you (and you believe them) that your white neighbors hate you, then you are likely to start "experiencing" their hate in the way they look at you, their tone of voice, and other ambiguous events that you would not otherwise see as hateful.

So our justification for accepting progressive ideology turns on the reliability of sources who give us empirical evidence for that ideology—journalists, professors, artists, and other intellectuals who tell us such alleged facts as "Women earn less than men for the same work" and "Trayvon Martin was killed due to racism" and "Global warming is an existential threat."

There are an enormous number of empirical claims in that general vein, and I cannot check them all. But whenever I *do* check such a claim, it generally turns out to be false or radically misleading. I see no reason to think that the ones I do not have time to check would turn out to be much more reliable than the ones I have checked. So probably, empirical claims that support progressivism are in general highly unreliable.

If you are inclined toward progressive ideology, it is probably because of some empirical information you have received. You probably cannot remember all the progressive-friendly bits of information you have received that have led you to this point. Nevertheless, even without being able to identify them, you can infer that most of the progressive-friendly information you have received in your life has probably been false or heavily misleading. Hence, you should give up progressive ideology.

G. In Defense of America

Most of progressive ideology revolves around the evils of America and the West: America is racist, sexist, homophobic; we don't give fair opportunity to the poor; we don't take care of the disabled; we are destroying the planet.

I am not going to try to convince you of another ideology now; that is beyond the scope of this book.[354] Rather, I want to conclude by simply suggesting that America is a pretty good country if you compare it to other real societies, rather than hypothetical ideal societies. (Of course, every real society pales in comparison to the most perfect society you can imagine.)

In the previous chapter (§24.F.5), I mentioned that life in America today is *vastly* better than in the overwhelming majority of societies throughout human history. (The same is true of other Western democracies.) In America, virtually every measure of human wellbeing is near the historical peak for humans—overall life expectancy, infant mortality, the burden of infectious disease, crime, material wealth, literacy, education, access to art, freedom of speech, political liberty... If you can find a way to measure it, you'll probably find that it is *much* better in modern America than in the vast majority of societies in human history. Even America's poor are rich by historical standards, and *average* Americans are rich compared to the rest of the world. The median American today is in the 92nd percentile of world income.[355]

Perhaps this is why America is the most desired destination country in the world for people who want to migrate.[356] If the U.S. is such an unjust, oppressive society, why do 160 million people around the world want to come here—more than twice as many as any other country? During the cold war, the communist countries had to build walls to keep their people in. The U.S. builds walls to keep people *out*.

America's founding ideals are things that people on the left ought to appreciate: equality, democracy, respect for the rights of the individual.

---

[354] For the correct ideology, see my *The Problem of Political Authority* (2013).
[355] Median U.S. personal income, 2022: $40,480. St. Louis Federal Reserve 2023; World Inequality Database 2024.
[356] Pugliese and Ray 2023.

It is mainly the superiority of these values that explains why Americans are so much better off than most people in history. In the history of civilization, almost everyone lived, in essence, under dictatorship. America was the first democracy in modern times, which led the rest of the world to see the superiority of democracy over other forms of government.

The injustices in America's past (e.g., slavery, institutionalized racism and sexism) are generally (a) things that were common throughout human history before modern times and (b) things that we have now put behind us. (Progressives disagree with (b); see section F above.) America's founders were hypocritical in that they failed to live up to their stated ideals, especially that of equality. But the rest of the world at the time outright rejected those ideals. Which is worse: to be inconsistent in one's support for equality, or to consistently reject equality?

The fact that we have progressives protesting alleged inequities today is a testament to America's superior values. Most societies in history did not have that sort of protest, not because there weren't any inequities to protest (they had *much* more inequality), but because (a) they did not value equality, and (b) people who disagreed with the government could be thrown in jail, or worse.

You might argue that America still acts as a hegemonic power today, sometimes entering unjust wars, such as the 2003 Iraq War. Some progressives would even label America an imperial power. These complaints have some basis. But let's get real about human nature and human history. Human beings throughout history have been conquering each other, enslaving each other, building empires. Frankly, most of the societies that *didn't* conquer other societies were probably just not strong enough to do so. And most of the empires of the past were utterly brutal; America is like a sweet little lamb by comparison. Most societies in history, and many that exist today, would, if given the sort of power America now possesses, immediately use it to subjugate the rest of the world and wipe out all who resisted. If America is an empire, it's about the mildest empire the world has seen.

And why does America have so much power? The answer is that America *makes the most of human talents*. The society does not guarantee you success, but it *lets* you *compete* for success. Granted, not everyone has a perfectly equal opportunity. But the poor have much *more* opportunity in the U.S. than in the vast majority of other societies today and throughout history. Consider that the median household income in

Nigeria is just $930, yet in the U.S., households headed by black immigrants have a median annual income of $57,200, over sixty times higher.[357]

We make the most of people's talents in any area, whether it be business, or art, or science, or athletics. The U.S., with just 4% of the world's population, has been the home of nearly *half* of all the world's Nobel prize-winners (411 out of 860; second place goes to the U.K., with 137).[358] Seven of the world's top ten universities are American, the other three being British.[359] In the 2020 Olympic games, Americans took home 113 medals, compared to 88 for the #2 country (China, which has four times as many people).[360] America has six of the world's ten most profitable companies (including all of the top three), eleven of the twenty largest companies, and seventeen of the world's twenty most valuable brands.[361] Of the ten best-selling movies *outside of America*, all ten are American-made. America has six of the ten most popular authors in the world, and ten of the twenty most popular musical artists of all time.[362] These are just a few quick indicators of success in making the most of people's talents. If you don't like these indicators, I invite you to find your own. I challenge you to find an area of human endeavor and a measure of success in that area such that the U.S. is not doing excellently in that area. In most cases, the U.S. will be *the* dominant force.

When it comes to economics, leftists often claim that American success is due to exploiting the poor nations. But how would they explain American success in music, writing, filmmaking, science, and athletics? The simplest explanation is that we have a society set up to maximize human achievement. Can't we just admit that the U.S. is doing something right?

---

[357] Tamir and Anderson 2022, p. 28; Lindner 2024.
[358] Wikipedia, "List of Nobel Laureates by Country".
[359] Times Higher Education 2024. The Center for World Class Universities (2024) lists *eight* of the top ten universities as American, the other two being British, based on objective, quantitative measures.
[360] USA Today 2021.
[361] Johnston 2024; Murphy and Schifrin 2024; Swant 2020.
[362] The Numbers 2024; Hayat 2023; Wikipedia, "List of Best-Selling Music Artists".

H. The Road to Progress

None of this is to discourage efforts at improving America. However well things are going, they could always go better. Indeed, part of America's success is down to the widespread confidence of Americans in our ability to improve things.

The way to improve things is not to lament how evil we are, to undermine our basic institutions, or to attack our values. The way to improve things is to think about what could be done, starting from our current institutions and without abandoning our basic values, to make things a little better. Then think about the next improvement after that, and so on. For instance, if you are concerned about the lesser success of black Americans compared to whites, the answer is not to start attacking whites. The answer is to think about what practical steps could be taken to help black communities. Perhaps charter schools or school choice could improve education. Perhaps funding for security guards could make these communities safer.

Whatever you think of those ideas, notice how they are practical ideas geared towards directly helping people. Inner city kids will not be helped to complete school and avoid gangs by white progressives in the suburbs holding self-indulgent "education" sessions to feel their white privilege, nor by Twitter mobs shaming someone for failing to post a black square on their Twitter page. If you care about black people, think about how to actually help them. If you don't like my suggestions, come up with your own practical proposals. If you don't want to do that, or you don't want to do the work to try to get the government to adopt such proposals, then just admit that you don't care enough to help.

I. Conclusion

Contemporary woke progressivism is not what it purports to be. It is not a tool for helping women and minorities. It is better understood as a quasi-religious, intellectual virus that has infected the minds of a large portion of Western intellectual elites. Like other religions, the progressive mind virus spreads itself by taking advantage of the human psychological needs for meaning and community, and it deploys intellectual defense mechanisms designed to short circuit critical examination of its tenets. Like other religions, progressivism comes with its own mythology. It is a mythology in which such characters as Michael Brown and Trayvon Martin are held up as martyrs, while the "cishet" (cisgender, heterosexual) white man is held up as the world's great villain.

Most of our society's institutions for creating and spreading knowledge have already been corrupted by this virus. Mainstream journalists, academic researchers, and political leaders can be seen shamelessly lying, spinning news, or suppressing information explicitly for the purpose of promoting the progressive agenda. Of this, we have seen many examples in the preceding pages.

Why not let people have their mythology? Two reasons: One, because it is factually false. White people are not holding back blacks from succeeding. Men are not holding back women. The rich are not holding back the poor. Humans are not about to destroy the Earth. None of that is true. And we need to know what is true if we are to make progress on any of the actual, real problems we face.

Two, the progressive quasi-religion is an extremely divisive and malevolent force in our society. Progressivism actively sows discord by teaching us to identify with some group other than the whole society, then teaching us that *another* group within our society is *our* group's enemy. Contemporary progressivism teaches us to distrust our society's norms and institutions. And the belief system defenses deployed by progressivism directly attack the norms of free expression and rational inquiry that are necessary not only for identifying truth but for peacefully negotiating disagreements in a pluralistic society.

All of this is not just bad from the standpoint of conservative values. Contemporary progressivism is counterproductive to the values that progressivism itself has traditionally stood for. Heightened racial consciousness promotes segregation, not equality. Suppression of dissent promotes stagnation and tyranny, not freedom and progress. Those who value equality, freedom, and progress should celebrate contemporary America. America is among the freest, most egalitarian, and most open-to-progress societies in history—not to mention one of the societies with the highest levels of human wellbeing.

I don't know if there is a way to stop the spread of woke progressivism, since it seems to have taken over our educational system, and the virus, once lodged in a person's mind, deactivates one's truth-seeking capacities. But I suppose that it is up to those of us who have not yet been infected to try to stop the spread, and the only way I can see to do that is through exposing the various myths that progressive information sources have been using to propagate their belief system.

My hope is that this book will act as a kind of inoculation. Some of the myths I have addressed will probably fade from collective memory within a few years, particularly those in Part I. I nevertheless think it is instructive to look at how mainstream information sources treated those myths—and to remember that when the next big progressive claim comes along. This, I hope, will give you a resistance against being taken in by whatever pieces of propaganda arise in the future.

References

Abaluck, Jason et al. 2022. "Impact of Community Masking on COVID-19: A Cluster-Randomized Trial in Bangladesh", *Science* 375:eabi9069.

Abramowitz, Stephen, Beverly Gomes, and Christine Abramowitz. 1975. "Publish or Politic: Referee Bias in Manuscript Review", *Journal of Applied Social Psychology* 5:187–200.

Aggeler, Madeleine. 2020, May 28. "A Black Man Asked a White Woman to Leash Her Dog. She Called the Cops.", *The Cut*, https://www.thecut.com/2020/05/amy-cooper-central-park-dog-video.html.

Ahmad, Unber. 2017, June 8. "Implicit Bias in the Workplace", Training Industry, https://trainingindustry.com/articles/diversity-equity-and-inclusion/implicit-bias-in-the-workplace/.

Ahmed, Nafeez. 2019, June 3. "New Report Suggests 'High Likelihood of Human Civilization Coming to an End' Starting in 2050", *Vice*, https://www.vice.com/en/article/597kpd/new-report-suggests-high-likelihood-of-human-civilization-coming-to-an-end-in-2050.

Alcantara, Chris, Youjin Shin, Leslie Shapiro, Adam Taylor and Armand Emamdjomeh. 2020. "Tracking Covid-19 Cases and Deaths Worldwide", *Washington Post*, https://www.washingtonpost.com/graphics/2020/world/mapping-spread-new-coronavirus/.

Alexander, Scott. 2014, Dec. 12. "Beware the Man of One Study" (blog post), *Slate Star Codex*, https://slatestarcodex.com/2014/12/12/beware-the-man-of-one-study/.

Allison, Stephen, Megan Warin, and Tarun Bastiampillai. 2013. "Anorexia Nervosa and Social Contagion: Clinical Implications", *Australian & New Zealand Journal of Psychiatry* 48:116–20.

AlShebli, Bedoor, Kinga Makovi, and Talal Rahwan. 2020a. "The Association Between Early Career Informal Mentorship in Academic Collaborations and Junior Author Performance", *Nature Communications* 11:5855.

————. 2020b. "Retraction Note: The Association Between Early Career Informal Mentorship in Academic Collaborations and Junior Author Performance", *Nature Communications* 11:6446.

Alvarez, Lizette. 2012, July 12. "More Records Released in Trayvon Martin Case", *New York Times*, https://www.nytimes.com/2012/07/13/us/more-records-released-in-trayvon-martin-case.html.

American Bar Association. n.d. "Achieving an Impartial Jury Toolbox", https://www.americanbar.org/content/dam/aba/publications/criminaljustice/voirdire_toolchest.authcheckdam.pdf.

American Psychiatric Association. 2013. *Diagnostic and Statistical Manual of Mental Disorders*, 5th ed. American Psychiatric Publishing.

American Psychological Association. 2011. "Answers to Your Questions About Transgender People, Gender Identity, and Gender Expression", https://www.apa.org/topics/lgbtq/transgender.pdf.

Armstrong, Ari. 2023. Getting Over Jesus: Finding Meaning and Morals Without God. Self in Society.

Bach, Theodore. 2012. "Gender Is a Natural Kind with a Historical Essence", *Ethics* 122:231–72.

Baker, Sinéad. 2021, March 12. Conservative Stars Like Tucker Carlson and Candace Owens Keep Claiming George Floyd Wasn't Killed by Police", *Insider*, https://www.insider.com/conservative-stars-claiming-george-floyd-death-drugs-not-police-2021-3.

Balko, Radley. 2020, June 10. "There's Overwhelming Evidence that the Criminal-Justice System Is Racist. Here's the Proof", *Washington Post*, https://www.washingtonpost.com/graphics/2020/opinions/systemic-racism-police-evidence-criminal-justice-system/.

Baltimore Ravens. 2020, August 27. "Ravens Make Statement, Demands for Social Justice", https://www.baltimoreravens.com/news/ravens-make-statement-demands-for-social-justice.

Banaji, Mahzarin and Anthony Greenwald. 2013. *Blindspot: Hidden Biases of Good People*. Random House.

Bargh, John, Mark Chen, and Lara Burrows. 1996. "Automaticity of Social Behavior: Direct Effects of Trait Construct and Stereotype Activation on Action", *Journal of Personality and Social Psychology* 71:230–44.

Barone, Vincent. 2020, Aug. 26. "Suspected Teen Gunman Kyle Rittenhouse Spotted Cleaning Kenosha Graffiti Before Shooting", *New York Post*, https://nypost.com/2020/08/26/suspected-kenosha-gunman-kyle-rittenhouse-spotted-cleaning-graffiti/.

Based Logic. 2020, Aug. 28. "Joseph Rosenbaum Begging, 'Shoot Me NiQQA', Before Being Shot" (video), https://youtu.be/5v-oEdnLNB8.

Bauer, Patricia. 2020. "Retraction of 'Declines in Religiosity Predict Increases in Violent Crime—but Not Among Countries with Relatively High Average IQ'", *Psychological Science* 31:905.

Baum, Dan. 2016, Apr. "Legalize It All: How to Win the War on Drugs", *Harper's*, https://harpers.org/archive/2016/04/legalize-it-all/.

Baumeister, Roy, Ellen Bratslavsky, Mark Muraven, and Dianne Tice. 1998. "Ego Depletion: Is the Active Self a Limited Resource?", *Journal of Personality and Social Psychology* 74: 1252–65.

Baumeister, Roy. 2022, Mar. 23. "What's the Best-Replicated Finding in Social Psychology?", *Psychology Today*, https://www.psychologytoday.com/intl/blog/cultural-animal/202203/what-s-the-best-replicated-finding-in-social-psychology.

Bedford, Daniel and John Cook. 2013. "Agnotology, Scientific Consensus, and the Teaching and Learning of Climate Change: A Response to Legates, Soon and Briggs", *Science & Education* 22:2019–30.

Bem, Daryl. 2011. "Feeling the Future: Experimental Evidence for Anomalous Retroactive Influences on Cognition and Affect", *Journal of Personality and Social*

Psychology 100:407–25.

Biden, Joseph. 2020, Aug. 9. Tweet: https://twitter.com/JoeBiden/status/1292505925685633025.

———. 2022, July 20. Speech at Brayton Point Power Station, Somerset, Massachusetts, https://youtu.be/djYgIyM-DxA. Transcript: https://www.whitehouse.gov/briefing-room/speeches-remarks/2022/07/20/remarks-by-president-biden-on-actions-to-tackle-the-climate-crisis/.

Blake, Jacob and Michael Strahan. 2021. "Jacob Blake Tells His Story After Being Shot 7 Times by Police" (video interview), ABC News, Nightline, https://youtu.be/JjyJTaOr5vc.

Blake, John. 2023, Sept. 11. "Here's Why Many Black People Despise Clarence Thomas. (It's Not Because He's a Conservative.)", CNN, https://www.cnn.com/2023/09/11/politics/clarence-thomas-black-people-blake-cec/index.html.

BLM (Black Lives Matter) website (a). "About", https://blacklivesmatter.com/about/, accessed June 13, 2023.

——— (b). "Herstory", https://blacklivesmatter.com/herstory/, accessed July 5, 2023.

Boler, Jean. 2018, Dec. 17. "Women Don't Lie About Sexual Assault, Why Are They Treated Like They Do?", Schaefer Halleen, LLC (law firm) web page, https://www.schaeferhalleen.com/women-dont-lie-sexual-assault/.

Brandom, Russell. 2020, Aug. 27. "Facebook Is Blocking Searches for the Name of Kenosha Shooter", *The Verge*, https://www.theverge.com/2020/8/27/21404518/facebook-search-kyle-rittenhouse-blocked-kenosha-shooting.

Bricker, Jesse, Sarena Goodman, Kevin Moore, and Alice Volz. 2020, Sept. 28. "Wealth and Income Concentration in the SCF: 1989–2019", Board of Governors of the Federal Reserve System, https://www.federalreserve.gov/econres/notes/feds-notes/wealth-and-income-concentration-in-the-scf-20200928.html.

Brint, Steven and Komi Frey. 2023. "Is the University of California Drifting Toward Conformism? The Challenges of Representation and the Climate for Academic Freedom", UC Berkeley Research and Occasional Papers Series: CSHE.5.2023, https://escholarship.org/uc/item/3pt9m168.

Brown University, Harriet W. Sheridan Center for Teaching and Learning. n.d. "Strategies and Resources About Stereotype Threat", https://www.brown.edu/sheridan/teaching-learning-resources/inclusive-teaching/stereotype-threat, accessed June 26, 2023.

Brown, Anna. 2022, June 7. "About 5% of Young Adults in the U.S. Say Their Gender Is Different from Their Sex Assigned at Birth", Pew Research Center, https://www.pewresearch.org/short-reads/2022/06/07/about-5-of-young-adults-in-the-u-s-say-their-gender-is-different-from-their-sex-assigned-at-birth/.

Brown, Gillian and Kim Alexandersen. 2020. "Gender Equality and Gender Gaps in Mathematics Performance", *Trends in Cognitive Sciences* 24:591–3.

Brzezinski, Mika. 2020, May 1. Interview with Joe Biden, *Morning Joe* (television show), https://youtu.be/seu_C08yAAM.

Buffett, Warren. 2011, Aug. 14. "Stop Coddling the Super-Rich", *New York Times*, https://www.nytimes.com/2011/08/15/opinion/stop-coddling-the-super-rich.html.

Bunn, Curtis. 2022, Mar. 3. "Report: Black People Are Still Killed by Police at a Higher Rate than Other Groups", NBC News, https://www.nbcnews.com/news/nbcblk/report-black-people-are-still-killed-police-higher-rate-groups-rcna17169.

Bush, Cori. 2021, Nov. 19. Tweet: https://twitter.com/CoriBush/status/1461776152255774722.

Callimachi, Rukmini. 2020, August 30. "Breonna Taylor's Life Was Changing. Then the Police Came to Her Door.", *The New York Times*, https://www.nytimes.com/2020/08/30/us/breonna-taylor-police-killing.html.

Cantor, David, et al. 2020. "Report on the AAU Campus Climate Survey on Sexual Assault and Misconduct", Westat (research firm), https://www.aau.edu/sites/default/files/%40%20Files/Climate%20Survey/AAU_Campus_Climate_Survey_12_14_15.pdf.

Cantor, James. 2011. "New MRI Studies Support the Blanchard Typology of Male-to-Female Transsexualism", *Archives of Sexual Behavior* 40:863–4.

Caplan, Bryan. 2007. The Myth of the Rational Voter: Why Democracies Choose Bad Policies. Princeton University Press.

———. 2011. Selfish Reasons to Have More Kids. Basic Books.

Carleton College, Science Education Research Center. n.d. "What Is Stereotype Threat?", https://serc.carleton.edu/sage2yc/stereotype/stereotype.html.

Carleton, Tamma et al. 2022. "Valuing the Global Mortality Consequences of Climate Change Accounting for Adaptation Costs and Benefits", *The Quarterly Journal of Economics* 137:2037–2105.

Carloni, Dorian. 2021. "Revisiting the Extent to Which Payroll Taxes Are Passed Through to Employees", Congressional Budget Office Working Paper 2021-06, https://www.cbo.gov/publication/57089.

Carlson, Tucker and Andrew Baker. 2021, Apr. 13. "Tucker Carlson's Lies About George Floyd's Death v. Professional Testimony of Dr. Baker Under Oath" (video), https://youtu.be/LwPPvxhL0VE.

Carlsson, Rickard and Jens Agerström. 2016. "A Closer Look at the Discrimination Outcomes in the IAT Literature", *Scandinavian Journal of Psychology* 57:278–87.

Carpenter, Siri. 2000. *Implicit Gender Attitudes*, PhD thesis, Yale University, https://www.researchgate.net/publication/35162810_Implicit_gender_attitudes.

Carr, Stewart. 2021, Oct. 17. "More Than 200 Academics Call Out UK Universities for Allowing 'Trans Activist Bullies' to Create 'Hostile Environment for Staff and Students Who Recognise that Sex Matters' in Open Letter of Support for Feminist Professor", *Daily Mail*, https://www.dailymail.co.uk/news/article-10100555/Over-200-academics-call-trans-activist-bullies-letter-support-feminist-professor.html.

Carson, David. 2022, Aug. 9. "Photos: Eighth Anniversary of Michael Brown Shooting in Ferguson", *St. Louis Post-Dispatch*, https://www.stltoday.com/news/multimedia/photos-eighth-anniversary-of-michael-brown-shooting-in-ferguson/collection_d63432a1-51e3-5589-aac4-55a6995925a3.html.

Castanet News. 2014, Dec. 4. "Raw Footage of Officers Taking Down Eric Garner" (video), https://youtu.be/dzHwiGS48Og.

Castillejo, Esther and Allie Yang. 2020, Aug. 10. "Fauci to David Muir: 'Universal Wearing of Masks' Essential to Combat COVID-19 Spread", ABC News, https://abcnews.go.com/US/fauci-david-muir-universal-wearing-masks-essential-combat/story?id=72294374.

CBS News. 2015, Mar. 4. "DOJ Clears Darren Wilson in Michael Brown Killing", https://www.cbsnews.com/news/darren-wilson-cleared-in-michael-brown-ferguson-killing-by-justice-department/.

———. 2019, Aug. 19. "NYPD Officer Daniel Pantaleo Fired Over 2014 Eric Garner Chokehold Death", https://www.cbsnews.com/news/nypd-officer-daniel-pantaleo-fired-today-eric-garner-chokehold-death-2019-08-19/.

Ceci, Stephen, Douglas Peters, and Jonathan Plotkin. 1985. "Human Subjects Review, Personal Values, and the Regulation of Social Science Research", *American Psychologist* 40:994–1002.

Center for World Class Universities. 2024. "2024 Academic Ranking of World Universities", https://www.shanghairanking.com/rankings/arwu/2024.

Chandler, Michael (writer & director). 1999, Oct. 5. "Secrets of the SAT" (television episode), *Frontline*, PBS, https://youtu.be/GeTFZN0DsLM.

Chetty, Raj, Nathaniel Hendren, Patrick Kline, and Emmanuel Saez. 2014. "Where Is the Land of Opportunity: The Geography of Intergenerational Mobility in the United States", *Quarterly Journal of Economics* 129:1553–1623.

Chicago Sun-Times. 2020, Aug. 27. "GRAPHIC: Video Allegedly Shows 17-Year-Old Kyle Rittenhouse Shooting 3 People, 2 Fatally in Kenosha", https://youtu.be/iryQSpxSlrg.

Clark, Cory, Bo Winegard, Jordan Beardslee, Roy Baumeister, and Azim Shariff. 2020. "Declines in Religiosity Predict Increases in Violent Crime—but Not Among Countries with Relatively High Average IQ", *Psychological Science* 31:170–83.

CNBC. 2019, Dec. 28. "The 10 Most Dangerous Jobs in America", https://www.cnbc.com/2019/12/27/the-10-most-dangerous-jobs-in-america-according-to-bls-data.html.

Cofnas, Nathan. 2017, July 13. "Dadaist Science", *Washington Examiner*, https://www.washingtonexaminer.com/magazine/1489797/dadaist-science/.

Collin, Liz (producer). 2023. *The Fall of Minneapolis* (documentary film). Alpha News. https://youtu.be/eFPi3EigjFA.

Collins, Chuck and Bob Lord. 2021, Mar. 18. "The Rich Are Not Remotely Paying Their Fair Share", Common Dreams, https://www.commondreams.org/views/2021/03/18/rich-are-not-remotely-paying-their-fair-share.

Connor, Paul, Matthew Weeks, Jack Glaser, Serena Chen, and Dacher Keltner. 2023. "Intersectional Implicit Bias: Evidence for Asymmetrically Compounding Bias and the Predominance of Target Gender", *Journal of Personality and Social Psychology* 124:22–48.

Cook, John, Dana Nuccitelli, Sarah Green, Mark Richardson, Bärbel Winkler, Rob Painting, Robert Way, Peter Jacobs, and Andrew Skuce. 2013. "Quantifying the Consensus on Anthropogenic Global Warming in the Scientific Literature", *Environmental Research Letters* 8:024024.

Cooper, Amy and Christian Cooper. 2020. "Amy Cooper Full Video", https://youtu.be/W0FByIEijXI.

Cost, Ben. 2023, Mar. 22. "NYC Audubon Society Changing Name Due to 'White Supremacy' Legacy", *The New York Post*, https://nypost.com/2023/03/22/nyc-audubon-society-changing-white-supremacy-legacy-name/.

Crichton, Michael. 2003, Jan. 17. "Aliens Cause Global Warming", Caltech Michelin Lecture. Transcript: https://stephenschneider.stanford.edu/Publications/PDF_Papers/Crichton2003.pdf.

Crippen, Alex. 2007, Oct. 31. "Warren Buffett and NBC's Tom Brokaw: The Complete Interview", CNBC, https://www.cnbc.com/id/21553857.

Crump, Benjamin. 2019. Open Season: Legalized Genocide of Colored People. HarperCollins.

Dal Bo, Ernesto. 2006. "Regulatory Capture: A Review", *Oxford Review of Economic Policy* 22:203–25.

Daley, Nathan. 2021, Nov. 7. "New Evidence: FBI Drone Footage In The Kyle Rittenhouse Shooting" (video), https://youtu.be/lWNrm6jdvMA.

Dawson, John and John Seater. 2013. "Federal Regulation and Aggregate Economic Growth", *Journal of Economic Growth* 18: 137–77.

Dayton, Carl. n.d. "How Many People Get Struck By Lightning Outdoors?", Outdoor Meta, http://outdoormeta.com/how-many-people-struck-lightning/.

de Blasio, Bill. 2020, May 26. Tweet: https://twitter.com/NYCMayor/status/1265265665755230209. (Twitter account subsequently taken over by de Blasio's successor.)

De Pinto, Jennifer, Sarah Dutton, Anthony Salvanto, and Fred Backus. 2014, Dec. 10. "Michael Brown and Eric Garner: The Police, Use of Force and Race", CBS News, https://www.cbsnews.com/news/michael-brown-and-eric-garner-the-police-use-of-force-and-race/.

De Zutter, André, Robert Horselenberg, and Peter van Koppen. 2018. "Motives for Filing a False Allegation of Rape", *Archives of Sexual Behavior* 47:457–64.

Dechezleprêtre, Antoine, Adrien Fabre, Tobias Kruse, Bluebery Planterose, Ana Sanchez Chico, and Stefanie Stantcheva. 2022. "Fighting Climate Change: International Attitudes Toward Climate Policies", OECD Economics Department Working Papers No. 1714, https://www.oecd-ilibrary.org/economics/fighting-climate-change-international-attitudes-toward-climate-policies_3406f29a-en.

DiAngelo, Robin. 2011. "White Fragility", *International Journal of Critical Pedagogy* 3:54–70.

———. 2018. White Fragility: Why It's So Hard for White People to Talk about Racism. Beacon Press.

Doran, Peter and Maggie Kendall Zimmerman. 2009. "Examining the Scientific Consensus on Climate Change", *Eos* 90:22-3.

Doyle, Jude. 2017, Nov. 29. "Despite What You May Have Heard, 'Believe Women' Has Never Meant 'Ignore Facts'", *Elle*, https://www.elle.com/culture/career-politics/a13977980/me-too-movement-false-accusations-believe-women/.

Duarte, José, Jarret Crawford, Charlotta Stern, Jonathan Haidt, Lee Jussim, and Philip Tetlock. 2015. "Political Diversity Will Improve Social Psychological Science", *Behavioral and Brain Sciences* 38:e130.

Eagly, Alice and Antonio Mladinic. 1989. "Gender Stereotypes and Attitudes Toward Women and Men", *Personality and Social Psychology Bulletin* 15:543–58.

———. 1994. "Are People Prejudiced Against Women? Some Answers from Research on Attitudes, Gender Stereotypes, and Judgments of Competence", *European Review of Social Psychology* 5:1–35.

Eagly, Alice, Antonio Mladinic, and Stacey Otto. 1991. "Are Women Evaluated More Favorably Than Men? An Analysis of Attitudes, Beliefs and Emotions", *Psychology of Women Quarterly* 15:203–16.

Easterbrook, Gregg. 2006, June 1. "Case Closed: The Debate about Global Warming Is Over", The Brookings Institution, https://www.brookings.edu/articles/case-closed-the-debate-about-global-warming-is-over/.

Ebell, Myron and Steven Milloy. 2019, Sept. 18. "Wrong Again: 50 Years of Failed Eco-pocalyptic Predictions", Competitive Enterprise Institute blog, https://cei.org/blog/wrong-again-50-years-of-failed-eco-pocalyptic-predictions/.

Ekins, Emily. 2019. "What Americans Think About Poverty, Wealth, and Work: Findings from the Cato Institute 2019 Welfare, Work, and Wealth National Survey", Cato Institute, http://www.cato.org/publications/survey-reports/what-americans-think-about-poverty-wealth-work.

Elder, Larry. 2018. "If Tough Anti-Drug Laws Are 'Racist,' Blame Black Leaders", RealClearPolitics, https://www.realclearpolitics.com/articles/2018/06/14/_if_tough_anti-drug_laws_are_racist_blame_black_leaders_137273.html.

England, Deborah and Kelly Martin. 2022. "Crack vs. Powder Cocaine: One Drug, Two Penalties", Nolo, https://www.criminaldefenselawyer.com/resources/crack-vrs-powder-cocaine-one-drug-two-penalties.htm.

Eugene, Diamond. 2012, Mar. 19. Letter to Sybrina Fulton. https://www.gettyimages.com/detail/news-photo/the-evidence-letter-that-witness-rachel-jeantel-wrote-to-news-photo/171648991.

Evon, Dan. 2018, Aug. 6. "Are These 'I'd Rather Be a Russian Than a Democrat' Shirts Real?", Snopes, https://www.snopes.com/fact-check/russian-than-democrat-shirts/.

Farrell, William. 2005. Why Men Earn More: The Startling Truth Behind the Pay Gap—and What Women Can Do About It. Independently published.

Fauci, Anthony and Jon LaPook. 2020, Mar. 8. "March 2020: Dr. Anthony Fauci Talks with Dr Jon LaPook About Covid-19" (excerpt from interview with *60 Minutes*), https://youtu.be/PRa6t_e7dgI.

FBI. 2020. *Crime in the United States 2019*, Expanded Homicide Data Table 3, https://ucr.fbi.gov/crime-in-the-u.s/2019/crime-in-the-u.s.-2019/tables/expanded-homicide-data-table-3.xls.

Fileva, Iskra. 2019. "The Gender Puzzles", *European Journal of Philosophy* 29:182–98.

Fisher, Bonnie, Francis Cullen, and Michael Turner. 2000. "The Sexual Victimization of College Women", U.S. Department of Justice, Bureau of Justice Statistics, https://www.ojp.gov/pdffiles1/nij/182369.pdf.

Forbes. 2018, Apr. 10. "10 Empowering Quotes For Women On Equal Pay Day", https://www.forbes.com/sites/forbes-summit-talks/2018/04/10/10-empowering-quotes-from-female-leaders-on-equal-pay-day/?sh=aabb0f518f3f.

Forliti, Amy, Tammy Webber, and Michael Tarm. 2021, Nov. 4. "Watch: Kyle Rittenhouse Trial for Kenosha Shooting Continues—Day 3", *PBS News Hour*, https://www.pbs.org/newshour/nation/watch-kyle-rittenhouse-trial-for-kenosha-shooting-continues-day-3.

Forscher, Patrick, Calvin Lai, Jordan Axt, Charles Ebersole, Michelle Herman, Patricia Devine, and Brian Nosek. 2019. "A Meta-Analysis of Procedures to Change Implicit Measures", *Journal of Personality and Social Psychology* 117:522–59.

Fortner, Michael. 2013. "The Carceral State and the Crucible of Black Politics: An

Urban History of the Rockefeller Drug Laws", *Studies in American Political Development* 27:14–35.

FOX 9 Minneapolis-St. Paul. 2023, Apr. 13. "Derek Chauvin Settlements Approved, Bodycam Videos Released for Pair of 2017 Complaints", https://youtu.be/mjuDd_iFq3A.

Francescani, Chris. 2012, Apr. 25. "George Zimmerman: Prelude to a Shooting", Reuters, https://www.reuters.com/article/us-usa-florida-shooting-zimmerman -idUSBRE83O18H20120425.

Frankovic, Kathy. 2021, Nov. 18. "More Americans Think Kyle Rittenhouse Should Be Convicted Than Say He Will Be", YouGov, https://today.yougov.com/topics/politics/articles-reports/2021/11/18/kyle-rittenhouse-perception-guilt-poll.

Friedman, David. 2014. *The Machinery of Freedom: Guide to a Radical Capitalism*, 3rd ed. Independently published.

———. 2023a, Jan. 27. "My First Post Done Again", https://daviddfriedman.substack.com/p/my-first-post-done-again.

———. 2023b, Apr. 14. "A Climate Falsehood You Can Check for Yourself", https://daviddfriedman.substack.com/p/a-climate-falsehood-you-can-check.

Fryer, Roland. 2006. "Acting White: The Social Price Paid by the Best and Brightest Minority Students", *Education Next* 6(1): 52–9.

———. 2019. "An Empirical Analysis of Racial Differences in Police Use of Force", *Journal of Political Economy* 127:1210–61.

Fung, Katherine. 2021, Feb. 22. "Best-Selling Controversial Book on Transgender People Removed From Amazon 3 Years After Publication", *Newsweek*, https://www.newsweek.com/best-selling-controversial-book-transgender-people-removed-amazon-3-years-after-publication-1571087.

Gabbatt, Adam. 2021, May 3. "Biden Says It's Time for Richest Americans to Pay 'Their Fair Share' of Taxes", *The Guardian*, https://www.theguardian.com/us-news/2021/may/03/joe-biden-taxes-corporations-richest-americans.

Galak, Jeff, Robyn LeBoeuf, Leif Nelson, and Joseph Simmons. 2012. "Correcting the Past: Failures to Replicate", *Journal of Personality and Social Psychology* 103: 933–48.

Ganley, Colleen. 2018, Aug. 14. "Are Boys Better Than Girls at Math?", *Scientific American*, https://www.scientificamerican.com/article/are-boys-better-than-girls-at-math/.

Gardner, Matthew and Steve Wamhoff. 2021. "55 Corporations Paid $0 in Federal Taxes on 2020 Profits", Institute on Taxation and Economic Policy, https://itep.org/55-profitable-corporations-zero-corporate-tax/.

Gateway Foundation. 2022, Jan. 3. "Racism in the War on Drugs", https://www.gatewayfoundation.org/addiction-blog/racism-war-on-drugs/.

Gawronski, Bertram, Mike Morrison, Curtis E. Phills, and Silvia Galdi. 2017. "Temporal Stability of Implicit and Explicit Measures: A Longitudinal Analysis", *Personality and Social Psychology Bulletin* 43:300–312.

Gayla, Marella. 2017, June 21. "A Federal Court Asks Jurors to Confront Their Hidden Biases", The Marshall Project, https://www.themarshallproject.org/2017/06/21/a-federal-court-asks-jurors-to-confront-their-hidden-biases.

Gelman, Andrew. 2020, June 22. "Retraction of Racial Essentialist Article That Appeared in *Psychological Science*", https://statmodeling.stat.columbia.edu/

2020/06/22/retraction-of-racial-essentialist-article-that-appeared-in-psychological-science/.

Gerald, Wayne. 2019, Nov. 26. "Scripted Journalists (Media) All Saying the Same Thing—Compilation", https://youtu.be/yshJn7lgVsY.

Ghorayshi, Azeen. 2017, July 27. "A Landmark Lawsuit About An Intersex Baby's Genital Surgery Just Settled For $440,000", Buzzfeed, https://www.buzzfeednews.com/article/azeenghorayshi/intersex-surgery-lawsuit-settles.

———. 2022, June 10. "Report Reveals Sharp Rise in Transgender Young People in the U.S.", *New York Times*, https://www.nytimes.com/2022/06/10/science/transgender-teenagers-national-survey.html.

Gilbert, Joel, director. 2019. *The Trayvon Hoax: Unmasking the Witness Fraud that Divided America* (documentary film), https://youtu.be/QAw5ykIPOBM.

Gilbert, Neil. 1997. "Advocacy Research and Social Policy" in *Crime and Justice: A Review of Research*, ed. Michael Tonry. University of Chicago Press.

Giorgis, Hannah. 2014, Nov. 10. "Beyond 'Hands Up, Don't Shoot': What if There's No Indictment in Ferguson?", *The Guardian*, https://www.theguardian.com/commentisfree/2014/nov/10/no-indictment-ferguson-no-justice-michael-brown.

Goldhill, Olivia. 2017, Dec. 3. "The World Is Relying on a Flawed Psychological Test to Fight Racism", *Quartz*, https://qz.com/1144504/the-world-is-relying-on-a-flawed-psychological-test-to-fight-racism.

Goldman, Bruce. 2017, May 22. "Two Minds: The Cognitive Differences Between Men and Women", *Stanford Medicine Magazine*, https://stanmed.stanford.edu/how-mens-and-womens-brains-are-different/.

Gorman, Michele. 2015, Sept. 21. "1 in 4 Women Experienced Sexual Assault While in College, Survey Finds", *Newsweek*, https://www.newsweek.com/1-4-women-sexual-assault-college-374793.

Govtrack (a). "To Pass H.R. 18583", https://www.govtrack.us/congress/votes/91-1970/s584.

——— (b). "To Pass H.R. 18583, Comprehensive Drug Abuse Prevention and Control Act of 1970", https://www.govtrack.us/congress/votes/91-1970/h355.

——— (c). "To Pass HR 5484", https://www.govtrack.us/congress/votes/99-1986/h787.

——— (d). "H.R. 3355 (103rd): Violent Crime Control and Law Enforcement Act of 1994", https://www.govtrack.us/congress/votes/103-1994/s295.

——— (e). "H.R. 3355 (103rd): Violent Crime Control and Law Enforcement Act of 1994", https://www.govtrack.us/congress/votes/103-1994/h416.

Grace, Nancy. 2006, Mar. 31. "Was Young Woman Assaulted by Duke Lacrosse Team?" (television episode). Transcript at https://transcripts.cnn.com/show/ng/date/2006-03-31/segment/01.

Graveley, Michael. 2021. "Report on the Officer Involved Shooting of Jacob Blake", County of Kenosha, District Attorney's office. https://www.kenoshacounty.org/DocumentCenter/View/11827/Report-on-the-Officer-Involved-Shooting-of-Jacob-Blake.

Green, Richard. 1987. The "Sissy Boy Syndrome" and the Development of Homosexuality. Yale University Press.

Greenwald, Anthony, Andrew Poehlman, Eric Uhlmann, and Mahzarin Banaji.

2009. "Understanding and Using the Implicit Association Test: III. Meta-Analysis of Predictive Validity", *Journal of Personality and Social Psychology* 97:17–41.

Greenwald, Anthony, Debbie McGhee, and Jordan Schwartz. 1998. "Measuring Individual Differences in Implicit Cognition: The Implicit Association Test", *Journal of Personality and Social Psychology* 74:1464–80.

Grosskreutz, Gaige. 2021, Nov. 8. Testimony in the Kyle Rittenhouse trial. Posted by FOX6 News Milwaukee as "Kyle Rittenhouse Trial: Gaige Grosskreutz Testifies" (video), https://youtu.be/Bv21bE9PWtE.

Guillamon, Antonio, Carme Junque, and Esther Gómez-Gil. 2016. "A Review of the Status of Brain Structure Research in Transsexualism", *Archives of Sexual Behavior* 45:1615–48.

Gutman, Matt. 2012, Mar. 28. "Trayvon Martin Video Shows No Blood or Bruises on George Zimmerman", ABC News, https://abcnews.go.com/WNT/trayvon-martin-case-exclusive-surveillance-video-george-zimmerman/story?id=16022897.

Haan, Kathy. 2023, Feb. 27, "Gender Pay Gap Statistics in 2023", *Forbes*, https://www.forbes.com/advisor/business/gender-pay-gap-statistics/.

Hager, Amber. n.d. "Supporting Gender Identity: A Beginner's Guide for Friends, Family, and University Staff", University of San Francisco, https://myusf.usfca.edu/caps/supporting-gender-identity.

Hagger, Martin and Nikos Chatzisarantis. 2016. "A Multilab Preregistered Replication of the Ego-Depletion Effect", *Perspectives on Psychological Science* 11:546–73.

Haidt, Jonathan. 2011, Feb. 17. "Discrimination Hurts Real People", YourMorals Blog, https://ymblog.jonathanhaidt.org/2011/02/discrimination-hurts-real-people/.

Harris, Kamala. 2019, Aug. 9. Tweet: https://twitter.com/KamalaHarris/status/1159893277954514944.

Hayat, Ahsan. 2023. "The World's 10 Most Successful Authors", Wonders List, https://www.wonderslist.com/10-most-successful-authors/.

Hayes, Akeem Ali Douglas ("Guap"). 2021, Nov. 19. Tweet: https://twitter.com/guapdad4000/status/1461767563503759362.

Hazlett, Thomas Winslow. 1997, Jan. 1. "Looking for Results: An Interview with Ronald Coase", *Reason*, https://reason.com/archives/1997/01/01/looking-for-results/.

Hemenway, David. 1997. "Survey Research and Self-Defense Gun Use: An Explanation of Extreme Overestimates", *Journal of Criminal Law and Criminology* 87:1430–45.

Henderson, David. 2014, Mar. 1. "1.6%, Not 97%, Agree that Humans are the Main Cause of Global Warming", EconLog, https://www.econlib.org/archives/2014/03/16_not_97_agree.html.

Hendricks, Perry. 2024a, Feb. 19. "Diversity Statements Are Discriminatory and a Waste of Time", Blog of the American Philosophical Association, https://blog.apaonline.org/2024/02/19/diversity-statements-are-discriminatory-and-a-waste-of-time/.

———. 2024b. "Abortion Restrictions Are Good for Black Women" (unpublished ms.), https://philpapers.org/archive/HENARA-5.pdf.

Herman, Jody, Andrew Flores, and Kathryn O'Neill. 2022. *How Many Adults and Youth Identify as Transgender in the United States?*, Williams Institute, UCLA, https://williamsinstitute.law.ucla.edu/wp-content/uploads/Trans-Pop-Update-Jun-2022.pdf.

Herman, Jody, Andrew Flores, Taylor Brown, Bianca Wilson, and Kerith Conron. 2017. *Age of Individuals Who Identify as Transgender in the United States*, Williams Institute, UCLA, https://williamsinstitute.law.ucla.edu/wp-content/uploads/Age-Trans-Individuals-Jan-2017.pdf.

Hollander, Jenny. 2017, Nov. 21. "Nice Guys Aren't Nice If They're Assaulting Other Women", *Bustle*, https://www.bustle.com/p/why-believe-women-means-believing-women-without-exception-5532903. Originally titled "Why 'Believe Women' Means Believing Women Without Exception".

Hooke, Angus and Lauren Alati. 2022. "What Will the World Economy Look Like in 2100?", UBSS Scholarship Series, Issue 3, Article 15, https://www.ubss.edu.au/articles/2022/july/what-will-the-world-economy-look-like-in-2100/.

Hudak, John. 2021 July 7. "Reversing the War on Drugs: A Five-point Plan", The Brookings Institution, https://www.brookings.edu/articles/reversing-the-war-on-drugs-a-five-point-plan/.

Huemer, Michael. 2004. "America's Unjust Drug War", pp. 133–44 in *The New Prohibition*, ed. Bill Masters. Accurate Press.

———. 2008. "The Drug Laws Don't Work", *The Philosophers' Magazine* no. 41:71–5.

———. 2013. *The Problem of Political Authority*. Palgrave Macmillan.

———. 2015. "Why People Are Irrational About Politics," pp. 456–67 in *Philosophy, Politics, and Economics*, ed. Jonathan Anomaly, Geoffrey Brennan, Michael Munger, and Geoffrey Sayre-McCord. Oxford University Press. https://spot.colorado.edu/~huemer/papers/irrationality.htm.

———. 2020, Jan. 11. "Outlaw Universities", Fake Noûs, https://fakenous.substack.com/p/outlaw-universities.

———. 2021. *Justice Before the Law*. Palgrave Macmillan.

———. 2022. *Understanding Knowledge*. Independently published.

———. 2023, Mar. 4. "Why Not Shibboleths", Fake Noûs, https://fakenous.substack.com/p/whats-wrong-with-shibboleths.

———. 2024. "How to Be Irrational," pp. 94–108 in *Seemings: New Arguments, New Angles*, ed. Scott Stapleford, Kevin McCain, and Matthias Steup. Routledge.

Human Rights Watch. 2017. *"I Want to Be Like Nature Made Me": Medically Unnecessary Surgeries on Intersex Children in the US*, https://www.hrw.org/sites/default/files/report_pdf/lgbtintersex0717_web_0.pdf.

Hunter, George and Hayley Harding. 2021, Sept. 27. "Detroit Remains Among Nation's Most Violent Big Cities, FBI Statistics Show," *The Detroit News*, https://www.detroitnews.com/story/news/local/michigan/2021/09/27/detroit-most-violent-big-us-cities-fbi-uniform-crime-report-2020/5883984001/.

Hyytinen, Ari, Pekka Ilmakunnas, Edvard Johansson, and Otto Toivanen. 2019. "Heritability of Lifetime Earnings", *Journal of Economic Inequality* 17:319–35.

Inbar, Yoel and Joris Lammers. 2012. "Political Diversity in Social and Personality Psychology", *Perspectives on Psychological Science* 7:496–503.

Intersex Society of North America. 2008. "What's Wrong with the Way Intersex

Has Traditionally Been Treated?", https://isna.org/faq/concealment/.

Ioannidis, John. 2005. "Why Most Published Research Findings Are False", *PLoS Medicine* 2:e124.

IPCC (Intergovernmental Panel on Climate Change). 2018. *Global Warming of 1.5°C.* https://www.ipcc.ch/sr15/.

———. 2023a. *Climate Change 2023: Synthesis Report.* https://www.ipcc.ch/report/ar6/syr/.

———. 2023b. "Fact Sheet—Health", https://www.ipcc.ch/report/ar6/wg2/downloads/outreach/IPCC_AR6_WGII_FactSheet_Health.pdf.

———. 2023c. *Sixth Assessment Report*, Chapter 9: Ocean, Cryosphere and Sea Level Change, https://www.ipcc.ch/report/ar6/wg1/chapter/chapter-9/.

Jacobson, Louis. 2021, April 12. "Fact-Checking Joe Biden on How Little Some Corporations Pay in Taxes", Politifact, https://www.politifact.com/factchecks/2021/apr/12/joe-biden/fact-checking-joe-biden-corporation-taxes/.

Jacobson, Roi and Daphna Joel. 2021. "Gender Identity and Sexuality in an Online Sample of Intersex-Identified Individuals: A Descriptive Study", *Psychology & Sexuality* 12:248–60.

James, Lois, Stephen James, and Bryan Vila. 2016. "The Reverse Racism Effect", *Criminology and Public Policy* 15:457–79.

Janis, Irving. 1972. Victims of Groupthink: A Psychological Study of Foreign-Policy Decisions and Fiascoes. Houghton, Mifflin.

Jefferson, Melissa ("Lizzo"). 2021, Nov. 19. Tweet: https://twitter.com/lizzo/status/1461818116757807105. Quoted by Jessica Napoli, Fox News, Nov. 19, 2021, https://www.foxnews.com/entertainment/celebs-react-kyle-rittenhouses-not-guilty-verdict.

Jefferson, Tom et al. 2023. "Physical Interventions to Interrupt or Reduce the Spread of Respiratory Viruses", *Cochrane Database of Systematic Reviews*, Issue 1, Article No. CD006207.

Jencks, Christopher and Meredith Phillips. 1998, Mar. 1. "The Black-White Test Score Gap: Why It Persists and What Can Be Done", Brookings Institution, https://www.brookings.edu/articles/the-black-white-test-score-gap-why-it-persists-and-what-can-be-done/.

John, Leslie, George Loewenstein, and Drazen Prelec. 2012. "Measuring the Prevalence of Questionable Research Practices With Incentives for Truth Telling", *Psychological Science* 23:524–32.

Johnson, Daniel. 2021, Aug. 5. "'Central Park Karen' Defends Her Actions in First Interview Since Fleeing U.S.", *National Post*, https://nationalpost.com/news/central-park-karen-defends-her-actions-in-first-interview-since-fleeing-u-s.

Johnson, Derrick. 2021, Nov. 19. Tweet: https://twitter.com/DerrickNAACP/status/1461763568223858700.

Johnson, K.C. n.d. "Durham in Wonderland" (blog), https://durhamwonderland.blogspot.com.

Johnston, Matthew. 2024, June 19. "10 Most Profitable Companies in the World", Investopedia, https://www.investopedia.com/the-world-s-10-most-profitable-companies-4694526.

Jussim, Lee, Jarret Crawford, Stephanie Anglin, John Chambers, Sean Stevens, and Florette Cohen. 2015. "Stereotype Accuracy: One of the Largest and Most

Replicable Effects in All of Social Psychology", pp. 31-63 in *Handbook of Prejudice, Stereotyping, and Discrimination*, 2nd ed., ed. Todd Nelson. Psychology Press.

Kaltiala-Heino, Riittakerttu, Hannah Bergman, Marja Työläjärvi, and Louise Frisén. 2018. "Gender Dysphoria in Adolescence: Current Perspectives", *Adolescent Health, Medicine, and Therapeutics* 9:31–41.

Kanin, Eugene. 1994. "False Rape Allegations", *Archives of Sexual Behavior* 23:81–92.

KARE (Minneapolis Television News Channel). 2020. "Raw Video: Jacob Blake Police Shooting", https://youtu.be/K0DSTV7XT1E.

Kavanagh, Rebecca. 2020, Aug. 26. Twitter video, https://twitter.com/DrRJKavanagh/status/1298532736790077440.

Kaye, Randi. 2013, June 27. "Jeantel Had Friend Write Letter to Martin's Mom", CNN, https://youtu.be/NhRXvP04Ogw.

Kelly, Jack. 2019, Oct. 22. "The Number Of Millionaires Has Boomed—Here's Where Your Net Worth Ranks Compared To Others", *Forbes*, https://www.forbes.com/sites/jackkelly/2019/10/22/the-number-of-millionaires-has-boomedheres-where-your-net-worth-ranks-compared-to-others/.

Kemp, Luke et al. 2022. "Climate Endgame: Exploring Catastrophic Climate Change Scenarios", *PNAS* 119:e2108146119, https://www.pnas.org/doi/full/10.1073/pnas.2108146119.

Kendi, Ibram. 2017, May 28. "The 11 Most Racist U.S. Presidents", *Huffington Post*, https://www.huffpost.com/entry/would-a-president-trump-m_b_10135836.

King, Gayle. 2020, Oct. 28. "Jurors Speak with CBS About Breonna Taylor Case", (video interview), CBS Mornings, part 1: https://youtu.be/JpOmtbTT0F8; part 2: https://youtu.be/tcirSxGq7yE.

Klar, Rebecca. 2022, Mar. 21. "Twitter Suspends Babylon Bee for Misgendering Rachel Levine", The Hill, https://thehill.com/policy/technology/599051-twitter-suspends-babylon-bee-for-misgendering-rachel-levine/.

Kleck, Gary. 1997. Targeting Guns: Firearms and Their Control. Aldine de Gruyter.

Knowles, Hannah and Marisa Iati. 2020, Sept. 29. "Kentucky Attorney General Says He Did Not Present Homicide Charges to Grand Jury in Breonna Taylor Case", *Washington Post*, https://www.washingtonpost.com/nation/2020/09/28/breonna-taylor-grand-juror/.

Kochhar, Rakesh. 2023, Mar. 1. "The Enduring Grip of the Gender Pay Gap", Pew Research Center, https://www.pewresearch.org/social-trends/2023/03/01/the-enduring-grip-of-the-gender-pay-gap/.

Korot, Edward, Nikolas Pontikos, Xiaoxuan Liu, Siegfried Wagner, Livia Faes, Josef Huemer, Konstantinos Balaskas, Alastair Denniston, Anthony Khawaja, and Pearse Keane. 2021. "Predicting Sex From Retinal Fundus Photographs Using Automated Deep Learning", *Scientific Reports* 11:10286.

Koss, Mary, Christine Gidycz, and Nadine Wisniewski. 1987. "The Scope of Rape: Incidence and Prevalence of Sexual Aggression and Victimization in a National Sample of Higher Education Students", *Journal of Consulting and Clinical Psychology* 55:162–70.

Kovaleski, Serge and Campbell Robertson. 2012, May 17. "New Details Are Released in Shooting of Trayvon Martin", *New York Times*, https://www.nytimes.com/2012/05/18/us/new-details-are-released-in-shooting-of-teenager.html.

Kraus, Jame. 2021, Nov. 15. Closing statement in the Kyle Rittenhouse trial. Posted by Law & Crime Network as "WI v. Kyle Rittenhouse Trial Day 10— Prosecution Rebuttal Closing Argument by Jame Kraus" (video), https://youtu.be/-2vMnM0xnhw.

Krol, Aaron. 2023, Oct. 20. "Will Climate Change Drive Humans Extinct or Destroy Civilization?", Ask MIT Climate, https://climate.mit.edu/ask-mit/will-climate-change-drive-humans-extinct-or-destroy-civilization.

Krumholz, Willis. 2019, Oct. 7. "Family Breakdown and America's Welfare System", Institute for Family Studies blog, https://ifstudies.org/blog/family-breakdown-and-americas-welfare-system.

Kurtzleben, Danielle. 2010, Aug. 3. "Data Show Racial Disparity in Crack Sentencing", *U.S. News & World Report*, https://www.usnews.com/news/articles/2010/08/03/data-show-racial-disparity-in-crack-sentencing.

Kutner, Max. 2015, Mar. 21. "Who Kills Police Officers?", *Newsweek*, https://www.newsweek.com/who-kills-police-officers-315701.

Labatt, Henry J. 1860. *The California Practice Act*, 3rd ed. H.H. Bancroft & Co.

Lane, Kristin, Mahzarin Banaji, Brian Nosek, and Anthony Greenwald. 2007. "Understanding and Using the Implicit Association Test: IV", pp. 59–102 in *Implicit Measures of Attitudes: Procedures and Controversies*, ed. Bernd Wittenbrink and Norbert Schwarz. Guilford Press.

Langan, Patrick. 1994, Fall. "No Racism in the Justice System", *The Public Interest* 117:48–51.

Larkin, Paul. 2015. "Public Choice Theory and Occupational Licensing", *Harvard Journal of Law & Public Policy* 39:209–331.

Larotonda, Matthew and Chris Good. 2015, Mar. 6. "Obama Says 'We May Never Know What Happened' in Ferguson, But Defends DOJ", ABC News, https://abcnews.go.com/Politics/obama-happened-ferguson-defends-doj/story?id=29441456.

Larrimore, Jeff, Jacob Mortenson, and David Splinter. 2015. "Income and Earnings Mobility in U.S. Tax Data", Finance and Economics Discussion Series 2015-061, Board of Governors of the Federal Reserve System, http://dx.doi.org/10.17016/FEDS.2015.061.

Lawrence, Anne. 2017. "Autogynephilia and the Typology of Male-to-Female Transsexualism: Concepts and Controversies", *European Psychologist* 22:39–54, http://www.annelawrence.com/autogynephilia_&_MtF_typology.html.

Lee, Michelle. 2015, Jan. 9. "Are Black or White Offenders More Likely to Kill Police?", *Washington Post*, https://www.washingtonpost.com/news/fact-checker/wp/2015/01/09/are-black-or-white-offenders-more-likely-to-kill-police/.

Levine, Mark. 2020, May 25. Tweet: https://twitter.com/MarkLevineNYC/status/1265086830648668163.

Levine, Sam. 2014, Dec. 3. "Peter King Says Eric Garner Would Not Have Died From Chokehold Were He Not Obese", *Huffington Post*, https://www.huffpost.com/entry/peter-king-eric-garner_n_6265748.

Lewis, Nathaniel and Matt Bruenig. 2017, Oct. 10. "The Wealthiest 1% Inherited an Average of $4.8 Million", People's Policy Project blog, http://www.peoplespolicyproject.org/2017/10/10/the-wealthiest-1-inherited-an-average-of-4-8-million/.

Lieb, David and Holbrook Mohr. 2014, Nov. 27. "For Some, Location of Brown's Hands Irrelevant", Associated Press, https://www.wcvb.com/article/for-some-location-of-brown-s-hands-irrelevant/8212614.

Lindner, Jannik. 2024. "Average Income in Nigeria Statistics", WorldMetrics, https://worldmetrics.org/average-income-in-nigeria/.

Lindsay, James, Peter Boghossian, and Helen Pluckrose. 2018. "Project Fact Sheet", https://leiterreports.typepad.com/files/project-summary-and-fact-sheet.pdf.

Lipsky, Michael. 2016, Apr. 12. "Why Regulation Is Necessary and Proper for a Well-Functioning Democracy and Market Economy", Scholars Strategy Network, https://scholars.org/contribution/why-regulation-necessary-and-proper-well.

Lisak, David, Lori Gardinier, Sarah Nicksa, and Ashley Cote. 2010. "False Allegations of Sexual Assault: An Analysis of Ten Years of Reported Cases", *Violence Against Women* 16:1318–34.

Littman, Lisa. 2018. "Parent Reports of Adolescents and Young Adults Perceived to Show Signs of a Rapid Onset of Gender Dysphoria", *PLoS One* 13:e0202330.

Livingston, Gretchen and Anna Brown. 2017, May 18. "Public Views on Intermarriage", Pew Research Center, https://www.pewresearch.org/social-trends/2017/05/18/2-public-views-on-intermarriage/.

Lomborg, Bjørn. 2004. *Global Crises, Global Solutions*. Cambridge University Press.

———. 2007. "Global Priorities Bigger than Climate Change", TED lecture, https://youtu.be/Dtbn9zBfJSs.

———. 2009. Global Crises, Global Solutions: Costs and Benefits, 2nd ed. Cambridge Univ. Press.

———. 2013. How to Spend $75 Billion to Make the World a Better Place. Copenhagen Consensus Center.

Lopez, German. 2016, Mar. 29. "Was Nixon's War on Drugs a Racially Motivated Crusade? It's a Bit More Complicated", *Vox*, https://www.vox.com/2016/3/29/11325750/nixon-war-on-drugs.

Loury, Glenn and John McWhorter. 2023, Dec. 8. "The Truth about George Floyd's Death", The Glenn Show, https://youtu.be/0ffv4IUxkDU.

———. 2024, Feb. 16. "What the Controversial George Floyd Doc Didn't Tell Us", The Glenn Show, https://youtu.be/tCnK1UU3mks.

MacIntyre, C Raina et al. 2015. "A Cluster Randomised Trial of Cloth Masks Compared with Medical Masks in Healthcare Workers", *BMJ Open* 5:e006577.

Maddow, Rachel. 2012, April. Rachel Maddow television show, excerpted at https://youtu.be/ta7kLhnx_Uc.

Maloney, Carolyn. 2018, Sept. 26. Tweet: https://twitter.com/RepMaloney/status/1045005759728234497.

Mapping Police Violence. 2023. https://mappingpoliceviolence.org.

Marcus, Adam. 2020, June 18. "Authors of Article on IQ, Religiosity and Crime Retract It to Do 'a Level of Vetting We Should Have Done Before Submitting'", Retraction Watch (blog), https://retractionwatch.com/2020/06/18/authors-of-article-on-iq-religiosity-and-crime-retract-it-to-do-a-level-of-vetting-we-should-have-done-before-submitting/.

Martin, Tracy and Sybrina Fulton. 2012, Mar. 8. "Prosecute the Killer of our Son, 17-year-old Trayvon Martin" (petition), https://www.change.org/p/prosecute-the-killer-of-our-son-17-year-old-trayvon-martin.

May, Caroline. 2010, Sept. 09. "College Campus Rape Rate 10 Times Higher than Detroit's? Don't Believe Everything the Justice Department Tells You", *Daily Caller*, https://dailycaller.com/2010/09/09/college-campus-rape-rate-10-times-higher-than-detroits-dont-believe-everything-the-justice-department-tells-you/.

McAdams, Alexis. 2020, Sept. 2. "Kenosha Unrest Damages More Than 100 Buildings, at Least 40 Destroyed, Alliance Says", ABC News Chicago, https://abc7chicago.com/kenosha-shooting-protest-looting-fires/6402998/.

McBrayer, Justin. 2022, May 22. "Diversity Statements Are the New Faith Statements", *Inside Higher Ed*, https://www.insidehighered.com/views/2022/05/23/diversity-statements-are-new-faith-statements-opinion.

McBride, Jessica. 2021a, Nov. 20. "Gaige Grosskreutz: 5 Fast Facts You Need to Know", *Heavy*, https://heavy.com/news/gaige-grosskreutz/.

———. 2021b, Nov. 21. "Anthony Huber: 5 Fast Facts You Need to Know", *Heavy*, https://heavy.com/news/anthony-huber-rittenhouse-victim/.

———. 2021c, Nov. 21. "Joseph Rosenbaum: 5 Fast Facts You Need to Know", *Heavy*, https://heavy.com/news/joseph-rosenbaum/.

McFadden, Cynthia. 2010, Aug. 16. "Many Campus Assault Victims Stay Quiet, or Fail to Get Help," ABC News, https://abcnews.go.com/Nightline/college-campus-assaults-constant-threat/story?id=11410988.

McGinnis, Richard. 2021, Nov. 4. Testimony in Kyle Rittenhouse trial. Posted by Law & Crime Network, "WI v Kyle Rittenhouse Trial Day 3 - On The Stand - Richard McGinnis - Reporter On Scene", https://youtu.be/zPwCsnEqcb4.

McKenna, Kaylyn. 2023, Feb. 21. "10 Jobs You Didn't Know Need Licenses", *Business News Daily*, https://www.businessnewsdaily.com/2492-occupations-requiring-licenses.html.

McKnight, Hannah. n.d. "A Beginner's Guide to Crossdressing", https://hannahmcknight.org/a-beginners-guide-to-crossdressing/.

McLaughlin, Eliott. 2013, July 11. "Ex-Sanford Police Chief: Zimmerman Probe 'Taken Away from Us'", CNN, https://www.cnn.com/2013/07/10/justice/sanford-bill-lee-exclusive/index.html.

McLaughlin, Patrick, Jerry Ellig, and Dima Yazji Shamoun. 2014. "Regulatory Reform in Florida: An Opportunity for Greater Competitiveness and Economic Efficiency", *Florida State University Business Review* 13:95–130.

McLaughlin, Patrick, Matthew Mitchell, and Anne Philpot. 2017. "The Effects of Occupational Licensure on Competition, Consumers, and the Workforce", Mercatus Center, https://www.mercatus.org/research/public-interest-comments/effects-occupational-licensure-competition-consumers-and.

McWhorter, John. 2014, Oct. 8. "'Acting White' Remains a Barrier for Black Education", *Reason*, https://reason.com/2014/10/08/acting-white-remains-a-barrier-for-black/.

———. 2021. Woke Racism: How a New Religion Has Betrayed Black America. Portfolio.

Meadow, Tey. 2018, July 10. "The Loaded Language Shaping the Trans Conversation", *The Atlantic*, https://www.theatlantic.com/family/archive/2018/07/

desistance/564560/.

Midler, Bette. 2021, Nov. 19. Tweet: https://twitter.com/BetteMidler/status/1461776644268507140.

Miniño, Arialdi and Jiaquan Xu. 2024, Apr. 5. "QuickStats: Life Expectancy at Birth, by Sex — United States, 2019–2022", CDC, National Center for Health Statistics, https://blogs.cdc.gov/nchs/2024/04/05/7580/.

Moser, Charles. 2010. "Blanchard's Autogynephilia Theory: A Critique", *Journal of Homosexuality* 57:790–809.

Moynihan, Daniel P. 1965. *The Negro Family: The Case for National Action*. Office of Policy Planning and Research, U.S. Department of Labor.

Mueller, Sven et al. 2021. "The Neuroanatomy of Transgender Identity: Mega-Analytic Findings From the ENIGMA Transgender Persons Working Group", *Journal of Sexual Medicine* 18:1122–9.

Murphy, Andrea and Matt Schifrin. 2024, June 06. "The Global 2000 2024", *Forbes*, https://www.forbes.com/lists/global2000/.

Myers, Jeff and Pete Michels (directors). 2014. *Rick and Morty*, S1E7, "Raising Gazorpazorp".

Myers, Krista, Peter Doran, John Cook, John Kotcher, and Teresa Myers. 2021. "Consensus Revisited: Quantifying Scientific Agreement on Climate Change and Climate Expertise Among Earth Scientists 10 Years Later", *Environmental Research Letters* 16:104030.

Nagourney, Adam. 2010, Dec. 10. "In Tapes, Nixon Rails About Jews and Blacks", *The New York Times*, https://www.nytimes.com/2010/12/11/us/politics/11nixon.html.

National Organization for Women. 2021, May 12. Tweet: https://twitter.com/NationalNOW/status/1392515410679930881.

NBC News. 2013, June 27. "Zimmerman Testimony Focuses on Letter Given to Trayvon Martin's Mom", https://www.nbcnews.com/news/us-news/zimmerman-testimony-focuses-letter-given-trayvon-martins-mom-flna6C10475625. Image archived at http://web.archive.org/web/20131227012409/http://msnbcmedia.msn.com/i/MSNBC/Sections/NEWS/w8_letter.pdf.

NCSL (National Conference of State Legislatures). 2022. "The National Occupational Licensing Database", https://www.ncsl.org/labor-and-employment/the-national-occupational-licensing-database.

Netburn, Deborah. 2021, July 27. "A Timeline of the CDC's Advice on Face Masks", *Los Angeles Times*, https://www.latimes.com/science/story/2021-07-27/timeline-cdc-mask-guidance-during-covid-19-pandemic.

New York State Assembly. 2020, June 8. "Assembly Passes Eric Garner Anti-Chokehold Act" (press release), https://nyassembly.gov/Press/files/20200608a.php.

Nicolay, John and John Hay (eds.). 1920. *Abraham Lincoln: Complete Works*, vol. 1. Century Co.

Nir, Sarah Maslin. 2020a, May 26. "White Woman Is Fired After Calling Police on Black Man in Central Park", *New York Times*, https://www.nytimes.com/2020/05/26/nyregion/amy-cooper-dog-central-park.html.

———. 2020b, May 27. "The Bird Watcher, That Incident and His Feelings on the Woman's Fate", *New York Times*, https://www.nytimes.com/2020/05/27/

nyregion/amy-cooper-christian-central-park-video.html.

No to Racist Pseudoscience. 2018, Dec. 18. "Open Letter: No to Racist Pseudo-science at Cambridge", https://medium.com/@racescienceopenletter/open-letter-no-to-racist-pseudoscience-at-cambridge-472e1a7c6dca.

Noah, Trevor. 2020, May 29. "George Floyd, the Minneapolis Protests, Ahmaud Arbery & Amy Cooper", (video) https://www.facebook.com/thedailyshow/videos/271504123969416/.

Nordhaus, William. 2008. A Question of Balance: Weighing the Options on Global Warming Policies. Yale University Press.

North, Anna. 2020, May 26. "Amy Cooper's 911 Call Is Part of an All-Too-Familiar Pattern: She Is Just the Latest in a Long Line of White People Calling the Police on Black Americans", *Vox*, https://www.vox.com/2020/5/26/21270699/amy-cooper-franklin-templeton-christian-central-park.

Nosek, Brian. 2005. "Moderators of the Relationship Between Implicit and Explicit Evaluation", *Journal of Experimental Psychology: General* 134:565–84.

NSVRC (National Sexual Violence Resource Center). n.d. "Statistics", https://www.nsvrc.org/statistics, accessed June 5, 2023.

Obama, Barack. 2013, July 19. "President Obama Speaks on Trayvon Martin" (press conference video), https://youtu.be/MHBdZWbncXI. Transcript available at https://obamawhitehouse.archives.gov/the-press-office/2013/07/19/remarks-president-trayvon-martin.

———. 2015, Feb. 27. "Presidential Proclamation—Women's History Month", https://obamawhitehouse.archives.gov/the-press-office/2015/02/27/presidential-proclamation-women-s-history-month.

Ocasio-Cortez, Alexandria. 2019, Jan. 21. Interview by Ta-Nehisi Coates, MLK Now event, https://youtu.be/q3-QvoIfpxc.

Okun, Tema. 2020. "White Supremacy Culture", https://www.whitesupremacyculture.info/uploads/4/3/5/7/43579015/okun_-_white_sup_culture_2020.pdf.

Olson, Kristina, Lily Durwood, Rachel Horton, Natalie Gallagher, and Aaron Devor. 2022. "Gender Identity 5 Years After Social Transition", *Pediatrics* 150:e2021056082.

Open Science Collaboration. 2015. "Estimating the Reproducibility of Psychological Science", *Science* 349:aac4716.

Oransky, Ivan. 2020, June 27. "Editors in Chief Past and Present Apologize for Publishing Article That 'Feed[s] into Racist Narratives'", Retraction Watch, https://retractionwatch.com/2020/06/27/editors-in-chief-past-and-present-apologize-for-publishing-article-that-feeds-into-racist-narratives/.

Orfalea, Matt. 2021, November 19. "'Across State Lines' | MASHUP", https://youtu.be/hY1eoY_MMco.

Oswald, Debra and Richard Harvey. 2000. "Hostile Environments, Stereotype Threat, and Math Performance Among Undergraduate Women", *Current Psychology* 19:338–56.

Oswald, Frederick, Gregory Mitchell, Hart Blanton, James Jaccard, and Philip Tetlock. 2013. "Predicting Ethnic and Racial Discrimination: A Meta-Analysis of IAT Criterion Studies", *Journal of Personality and Social Psychology* 105:171–92.

Our World in Data. n.d. "Deaths per Year", https://ourworldindata.org/grapher/number-of-deaths-per-year.

Oxfam America. 2023. "Action Alert: Tax the Rich", https://www. oxfamamerica. org/take-action/action-alert-tax-the-rich/.

Pan, Jen and Paul Prescod. 2021. "The Absurdity of 'White Supremacy Culture'", Jacobin, https://youtu.be/vqV3ARvuymY.

Paoletta, Mark. 2022, May 11. "Forty Years of Attacks and Slurs Against Justice Thomas", *Newsweek*, https://www.newsweek.com/forty-years-attacks-slurs-against-justice-thomas-opinion-1705248.

PBS. 2015. "Growing Up Trans", *Frontline*, S2015E11, https://www.pbs.org/video/frontline-growing-up-trans/.

————. 2023, Mar. 20. "Dr. Fauci visits D.C. to battle vaccine hesistancy" [*sic*], *American Masters*, excerpt from S37E2, https://youtu.be/PBL8sAYytv0.

Pearce, Fred. 2010. The Climate Files: The Battle for the Truth About Global Warming. Guardian Books.

Perry, Mark. 2019, Sept. 23. "50 Years of Failed Doomsday, Eco-pocalyptic Predictions; the So-called 'experts' Are 0-50", American Enterprise Institute, https://www.aei.org/carpe-diem/50-years-of-failed-doomsday-eco-pocalyptic-predictions-the-so-called-experts-are-0-50/.

Pester, Patrick. 2021, Aug. 30. "Could Climate Change Make Humans Go Extinct?", *Live Science*, https://www.livescience.com/climate-change-humans-extinct.html.

Pew Research Center. 2013, July 22. "Big Racial Divide over Zimmerman Verdict", https://www.pewresearch.org/politics/2013/07/22/big-racial-divide-over-zimmerman-verdict/.

Pew Research Center. 2019, Dec. 17. "In A Politically Polarized Era, Sharp Divides In Both Partisan Coalitions" (polling report), "2. Views Of Government And The Nation", https://www.pewresearch.org/politics/2019/12/17/views-of-government-and-the-nation/.

Pinker, Steven. 2012. *The Better Angels of our Nature*. Penguin.

Piwowarczyk, Jim. 2021, Nov. 10. "New Drone Video presented in the Kyle Rittenhouse Trial", https://youtu.be/mSQYiurU6Us.

Post University Blog. 2021, Jan. 12. "Speeding Up the Process: How Long Does It Take to Earn a Bachelor's Degree?", https://post.edu/blog/speeding-up-the-process-how-long-does-it-have-to-take-to-earn-a-bachelors-degree/.

Powell, James. 2019. "Scientists Reach 100% Consensus on Anthropogenic Global Warming", *Bulletin of Science, Technology & Society* 37:183–4.

Pritzker, J.B. 2021, Nov. 19. Tweet: https://twitter.com/GovPritzker/status/1461802665986465797.

Public Health England. 2020, Feb. 25. "Guidance for Social or Community Care and Residential Settings on COVID-19", https://www.gov.uk/government/publications/guidance-for-social-or-community-care-and-residential-settings-on-covid-19/guidance-for-social-or-community-care-and-residential-settings-on-covid-19.

Pugliese, Anita and Julie Ray. 2023, Jan. 24. "Nearly 900 Million Worldwide Wanted to Migrate in 2021", Gallup, https://news.gallup.com/poll/468218/nearly-900-million-worldwide-wanted-migrate-2021.aspx.

Quillette. 2019, May 28. "Noah Carl: An Update on the Young Scholar Fired by a Cambridge College for Thoughtcrime", https://quillette.com/2019/05/28/noah-carl-an-update-on-the-young-scholar-fired-by-a-cambridge-college-for-thoughtcrime/.

Radcliffe, J.R. 2020, Aug. 24. "Prominent Figures React to the Jacob Blake Shooting in Kenosha, Including Joe Biden", *Milwaukee Journal Sentinel*, https://www.jsonline.com/story/news/2020/08/24/prominent-figures-react-jacob-blake-shooting-kenosha/3428435001/.

RAINN (Rape, Abuse, and Incest National Network). 2023. "Campus Sexual Violence: Statistics", https://www.rainn.org/statistics/campus-sexual-violence.

Ramsey Solutions. 2022, Apr. 11. "How Many Millionaires Actually Inherited Their Wealth?", https://www.ramseysolutions.com/retirement/how-many-millionaires-actually-inherited-their-wealth.

Redfield, Robert. 2020, Sept. 16. "Masks May Be More Effective Than Vaccines - CDC Director" (excerpt from U.S. Senate testimony), Reuters, https://youtu.be/cIVTOkfvmxk.

Reeves, Mel. 2021, Nov. 16. "Why It Seems Like Kyle Rittenhouse Shot Black People", *Minnesota Spokesman-Recorder*, https://spokesman-recorder.com/2021/11/16/%E2%80%8Bwhy-it-seems-like-kyle-rittenhouse-shot-black-people/.

Reeves, Richard. 2017, Feb. 1. "Race Gaps in SAT Math Scores Are as Big as Ever", Brookings Institution, https://www.brookings.edu/blog/brown-center-chalkboard/2017/02/01/race-gaps-in-sat-math-scores-are-as-big-as-ever/.

Reeves, Richard and Ember Smith. 2022, Oct. 12. "Boys Left Behind: Education Gender Gaps Across the US", Brookings Institution, https://www.brookings.edu/blog/up-front/2022/10/12/boys-left-behind-education-gender-gaps-across-the-us/.

Reuters Health. 2010, Sept. 2. "Soy May Ease Sleep Problems in Older Women", https://www.reuters.com/article/us-soy-sleep-idUSTRE6813N520100902.

Rivers, Glenn. 2020, Aug. 25. "Doc Rivers Emotional Postgame Interview on Jacob Blake Shooting", https://youtu.be/ahPuQSsiagw.

Roberson, Kate. 2024, May 31. "Journal Rejects 'White' 'Male' Author's Pro-Life Article", *The College Fix*, https://www.thecollegefix.com/journal-rejects-white-male-authors-pro-life-article/.

Rom, William. 2018. "Estimated Global Mortality from Present to 2100 from Climate Change", *International Journal of Humanities and Social Science Review* 4:1–8, https://legacy-assets.eenews.net/open_files/assets/2018/04/04/document_gw_09.pdf.

Roth, Philip, Craig Bevier, Philip Bobko, Fred Switzer, and Peggy Tyler. 2001. "Ethnic Group Differences in Cognitive Ability in Employment and Educational Settings: A Meta-Analysis", *Personnel Psychology* 54:297–330.

Rudman, Laurie and Stephanie Goodwin. 2004. "Gender Differences in Automatic In-Group Bias: Why Do Women Like Women More Than Men Like Men?", *Journal of Personality and Social Psychology* 87:494–509.

Ruibal, Sal. 2006, Mar. 29. "Rape Allegations Cast Pall at Duke", *USA Today*, https://usatoday30.usatoday.com/sports/college/lacrosse/2006-03-29-duke-fallout_x.htm.

Rumney, Philip. 2006. "False Allegations of Rape", *Cambridge Law Journal* 65:128–58.

Russo, Francine. 2016, Jan. 1. "Is There Something Unique about the Transgender Brain?", *Scientific American*, https://www.scientificamerican.com/article/is-there-something-unique-about-the-transgender-brain/.

Rutgers University, Department of Philosophy. n.d. "Stereotype Threat", https://philosophy.rutgers.edu/climate-v2/climate-issues-in-academic-philosophy/stereotype-threat.

Saad, Lydia. 2020, Nov. 13. "What Percentage of Americans Own Guns?", Gallup, https://news.gallup.com/poll/264932/percentage-americans-own-guns.aspx.

Saad, Nardine. 2020, Aug. 25. "'This Is Sickening': Cardi B, Beyoncé, Common Decry Jacob Blake Shooting", *Los Angeles Times*, https://www.latimes.com/entertainment-arts/story/2020-08-25/jacob-blake-shooting-celebrity-athlete-reactions.

Sacerdote, Bruce. 2007. "How Large Are the Effects from Changes in Family Environment? A Study of Korean American Adoptees", *The Quarterly Journal of Economics* 122:119–157.

Sackett, Paul, Chaitra Hardison, and Michael J. Cullen. 2004. "On Interpreting Stereotype Threat as Accounting for African American–White Differences on Cognitive Tests", *American Psychologist* 59:7–13.

Saide, Anondah, and Kevin McCaffree. 2021a. "How Informed Are Americans About Race and Policing?", Skeptic Research Center, CUPES-007, https://www.skeptic.com/research-center/reports/Research-Report-CUPES-007.pdf.

———. 2021b. "Why Are People Misinformed About Fatal Police Shootings?", Skeptic Research Center, CUPES-008, https://www.skeptic.com/research-center/reports/Research-Report-CUPES-008.pdf.

Sanchez, Ray. 2020, Sept. 4. "Jacob Blake's Shooting Shows America Has a Long Way to Go in Its Journey Toward a Racial Reckoning", CNN, https://www.cnn.com/2020/08/30/us/jacob-blake-shooting-one-week-later/index.html.

Sanders, Bernie. 2020, Aug. 24. Tweet: https://twitter.com/BernieSanders/status/1297924579613171720.

Santhanam, Laura, Vanessa Dennis, and Travis Daub. 2014, Nov. 25. "What Do the Newly Released Witness Statements Tell Us About the Michael Brown Shooting?", *PBS News Hour*, https://www.pbs.org/newshour/nation/newly-released-witness-testimony-tell-us-michael-brown-shooting.

Saplakoglu, Yasemin. 2021, Sept. 1. "Huge, Gold-Standard Study Shows Unequivocally that Surgical Masks Work to Reduce Coronavirus Spread", Live Science, https://www.livescience.com/randomized-trial-shows-surgical-masks-work-curbing-covid.html.

Savolainen, Jukka. 2024. "Unequal Treatment Under the Flaw: Race, Crime and Retractions", *Current Psychology* 43:16002–14.

Schimmack, Ulrich. 2020. "A Meta-Psychological Perspective on the Decade of Replication Failures in Social Psychology", *Canadian Psychology* 61:364–76, https://replicationindex.com/2020/01/05/replication-crisis-review/.

———. 2022, Feb. 15. "Publication Bias in the Stereotype Threat Literature", http://replicationindex.com/2022/02/15/rr22-stereotype-threat/.

Schmidtz, David. 2023. *Living Together: Inventing Moral Science*. Oxford Univ. Press.

Schumaker, Erin. 2020, June 5. "What the Latest Research Tells Us About Racial Bias in Policing," ABC News, https://abcnews.go.com/US/latest-research-tells-us-racial-bias-policing/story?id=70994421.

Schwarz, Joel. 1998, Sept. 29. "Roots of Unconscious Prejudice Affect 90 to 95

Percent of People, Psychologists Demonstrate at Press Conference", *UW News*, https://www.washington.edu/news/1998/09/29/roots-of-unconscious-prejudice-affect-90-to-95-percent-of-people-psychologists-demonstrate-at-press-conference/.

Searle, John. 1971. *The Campus War: A Sympathetic Look at the University in Agony*. World Publishing Co. https://www.ditext.com/searle/campus/campus.html.

Selby, Nick, Ben Singleton, and Ed Flosi. 2016. In Context: Understanding Police Killings of Unarmed Civilians. CIAI Press.

Serano, Julia. 2009. "Psychology, Sexualization and Trans-invalidations", keynote lecture, 8th Annual Philadelphia Trans-Health Conference, http://www.juliaserano.com/av/Serano-TransInvalidations.pdf.

Sharpton, Al. 2015. "Rev. Al Sharpton Comments on the Trayvon Martin Case" (press conference video), AP archive, https://youtu.be/ieLZdWbj-aI.

———. 2021, Nov. 19. "Statement by Reverend Sharpton & NAN on the Acquittal of Kyle Rittenhouse", https://nationalactionnetwork.net/newnews/statement-by-reverend-sharpton-nan-on-the-acquittal-of-kyle-rittenhouse/.

Shewach, Oren, Paul Sackett, and Sander Quint. 2019. "Stereotype Threat Effects in Settings with Features Likely Versus Unlikely in Operational Test Settings: A Meta-Analysis", *Journal of Applied Psychology* 104:1514–34.

Shortell, David. 2019, July 16. "Barr Sides Against Civil Rights Officials in Declining to Bring Charges Against NYPD Officer in Garner Case", CNN, https://edition.cnn.com/2019/07/16/politics/eric-garner-william-barr-nypd-officer-daniel-pantaleo/index.html.

Sieling, Mark. 1984. "Staffing Patterns Prominent in Female-Male Earnings Gap," *Monthly Labor Review* 107:29–33.

Singal, Jesse. 2017. "Psychology's Favorite Tool for Measuring Racism Isn't Up to the Job", *The Cut*, https://www.thecut.com/2017/01/psychologys-racism-measuring-tool-isnt-up-to-the-job.html.

Sirois, Martie. 2017, Apr. 2. "Are Trans Women Really Women? Why Chimamanda Ngozi Adichie's Answer Matters", *Huffington Post*, https://www.huffpost.com/entry/are-trans-women-really-women-why-chimamanda-ngozi_b_58e1878be4b0ca889ba1a763.

Skeptic Research Center. 2021. "Supplemental Materials for Report #: CUPES-007", https://www.skeptic.com/research-center/reports/Supplemental-CUPES-007.pdf.

Soave, Robby. 2020, May 19. "Feminists Who Now Claim They Never Meant 'Believe All Women' Are Gaslighting Us", *Reason*, https://reason.com/2020/05/19/believe-all-women-me-too-feminists-biden-reade/.

Spencer, Steven, Christine Logel, and Paul Davies. 2016. "Stereotype Threat", *Annual Review of Psychology* 67:415–37.

Spencer, Steven, Claude Steele, and Diane Quinn. 1999. "Stereotype Threat and Women's Math Performance", *Journal of Experimental Social Psychology* 35:4–28.

St. Louis Federal Reserve. 2023. "Median Personal Income in the United States", https://fred.stlouisfed.org/series/MEPAINUSA646N.

St. Louis University, Reinert Center for Transformative Teaching and Learning. n.d. "Resource Guide: Understanding Stereotype Threat", https://www.slu.edu/cttl/resources/resource-guides/understanding-stereoytpe-threat.pdf.

Statista. 2006. "Average Life Expectancy from Birth in Selected Regions and Time

Periods from 33CE to 1875 CE", https://www.statista.com/statistics/1069683/life-expectancy-historical-areas/.

———. 2023a. "Number of Occupational Injury Deaths in the U.S. from 2003 to 2020, by Gender", https://www.statista.com/statistics/187127/number-of-occupational-injury-deaths-in-the-us-by-gender-since-2003/.

———. 2023b. "Number of People Shot to Death by the Police in the United States from 2017 to 2023, by Gender", https://www.statista.com/statistics/585149/people-shot-to-death-by-us-police-by-gender/.

———. 2023c. "Number of Employer Firms in the United States in 2019, by Employment Size", https://www.statista.com/statistics/487741/number-of-firms-in-the-us-by-employment-size/.

Statistics How-To (website). n.d. "Test-Retest Reliability / Repeatability", https://www.statisticshowto.com/test-retest-reliability/.

Steele, Claude and Joshua Aronson. 1995. "Stereotype Threat and the Intellectual Test Performance of African Americans", *Journal of Personality and Social Psychology* 69:797–811.

Stellino, Molly. 2020, June 23. "Fact Check: Police Killed More Unarmed Black Men in 2019 than Conservative Activist Claimed", *USA Today*, https://www.usatoday.com/story/news/factcheck/2020/06/23/fact-check-how-many-unarmed-black-men-did-police-kill-2019/5322455002/.

Stenhouse, Neil et al. 2013. "Meteorologists' Views About Global Warming: A Survey of American Meteorological Society Professional Members", *Bulletin of the American Meteorological Society* 95:1029–40.

Stoet, Gijsbert, and David Geary. 2012. "Can Stereotype Threat Explain the Gender Gap in Mathematics Performance and Achievement?", *Review of General Psychology* 16:93–102.

Strachan, Laura. 2010, Sept. 10. "1 in 4 College Women Will Be Victims of Rape", FindLaw, https://www.findlaw.com/legalblogs/criminal-defense/1-in-4-college-women-will-be-victims-of-rape/.

Stricker, Lawrence and William Ward. 2004. "Stereotype Threat, Inquiring About Test Takers' Ethnicity and Gender, and Standardized Test Performance", *Journal of Applied Social Psychology* 34:665–93.

Stroessner, Steven et al. n.d. "FAQs", https://reducingstereotypethreat.org/support/, accessed June 26, 2023.

Stutzman, Rene and Amy Pavuk. 2012, Apr. 2. "Lawyer for Trayvon's Family: Wolfinger and Police Chief Met the Night Teen Was Killed", *Orlando Sentinel*. Removed from newspaper's website; archived at: https://web.archive.org/web/20120606225858/http://articles.orlandosentinel.com/2012-04-02/news/os-trayvon-martin-federal-review-justice-letter-20120402_1_chief-bill-lee-federal-review-federal-agency.

Swaine, Jon. 2014, Aug. 12. "Michael Brown Shooting: 'They Killed Another Young Black Man in America'", *The Guardian*, https://www.theguardian.com/world/2014/aug/12/ferguson-missouri-shooting-michael-brown-civil-rights-police-brutality.

Swant, Marty. 2020. "The World's Most Valuable Brands", *Forbes*, https://www.forbes.com/the-worlds-most-valuable-brands/#6e6ad8b1119c.

Tajfel, Henri, M.G. Billig, R.P. Bundy, and Claude Flament. 1971. "Social Categorization and Intergroup Behaviour", *European Journal of Social Psychology*

1:149–78.

Tamir, Christine and Monica Anderson. 2022. "One-in-Ten Black People Living in the U.S. Are Immigrants", Pew Research Center, https://www.pewresearch. org/wp-content/uploads/sites/20/2022/01/RE_2022.01.20_Black-Immigrants_FINAL.pdf.

Tanenbaum, Leora. 2018, Jan. 10. "Women Don't 'Cry Rape': Why It's So Unlikely any Woman Would Lie About Being Raped", *U.S. News and World Report*, https://www.usnews.com/opinion/civil-wars/articles/2018-01-10/ women-dont-lie-about-being-raped. Originally titled, "Women Don't Lie About Being Raped".

Tedeschi, Ted. 2022, Mar. 10. "Pain and Prejudice: UC Professor Reviews Origins of US Drug Policy, Proposes Strategies to Help End Opioid Epidemic", University of Cincinnati News, https://www.uc.edu/news/articles/2022/03/us-drug-policy-and-systemic-racism.html.

Temple Newhook, Julia et al. 2018. "A Critical Commentary on Follow-Up Studies and 'Desistance' Theories About Transgender and Gender-Nonconforming Children", *International Journal of Transgenderism* 19: 212–24.

The Numbers. 2024. "All Time International Box Office", https://www.the-numbers.com/box-office-records/international/all-movies/cumulative/all-time.

Thompson, Alexandra and Susannah Tapp. 2022. "Criminal Victimization, 2021", U.S. Department of Justice, Bureau of Justice Statistics, https://bjs.ojp.gov/ content/pub/pdf/cv21.pdf.

Thomson, Phil and John Halstead. 2022, Oct. 2. "How Violent Was the Pre-Agricultural World?", Social Science Research Network, https://ssrn.com/ abstract=4466809.

Thrasher, Steven. 2014, Aug. 12. "The Ghost of Mike Brown: Why Must a Dead Black Child Defend His Right to Life?", *The Guardian*, https://www. theguardian.com/commentisfree/2014/aug/12/mike-brown-ferguson-shooting-police-black.

Thunberg, Greta. 2019. No One Is Too Small to Make a Difference. Penguin Books.

Tierney, John. 2023. "The Misogyny Myth", *City Journal*, https://www.city-journal.org/article/the-misogyny-myth.

Times Higher Education. 2024. "World University Rankings 2024", https://www. timeshighereducation.com/world-university-rankings/2024/world-ranking.

Timothy, Maxwell. 2022, Aug. 3. "How Many Bots Are on Twitter and Does It Matter?", Make Use Of, https://www.makeuseof.com/how-many-bots-on-twitter/.

Trayvon Martin Shooting Call. 2012, Feb. 26. https://en.wikipedia.org/wiki/ File:Trayvon_Martin_Shooting_Call1.ogg.

Tremoglie, Christopher. 2022, July 22. "Of Course 'Trans Women' Are Not Women", *Washington Examiner*, https://www.washingtonexaminer.com/ opinion/of-course-trans-women-are-not-women.

Trevor Project. n.d. "Guide to Being an Ally to Transgender and Nonbinary Young People", https://www.thetrevorproject.org/resources/guide/a-guide-to-being-an-ally-to-transgender-and-nonbinary-youth/.

Trudeau, Justin. 2023, Mar. 8. Tweet: https://twitter.com/JustinTrudeau/status/

1633468198636113922.

TWAS (The World Academy of Sciences) Young Affiliates Network. 2020, Nov. 23. Open letter to *Nature Communications*. https://docs.google.com/forms/d/e/FAIpQLSfpyLtpNPcxgp1fhHHWrG3V3yoiad3vsY5Qh1BcYrBZGDLtkQ/viewform.

U.S. Congressional Budget Office. 2022. "The Distribution of Household Income, 2019", https://www.cbo.gov/publication/58353.

U.S. Department of Justice. 2002. "Federal Cocaine Offenses: An Analysis Of Crack And Powder Penalties", https://reason.com/wp-content/uploads/2021/05/Federal-Cocaine-Offenses-2002.pdf.

———. 2015. Department of Justice Report Regarding the Criminal Investigation Into the Shooting Death of Michael Brown by Ferguson, Missouri Police Officer Darren Wilson, https://www.justice.gov/sites/default/files/opa/press-releases/attachments/2015/03/04/doj_report_on_shooting_of_michael_brown_1.pdf.

———. 2020. *Crime in the United States, 2019*, Expanded Homicide Data Table 6, https://ucr.fbi.gov/crime-in-the-u.s/2019/crime-in-the-u.s.-2019/tables/expanded-homicide-data-table-6.xls.

———. 2022, Aug. 4. "Current and Former Louisville, Kentucky Police Officers Charged with Federal Crimes Related to Death of Breonna Taylor" (press release), https://www.justice.gov/opa/pr/current-and-former-louisville-kentucky-police-officers-charged-federal-crimes-related-death.

U.S. Department of Labor. n.d. "Federal Resources for Women", https://www.dol.gov/agencies/wb/federal-agency-resources.

U.S. Department of the Treasury. 2007. "Income Mobility in the U.S. from 1996 to 2005", https://home.treasury.gov/system/files/131/Report-Income-Mobility-2008.pdf.

U.S. Department of the Treasury, Office of Economic Policy; Council of Economic Advisers; and Department of Labor. 2015. "Occupational Licensing: A Framework for Policymakers", https://obamawhitehouse.archives.gov/sites/default/files/docs/licensing_report_final_nonembargo.pdf.

U.S. Office of Management and Budget. 2021. "2018, 2019, and 2020 Report to Congress on the Benefits and Costs of Federal Regulations and Agency Compliance with the Unfunded Mandates Reform Act", https://www.whitehouse.gov/wp-content/uploads/2021/01/2018_2019_2020-OMB-Cost-Benefit-Report.pdf.

U.S. Office of the Federal Register. 2023. "Code of Federal Regulations Actual Page Breakdown 1975–2021", https://uploads.federalregister.gov/uploads/2022/06/17142921/FR-Stats-2021-Cfr-Volumes-and-Pages-updated.pdf.

Uhlmann, Eric, Victoria Brescoll, and Elizabeth Paluck. 2006. "Are Members of Low Status Groups Perceived as Bad, or Badly Off? Egalitarian Negative Associations and Automatic Prejudice", *Journal of Experimental Social Psychology* 42:491–9.

University of Colorado Boulder, Center for Teaching and Learning. n.d. "Stereotype Threat", https://www.colorado.edu/center/teaching-learning/inclusivity/stereotype-threat.

University of Texas at Austin School of Social Work, Institute on Domestic Violence and Sexual Assault. 2017. "Cultivating Learning and Safe Environments", https://www.utsystem.edu/sites/default/files/sites/clase/files/2017-10/health-aggregate-R11-V4.pdf.

USA Today. 2021, Aug. 19. "Who Led Tokyo Olympics Medal Count? Here's How Each Country Performed at the Summer Games", https://www.usatoday.com/story/sports/olympics/2021/07/24/tokyo-olympics-2021-medal-count/8080071002/.

Valencia, Nick. 2015, Aug. 14. "Pistol-whipped Detective Says He Didn't Shoot Attacker Because of Headlines", CNN, https://www.cnn.com/2015/08/13/us/alabama-birmingham-police-detective-pistol-whipped/index.html.

Veale, Jaimie, David Clarke, and Terri Lomax. 2011. "Male-to-Female Transsexuals' Impressions of Blanchard's Autogynephilia Theory", *International Journal of Transgenderism* 13:131–9.

Venugopal, Arun. 2013, Aug. 15. "Black Leaders Once Championed the Strict Drug Laws They Now Seek to Dismantle", WNYC (New York Public Radio), https://www.wnyc.org/story/312823-black-leaders-once-championed-strict-drug-laws-they-now-seek-dismantle/.

Vohs, Kathleen, et al. 2021. "A Multisite Preregistered Paradigmatic Test of the Ego-Depletion Effect", *Psychological Science* 32:1566–81.

Walker, Jesse. 2004, May 24. "The Death of David Reimer", *Reason*, https://reason.com/2004/05/24/the-death-of-david-reimer/.

Wallace, George. 1963, Jan. 14. Governor's inaugural address, Montgomery, Alabama, https://viewingamerica.as.virginia.edu/1963-inaugural-address-governor-george-c-wallace.

Walsh, Matt. 2021. "Matt Walsh's Date with a Feminist", https://youtu.be/x3y_Wm8TjOY.

Warne, Russell. 2021, Aug. 7. "Send In The Clones: Stereotype Threat Needs Replication Studies" (weblog), https://russellwarne.com/2021/08/07/send-in-the-clones-stereotype-threat-needs-replication-studies/.

Warren, Elizabeth. 2019, Aug. 9. Tweet: https://twitter.com/ewarren/status/1159902078103445507.

———. 2021, Apr. 2. Tweet: https://twitter.com/SenWarren/status/1378010622030413835.

Watson, Emma. 2014, Sept. 20. "Emma Watson: Gender Equality Is Your Issue Too", UN Women, https://www.unwomen.org/en/news/stories/2014/9/emma-watson-gender-equality-is-your-issue-too.

Watts, Jonathan. 2018, Oct. 8. "We Have 12 Years to Limit Climate Change Catastrophe, Warns UN", *The Guardian*, https://www.theguardian.com/environment/2018/oct/08/global-warming-must-not-exceed-15c-warns-landmark-un-report.

Weiner, Jeff and Rene Stutzman. 2012, May 17. "Encounter Between George Zimmerman and Trayvon Martin 'Avoidable', Cops Said in Report", *Orlando Sentinel*. Removed from newspaper's website; archived at https://web.archive.org/web/20130715203718/http://articles.orlandosentinel.com/2012-05-17/news/os-george-zimmerman-evidence-released-20120517_1_special-prosecutor-angela-corey-new-evidence-documents/2.

Weiss, Bari. 2021, Aug. 3. "The Real Story of 'The Central Park Karen'", *Honestly* podcast, https://www.honestlypod.com/podcast/episode/256bac0b/the-real-story-of-the-central-park-karen.

Wemple, Erik. 2012, Mar. 31. "NBC to Do 'Internal Investigation' on Zimmerman Segment", *Washington Post*, https://www.washingtonpost.com/blogs/erik-wemple/post/nbc-to-do-internal-investigation-on-zimmerman-segment/2012/03/31/gIQAc4HhnS_blog.html.

Wikipedia. "Affilia", https://en.wikipedia.org/wiki/Affilia.

———. "Kenosha Unrest Shooting", https://en.wikipedia.org/wiki/Kenosha_unrest_shooting.

———. "Killing of Breonna Taylor", https://en.wikipedia.org/wiki/Killing_of_Breonna_Taylor.

———. "Killing of Eric Garner", https://en.wikipedia.org/wiki/Killing_of_Eric_Garner.

———. "Killing of Michael Brown", https://en.wikipedia.org/wiki/Killing_of_Michael_Brown.

———. "Killing of Trayvon Martin", https://en.wikipedia.org/wiki/Killing_of_Trayvon_Martin.

———. "List of African-American United States Representatives", https://en.wikipedia.org/wiki/List_of_African-American_United_States_representatives.

———. "List of African-American United States Senators", https://en.wikipedia.org/wiki/List_of_African-American_United_States_senators.

———. "List of Best-Selling Music Artists", https://en.wikipedia.org/wiki/List_of_best-selling_music_artists.

———. "List of Nobel Laureates by Country", https://en.wikipedia.org/wiki/List_of_Nobel_laureates_by_country.

———. "Murder of George Floyd", https://en.wikipedia.org/wiki/Murder_of_George_Floyd.

———. "Neuroscience of Sex Differences", https://en.wikipedia.org/wiki/Neuroscience_of_sex_differences.

———. "Noah Carl", https://en.wikipedia.org/wiki/Noah_Carl.

———. "Reactions to the Duke Lacrosse Case", https://en.wikipedia.org/wiki/Reactions_to_the_Duke_lacrosse_case.

———. "Shooting of Jacob Blake", https://en.wikipedia.org/wiki/Shooting_of_Jacob_Blake.

———. "Woman", https://en.wikipedia.org/wiki/Woman.

———. "Year 2000 problem", https://en.wikipedia.org/wiki/Year_2000_problem.

Williams, Paige. 2021, June 23. "Kyle Rittenhouse, American Vigilante", *The New Yorker*, https://www.newyorker.com/magazine/2021/07/05/kyle-rittenhouse-american-vigilante.

Williamson, Marianne. 2020, Aug. 23. Tweet: https://twitter.com/marwilliamson/status/1297760535107297290.

Willis, Raquel. 2017, Mar. 13. "Trans Women Are Women. This Isn't a Debate.", *The Root*, https://www.theroot.com/trans-women-are-women-this-isn-t-a-debate-1793202635.

Wilson, Frederica. 2012, Mar. 20. "Congresswoman Wilson's House Floor Speech on the Shooting Death of Trayvon Martin", https://youtu.be/BE4qGkA7Bxc.

Wingo, Ajume. 2003. *Veil Politics in Liberal Democratic States*. Cambridge Univ. Press.

Winter, Tom, James Novogrod, and Elizabeth Chuck. 2013, July 9. "Gunshot Wound Expert: Evidence Supports Zimmerman's Account of Fatal Encounter", NBC News, https://www.nbcnews.com/news/us-news/gunshot-wound-expert-evidence-supports-zimmermans-account-fatal-encounter-flna6C10580474.

Wisconsin Department of Justice. 2020, Sept. 12. Criminal background check on Gaige Grosskreutz, https://archive.md/H3THj.

Witchel, Selma. 2018. "Disorders of Sex Development", *Best Practice and Research Clinical Obstetrics and Gynaecology* 48:90–102.

Woodward, Calvin, Seth Borenstein, and Hope Yen. 2019, Mar. 16. "AP FACT CHECK: O'Rourke on Climate, Trump on 'No Collusion'", AP News, https://apnews.com/article/fe7c9d4a9f8f458c827677d31230f594.

World Health Organization. 2020, Mar. 30. Covid-19 Virtual Press Conference. Transcript: https://www.who.int/docs/default-source/coronaviruse/transcripts/who-audio-emergencies-coronavirus-press-conference-full-30mar2020.pdf.

World Inequality Database. 2024. https://wid.world/income-comparator/.

World Population Review. 2023. "Most Dangerous Cities in the United States 2023", https://worldpopulationreview.com/us-city-rankings/most-dangerous-cities-in-the-us.

YouGov. 2019. "International Climate Change Survey", https://d3nkl3psvxxpe9.cloudfront.net/documents/YouGov_-_International_climate_change_survey_d9Bf6E0.pdf.

Zepezauer, Frank. 1994. "Believe Her! The Woman Never Lies Myth", *Issues In Child Abuse Accusations* 6, http://www.ipt-forensics.com/journal/volume6/j6_2_4.htm.

Zimmerman, George. 2012. "Raw Video: George Zimmerman Reenacts Incident for Sanford Police", https://youtu.be/PX1sxARNq_c.

Zippia. 2019, Dec. 28. "Lumberjack Demographics and Statistics in the US", https://www.zippia.com/lumberjack-jobs/demographics/.

Made in United States
Troutdale, OR
10/20/2024

23931314R10170